009 WORKS ONE
049 PETER WEIBEL, JAN HOET
061 WORKS TWO
109 JOCHEN GERZ, KARL-HEINZ PETZINKA
WORKS THREE 121
XUYEN DAM, KAI RÖFFEN, TALENTS 161
CHRONICLE, 33PT 177

009  WORKS ONE

Das vorgegebene Thema der Editorial Modestrecke war Musik. Für meine Arbeit wählte ich die Discokugel als zentrales Objekt und Formgeber. Die selbst erstellten Outfits nehmen stets Bezug zu dem Objekt und setzen es in einen neuen Kontext. Somit ergibt sich eine Modeserie, die das Gefühl und die Stimmung von dem, was Musik bedeutet, verkörpert. Durch die vielseitigen Einsatzmöglichkeiten der Plättchen der Discokugel ergeben sich verschiedene Outfits, die ihrerseits in der Bildserie eine eigene Geschichte erzählen. **The set subject for the fashion editorial was music. As the central object and form-giver, I chose the disco ball for my work. The personally created outfits always relate to the object and place it in a new context. In this way, a fashion series develops which embodies the feeling and the atmosphere of the meaning of music. Through the diverse utilisation possibilities of the disco ball mirrors, various outfits are created, which for their part tell their own story in the picture series.**

»Mode«
Student: Michael Bader | Semester theme: Editorial for a fashion range | Semester: 6, Photo design
Type/Scope: Pictures | Mentoring: Kai Jünnemann | Free submission

Das Thema meiner Diplomarbeit ist die »A40«, die auch die Lebensader des Ruhrgebiets genannt wird. Sie zieht sich von Dortmund bis zur Bundesgrenze bei Straelen und verbindet auf einer Strecke von ca. 89 km fast alle großen Städte wie Dortmund, Gelsenkirchen, Bochum, Oberhausen und Duisburg miteinander. Sie führt vorbei an Wohnhäusern, an Bürofassaden, aber auch an kleinen Dörfern und ländlichen Gegenden. Gezeigt wird in meiner Arbeit das Leben rund um diese Verkehrsader. Welche interessanten Typen und welche skurrilen Landschaften gibt es hinter der Schallschutzmauer zu entdecken? Die gesamte Arbeit besteht aus 25 Portraits und 25 Landschaften. Diese sind zu einem Buch in annäherndem A3 Format gebunden. **The subject of my final student project is the motorway »A40«, which is also known as the lifeline of the Ruhr area. It stretches from Dortmund to the German border close to Straelen and joins almost all cities such as Dortmund, Gelsenkirchen, Bochum, Oberhausen and Duisburg over a distance of about 89 kilometers. It leads past residential buildings, office façades but also past small villages and rural areas. My work shows the life around this arterial road. What interesting characters and bizarre landscapes are there to be discovered behind the noise insulation wall? The entire work is made up of twenty-five portraits and twenty-five landscapes. These are bound in a book in an almost A3 format.**

»A40«
Student: Sebastian Mölleken | Semester theme: Diploma | Semester: 13, Photo design
Type/Scope: Book, 50 images | Mentoring: Prof. Jörg Winde

Idee ist es, ein Buch bzw. eine Bücherreihe zu entwickeln, die von den verschiedensten Lesern selbst zusammengestellt und erweitert werden kann. Die Inhalte dieses Buches sind in verschiedene Themenbereiche aufgeteilt, die jeweils ein Teilstück des Buches sind. Diese Teilstücke sind beliebig kombinierbar und lassen sich somit zu einem maßgeschneiderten, immer erweiterbaren Buch verbinden. So ist es möglich, das Buch auf die jeweiligen Bedürfnisse des Lesers abzustimmen und gleichzeitig aktualisierbar zu machen. Angewendet wird dieses erweiterbare System auf einen Umweltatlas für Deutschland. Dieser bietet einen Überblick über die ökologische und ökonomische Lage in Deutschland und visualisiert die wissenschaftlichen Informationen in diversen Karten und Grafiken. Die verschiedenen Themen, wie Klima oder Bevölkerung bilden jeweils ein Teilstück der gesamten Atlanten und funktionieren auch getrennt voneinander. The idea is to develop a book, or a series of books, which is compiled by the most diverse readers and is expandable. The book's content is divided into different subjects each of which makes up a part of the book. These parts can be merged at will and are thus combinable to make up a tailor-made ever-expandable book. This makes it possible to coordinate the book with readers' requirements whilst simultaneously allowing for its update. This expandable system is applied to an environmental atlas for Germany. This atlas offers an overview of the ecological and economic situation in Germany and visualises the scientific information in various maps and diagrams. The various subjects, such as climate or population, form an integral part of the entire atlas and also work independently of each other.

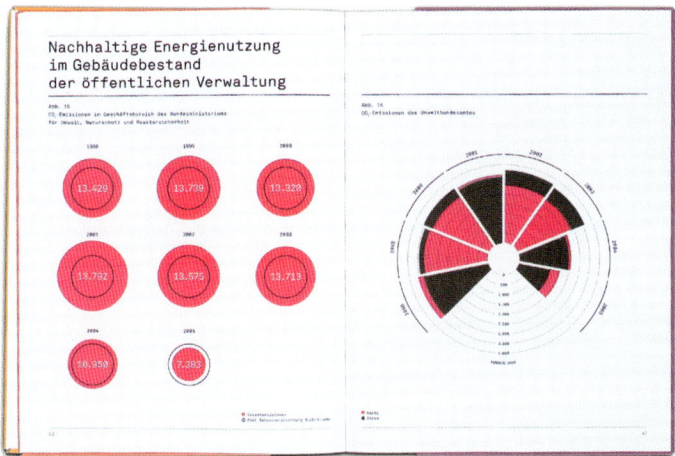

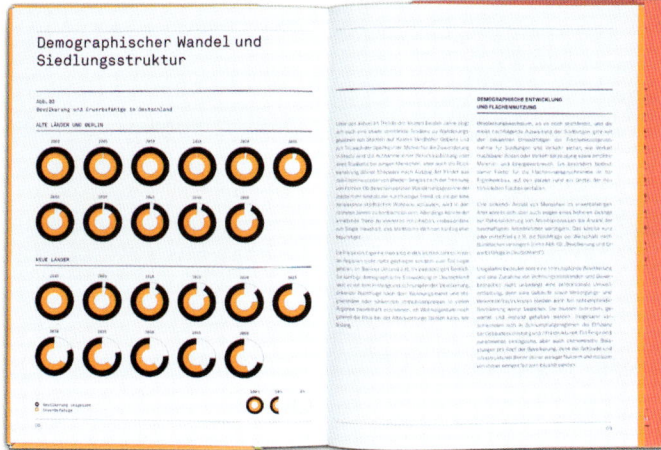

»Umweltatlas«
Student: Sebastian Emmel | Semester theme: What do tomorrow's books look like? | Semester: 7, Graphic design
Type/Scope: Book in 5 pieces | Mentoring: Prof. Sabine an Huef

HIRNGESPINSTER

»Hirngespinster« ist eine interaktive Installation, bei welcher der Benutzer mittels einer Lupe Animationen vom Buch aus startet. So verfügt jede illustrierte Seite über einen spezifischen Film. Gezeigt werden Szenen, die sich im Kopf einer halluzinierenden Person, die sich in der Realität befindet, abspielen. Das Buch ist in diesem Zusammenhang der Spiegel der realen Welt. Gewoben werden die Phantasien von den sogenannten Hirngespinstern: kleine Schwärme elektronischer Impulse, welche in unserem Kopf ihr Unwesen treiben. Auslöser der Animation sind Hirngespinster, welche sich im Bild tummeln. Um zu sehen was im Kopf der Person vorgeht, muss mit der Lupe nachgeforscht werden. »**Hirngespinster**« [phantasms] is an interactive installation, in which animations are set in motion from the book through the use of a magnifying glass. In this way, each illustrated page has a specific film. Scenes are shown taking place in the mind of a hallucinating person who is part of reality. In this context, the book is a reflection of the real world. Fantasies are woven by so-called Hirngespinster [phantasms]: small masses of electronic impulses, which do their mischief in our heads. The animation is triggered by the phantasms, which cavort in the picture. To see what goes on in the person's head, the observer must examine the scene more closely using the magnifying glass.

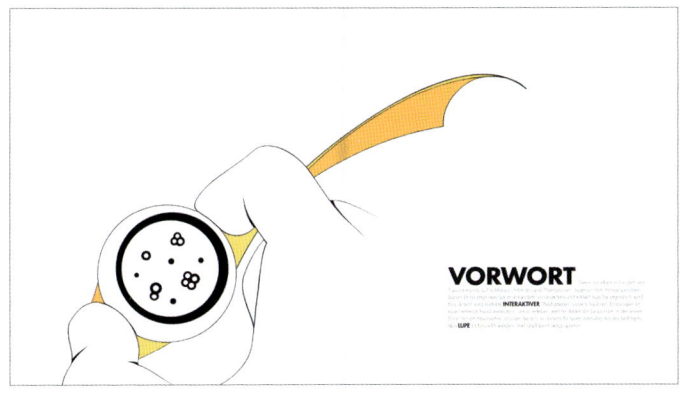

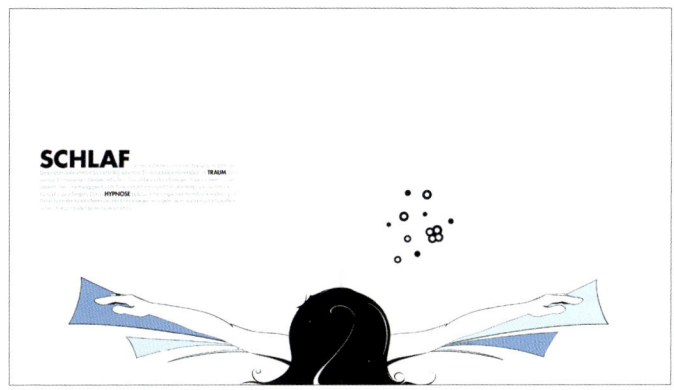

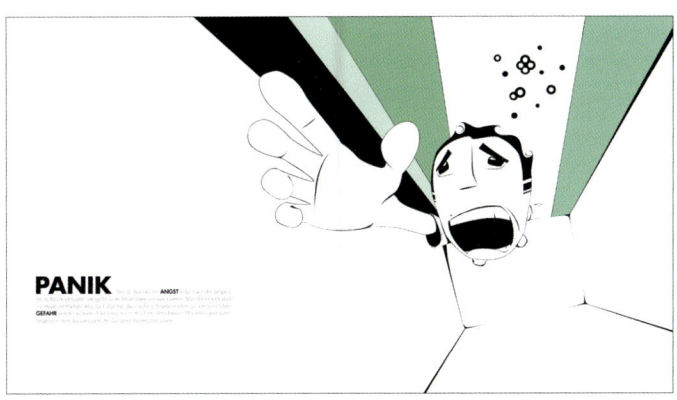
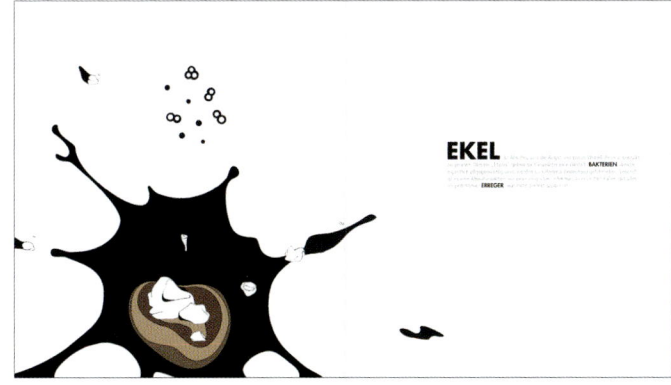

»Hirngespinster«
Student: Tristan Hohne | Semester theme: Diploma | Semester: 9, Graphic design
Type/Scope: Interactive installation, book, animation | Mentoring: Carsten Strübbe | Free submission

»Germarica«

Semester theme: Visual art battle | Type/Scope: 12 posters
Mentoring: Martin Schonhoff

Mit einer Designklasse aus Amerika wurde eine Art visueller Battle ausgetragen. Dabei hatte jeder deutsche Student ein gemeinsames Thema [z.B. Drogen, Politik, Musik, Kommunikation, Stereotypen etc.] mit einem amerikanischen Partner. Eine Datei galt es sich mehrmals gegenseitig zu schicken und zu erweitern. Abgesehen von dem visuellen Austausch bestand während dessen kein weiterer Kontakt zwischen den deutschen und den amerikanischen Studenten. Die deutschen Studenten führten ihre Gestaltung in den Farben Rot und Weiß durch, die amerikanischen in Blau und Weiß. Somit entstanden 12 Plakate, sechs pro Student. Im Anschluss wurde eine Broschüre zu jedem Thema gestaltet. Fotoshootings wurden organisiert und Video-Interviews mit den deutschen Studenten geführt. A kind of visual battle was fought with an American design class. In this battle, each German student shared a subject [e.g. drugs, politics, music, communication, stereotypes, etc.] with an American partner. The purpose was to mutually exchange and expand a file. Apart from the visual exchange, there was no other contact between the German and American students. The German students carried out their design in the colours red and white and the Americans in blue and white. Twelve posters – six per student – were created this way. In conclusion, a brochure was designed on each subject. Photo shootings were organised and video interviews were conducted with the German students.

»DBR1«
Student: Daniel Behn | Semester theme: Free subject | Semester: 5, Object and Interior design
Type/Scope: 1:1 Bookshelf | Mentoring: Prof. Xuyen Dam | Free submission

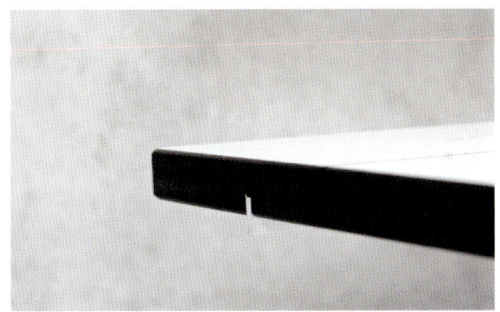

Dieses Systemmöbel lässt sich durch seine simple Modulbauweise individuell und ohne jegliche Werkzeuge oder Schrauben an jede beliebige Wohn- oder Nutzungssituation anpassen. Dem Nutzer steht eine Vielzahl an Modulen zur Verfügung, welche unzählig viele Kombinationen und Formen ermöglicht. Diese sind durch ein Schienen-Stecksystem jederzeit beliebig erweiter- und umbaubar. Die höhenverstellbaren Füße ermöglichen ein genaues Ausrichten und Nivellieren des Regals auch bei ungleicher Belastung. Das Resopal® beschichtete, schwarz durchfärbte MDF garantiert höchste Belastbarkeit und Verschleißresistenz. This piece of system furniture can be assembled without any tools or screws and adapts to any purpose or place within a given room thanks to its simple modular construction. The user has a choice of a variety of modules, which allow him to create innumerable combinations and forms. These can be expanded and rebuilt at any time in any manner through a rail push-fit system. The height of the feet is adjustable and enables accurate alignment and levelling of the shelf – even with an asymmetrical load. The black-imbued MDF with Resopal® coating guarantees the highest level of load-bearing capacity and resistance against wear and tear.

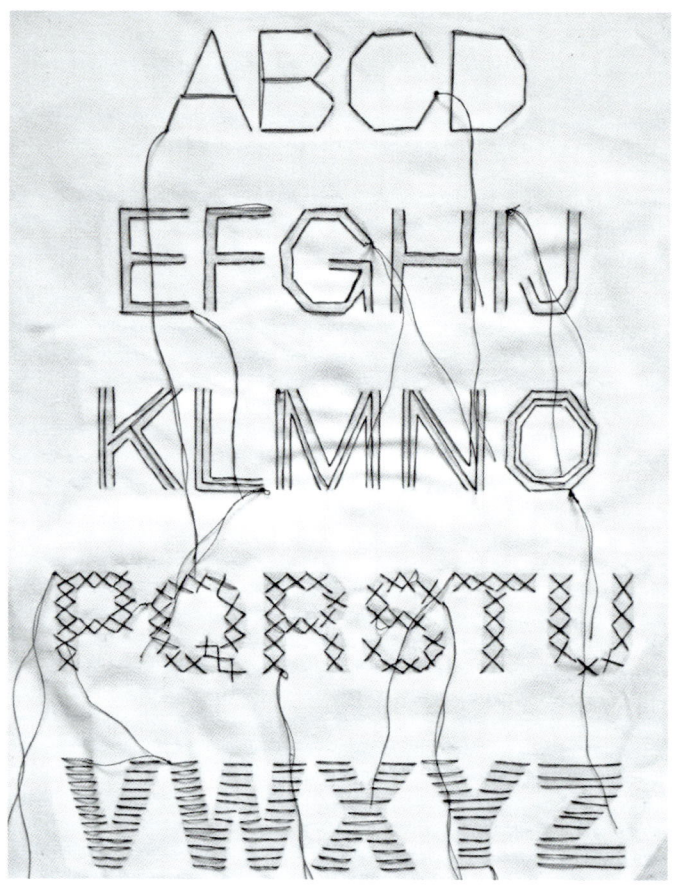

»Experimental Type«

Student: Sara Möbius | Semester theme: Free subject | Semester: 5, Graphic design
Type/Scope: Book | Mentoring: Prof. Xuyen Dam | Free submission

Unter dem selbstgestellten Thema »Experimentelle Typografie« ist ein 60-seitiges Buch entstanden, das aufzeigt, wie mit Typografie experimentell im Raum gespielt werden kann oder durch banale Gebrauchsgegenstände ein neues Typeface entsteht. Hierbei kamen Materialien wie z.B. Pappe, Zahnpasta, Holz, Stoff oder auch mal die Finger zum Einsatz. Ausgangspunkt für jede einzelne typografische Szenerie war die analoge Arbeit mit Papier und Schere. Durch das manuelle Zeichnen, Basteln und Schnitzen einzelner Fonts ließ sich ein Gespür für Form und Typografie entwickeln. **A sixty-page book was developed under the self-imposed subject »Experimental Typography«. The book shows how typography can be used experimentally and playfully in 3-D space or how a new typeface is created by mundane utensils. In this process, materials such as cardboard, toothpaste, wood, material and every now and again even fingers were used. The starting point for each individual typographic scenario was the analogue work with paper and scissors. A feeling for form and typography could develop through manually drawing, crafting and carving individual fonts.**

»milkydreams«
Student: Katharina Blasik | Semester theme: Free subject | Semester: 1, Graphic design
Type/Scope: Poster series, composite photographs | Mentoring: Arnim Kamps | Free submission

»Integration«

Student: Annika Schmermbeck | Semester theme: Stay abroad | Semester: 9, Photo design
Type/Scope: 5 pairs of images, 1 title image | Free submission

Diese Arbeit entstand während eines 18-monatigen Aufenthalts in Vietnam [Ho Chi Minh City]. Die Integration von Menschen mit unterschiedlicher Kultur besteht aus Annäherung, gegenseitiger Auseinandersetzung und Kommunikation, Finden von Gemeinsamkeiten und Feststellen von Unterschieden. Eine Übernahme wie z.B. der Sprache eröffnet die Möglichkeit einer Kommunikation mit anderen gesellschaftlichen Gruppen. Die Bereitschaft, fremde Bräuche und Sitten kennenzulernen und zu verstehen, bedeutet, nicht seine eigenen zu vergessen. Meine Arbeit ist eine fotografische Annäherung und Gegenüberstellung zweier Kulturen, welche unterschiedlicher nicht sein könnten. »Integration« fokussiert kulturelle Eckpfeiler wie Sprache und Religion; Gegenstände aus der Alltagskultur wie Mode und Esskultur werden thematisiert. Die Kollektion [er - couture] verbindet asiatische Elemente, Verarbeitungstechniken und Stoffe mit westlichem Design. **This work was developed during an eighteen-month stay in Vietnam [Ho Chi Minh City]. Integration of people of different cultures is made up of approaching each other, attempting to come to terms with each other and communicating, finding common ground, and determining differences. Adopting the language opens up communication with the other social groups. A willingness to learn about and understand strange habits and customs means not forgetting one's own. My work is a photographic approach and comparison of two cultures, which could not be more different. »Integration« focuses on cultural cornerstones such as language and religion; everyday cultural objects such as fashion and eating are also covered. The collection [er - couture] combines Asian elements, processing techniques and materials with Western design.**

Als sie mitten in den Wald gekommen waren, sprach der Vater: "Nun sammelt Holz, ihr Kinder, ich will ein Feuer anmachen, damit ihr nicht friert." Hänsel und Gretel trugen Reisig zusammen, einen kleinen Berg hoch. Das Reisig ward angezündet, und als die Flamme recht hoch brannte, sagte die Frau: "Nun legt euch ans Feuer, ihr Kinder, und ruht euch aus, wir gehen in den Wald und hauen Holz. Wenn wir fertig sind, kommen wir wieder und holen euch ab."

Hänsel und Gretel saßen um das Feuer, und als der Mittag kam, aß jedes sein Stücklein Brot. Und weil sie die Schläge der Holzaxt hörten, so glaubten sie, ihr Vater wär' in der Nähe. Es war aber nicht die Holzaxt, es war ein Ast, den er an einen dürren Baum gebunden hatte und den der Wind hin und her schlug. Und als sie so lange gesessen hatten, fielen ihnen die Augen vor Müdigkeit zu, und sie schliefen fest ein. Als sie endlich erwachten, war es schon finstere Nacht. Gretel fing an zu weinen und sprach:

"WIE SOLLEN WIR NUN AUS DEM WALD KOMMEN?"

Hänsel aber tröstete sie: "Wart nur ein Weilchen, bis der Mond aufgegangen ist, dann wollen wir den Weg schon finden." Und als der volle Mond aufgestiegen war, so nahm Hänsel sein Schwesterchen an der Hand und ging den Kieselsteinen nach, die schimmerten wie neugeschlagene Batzen und zeigten ihnen den Weg.

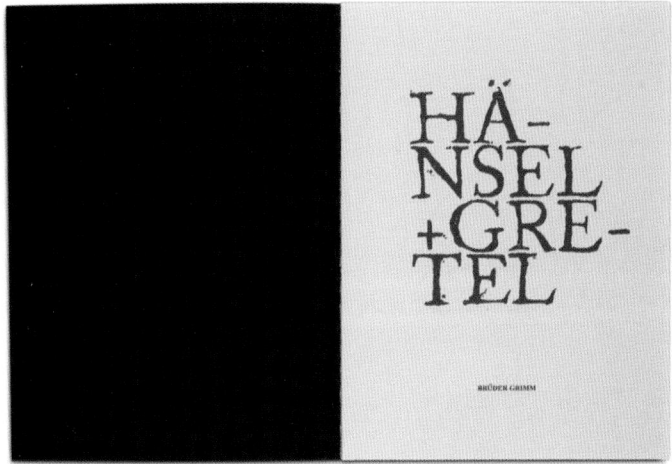

Dieses Buch ist ein Re-Design des Klassikers »Hänsel und Gretel« der Brüder Grimm. Durch die handgezeichneten Illustrationen und die ausdrucksstarke Typografie bekommt das traditionelle Märchen einen neuen, modernen Betrachtungsblickwinkel. **This book is a redesign of the classic »Hänsel und Gretel« by the Brothers Grimm. The hand-drawn illustrations and the very expressive typography give the traditional fairy tale a new, modern observational perspective.**

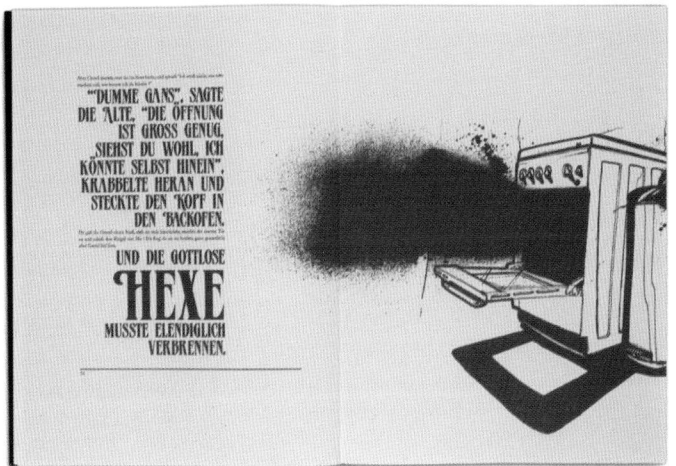
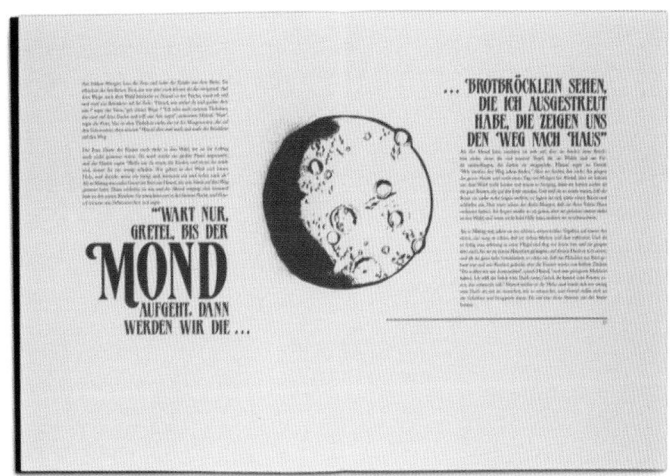

»Hänsel und Gretel«
Student: Christian Wohs | Semester theme: Re-Design of a publication | Semester: 3, Graphic design
Type/Scope: Book | Mentoring: Prof. Xuyen Dam | Free submission

»Loveparade 2008«
Student: Markus Mielek | Semester theme: Free subject | Semester: 13, Photo design
Type/Scope: 23 images | Mentoring: Prof. Caroline Dlugos | Free submission

Meine Arbeit beschäftigt sich mit der Loveparade, die im Juli 2008 in Dortmund stattfand. Die Fotostrecke setzt sich mit den unterschiedlichsten Menschen auseinander, die an diesem Tag an der Parade teilnahmen. Mir geht es hier um die Vielfalt der Personen und um ihre Intention, die Party zu besuchen. Zur Loveparade vereinigt sich ein weites Feld an Menschen jeglicher Couleur. Es sind Menschen, die der Subkultur der Elektro-Szene zugehörig sind. Raver, verkleidete junge Erwachsene, die feiern, Menschen, die ihren Fetisch offen ausleben können – Touristen und Schaulustige. In einem improvisierten Fotostudio direkt an der Loveparade lud ich Feiernde ein, um ohne jede Vorgabe für mich zu posieren. **My work dealt with the Loveparade, which took place in Dortmund in July 2008. The photo series deals with the most diverse people who took part in the parade that day. My concern here was the variety of the people and their intention to go to the party. The Loveparade unites a broad spectrum of people from all walks of life. These are people who belong to the sub-culture of the Electro Scene. Ravers, dressed-up young adults who celebrate, people who can openly live out their fetish, tourists and onlookers. I invited some revellers to an impromptu photographic studio directly on the Loveparade to come and – without any guidelines – to pose for me.**

Die Ausstellung zeigt schlafende Mädchen, abgewendete Körper und Gesichter, die sich unseren Blicken entziehen. Man sieht Räume, surrealistische Landschaften, Tiere und Stillleben. In Vitrinen werden Barytabzüge präsentiert. Ein Gedicht. Getrocknete Schmetterlinge und zwei Plastikkorsetts werden ausgestellt. »Hinter geschlossenen Lidern« mutet wie das Skelett einer Geschichte an. Es sind die Überreste einer Vergangenheit. Sich ähnelnde Motive tauchen auf, Bilder wiederholen sich, Symbole verweisen auf eine tiefere Deutungsebene. Zeit scheint hier nicht linear, sondern zyklisch zu verlaufen. Der Betrachter gerät in ein Spannungsfeld aus Traumwelt und Wirklickeit. Voyeurismus, Intimität, Heimlichkeiten, aber auch ein Ausgeschlossen sein und stille Melancholie bestimmen die Atmosphäre. Es ist eine Reise durch Gefühle und Gedanken, durch Raum und Zeit. Ein Herbarium menschlicher Erinnerung. Am Ende verschmelzen die Fragmente dieser Geschichte mit unseren eigenen Erinnerungen und eine neue, vollständigere Erzählung entsteht. **The exhibition shows sleeping girls, bodies turned away and faces, which are removed from our sight. The observer sees rooms, bizarre landscapes, animals, still lifes. Baryta prints are presented in glass cabinets. A poem. Dried butterflies and two plastic corsets are displayed. »Behind closed eyes« appears to be a skeleton of a story. These are the relics of a past. Similar motifs surface, images repeat themselves, symbols refer to a deeper level of meaning. Time seems to take on a cyclic rather than linear nature. The observer is caught in the middle of the contrast between a dream world and reality. Voyeurism, intimacy, secrecy, but also the feeling of exclusion and a quiet melancholia determine the atmosphere. It is a journey through feelings and thoughts, through space and time. A herbarium of human memories. In the end, the fragments of this story amalgamate with our own memories and a new, more complete narrative emerges.**

»Hinter geschlossenen Liedern«
Student: Kathi Ficek | Semester theme: Diploma | Semester: 9, Photo design
Type/Scope: 30 images and exhibition | Mentoring: Prof. Cindy Gates | Free submission

Epson art photo award 2009

»Monster«

Student: Christian Scharfe | Semester theme: Monster | Semester: 5, Photo design
Type/Scope: 3 images | Mentoring: Thomas Linke | Free submission

Durch gezielt eingesetzte Veränderungen werden aus Menschen angsteinflößende Kreaturen. Mir war wichtig, das Endprodukt nur aus dem Ausgangsfoto und einigen Texturen entstehen zu lassen. **Through systematic alterations, people are transformed into scary creatures. It was important to me to have the end product develop only from the initial photograph and some textures.**

Canto VII ist ein Projekt, inspiriert von den Werken Dante Alighieris, realisiert mit der Camera Obscura. Bei dieser Kamera wird das Bild auf dem Negativ durch eine kleine Öffnung in der Vorderseite eines lichtdichten Gehäuses erzeugt. Die so entstandenen Bilder haben eine besondere Optik, die in der Regel unscharf und weich bei gleichbleibender Tiefenschärfe ist. Hinzu kommt in meinen Fotografien die Wirkung der Farben, entstanden durch exotisches und zum großen Teil abgelaufenes und/oder falsch gelagertes Filmmaterial. Diese Faktoren gaben mir die Möglichkeit, Erinnerungsbilder aus Dantes Leben zu zeigen, die Erinnerung Dantes an seine geliebte, verlorene Heimat nach seiner Verbannung. **Canto VII** is a project inspired by Dante Alighieri's works realised with the camera obscura. The camera obscura creates an image on the negative by means of a small opening on the front side of a light-proof casing. The photographs thus created have a special optic, which is usually blurred and soft at a constant depth of field. In addition, my photographs show the effect of colours which came about through exotic and, for the large part, expired and/ or incorrectly stored film material. These factors gave me the possibility to show memory pictures from Dante's life: Dante's memory of his beloved, lost homeland after his banishment.

»Canto VII«
Student: Melanie Kutscha | Semester theme: Diploma | Semester: 9, Graphic design
Type/Scope: Book, 100 images, Poster series | Mentoring: Prof. Dieter Ziegenfeuter

Photos: Stefan Becker

Thema dieser Installation ist die »Erleuchtung«, die uns Bücher, Texte oder Gedichte bringen sollen. Diese Erleuchtung wollte ich visualisieren. Dazu habe ich ein transparentes Buch erstellt, dessen Textvorlage aus dem Roman »Alles ist Erleuchtet« von Jonathan Safran Foer stammt. Die im Roman stattfindende Erleuchtung wird im Titel bereits aufgegriffen und eignet sich daher optimal. Der komplette Inhalt des Romans ist auf transparenten Seiten abgedruckt und zwischen Plexiglasscheiben platziert, die wie Buchseiten modelliert wurden. Auf der Lichtsäule wird das transparente Buch unterleuchtet, was die Erleuchtung visuell darstellt. **The subject of this installation is the »illumination« we can find in books, texts or poetry. I wanted to visualise this illumination. To achieve this, I have compiled a transparent book, whose original text comes from the German translation of the novel Everything is Illuminated by Jonathan Safran Foer. The illumination that takes place in the novel is already taken up in the title, and therefore fits perfectly. The full content of the novel is printed on transparent pages and placed between sheets of acrylic glass which have been modelled to resemble pages of a book. The transparent book is lit up from below on the light pillar; thus visualising illumination.**

»Die Erleuchtung«
Student: Sergej Stele | Semester theme: Light | Semester: 1, Object and Interior design
Type/Scope: Lighting installation | Mentoring: Prof. Magareta Hesse | Free submission

Vielseitig kombinierbar passt sich »The Casket« an jede Wohnsituation an. Ob direkt an der Wand oder mitten im Raum, es entstehen immer interessante Kombinationen von edlem Schrankelement und praktischem Hocker. Die Elemente sind stapelbar und können beliebig gewendet werden. Die kompakte und quadratische Form ermöglicht es. Die Grundform ist aus Holz und mit einer strukturierten Vinyltapete bezogen, die Innenseiten des Würfels mit Aluminiumplatten kaschiert. Es entsteht ein einzigartiger Kontrast zwischen der matt-gerillten Struktur der Tapete und dem glänzend-glatten Aluminium. Die Quadrate werden zu ausgefallenen Sitzmöglichkeiten. EVA-Schaum-Platten [3 mm] auf der Sitzfläche dienen als Polster. »The Casket« multi-purpose combinations adapt to any living situation. Whether directly against the wall or in the middle of a room, one can always create interesting combinations ranging from noble cupboard elements to practical stools. The elements are stackable and can be used any way you like. This is made possible by the compact and square form. The basic form is made of wood and covered with structured vinyl wallpaper; the inside of the cube is clad with aluminium plates. This creates a unique contrast between the matt-grooved structure of the wallpaper and the shiny-smooth aluminium. The squares transform into unusual seating furniture. EVA foam sheets [3 mm] on the seat serve as cushioning.

»The Casket«

Student: Alicja Jelen | Semester theme: Object installation | Semester: 7, Object and Interior design
Type/Scope: 2 models | Mentoring: Axel Finke | Free submission

Ich stellte mich vor einen Club, um Menschen zu fotografieren, die von ihrer durchgemachten Nacht gezeichnet waren. Ich wollte einen Widerspruch zu ihrem Aussehen und ihrer Haltung herstellen. Durch das von mir gewählte Licht wollte ich sie als Heilige darstellen, die sie ganz und gar nicht sind. Ich habe den Leuten nichts außer deren Position vorgegeben, um möglichst viele verschiedene Reaktionen und Emotionen hervorrufen und festhalten zu können.

I positioned myself in front of a club to photograph people who bore the signs of having partied all night. I wanted to create a contrast to their appearance and their bearing. I therefore chose a lighting that would portray them as saints, which they most definitely were not. I did not ask for anything else except that they stand in a certain spot, so as to be able to evoke and capture the most reactions and emotions possible.

»Lichter der Nacht«
Student: Danilo Lehmann | Semester theme: Ligth Latiwes | Semester: 2, Photo design
Type/Scope: 11 images | Mentoring: Prof. Jörg Winde | Free submission

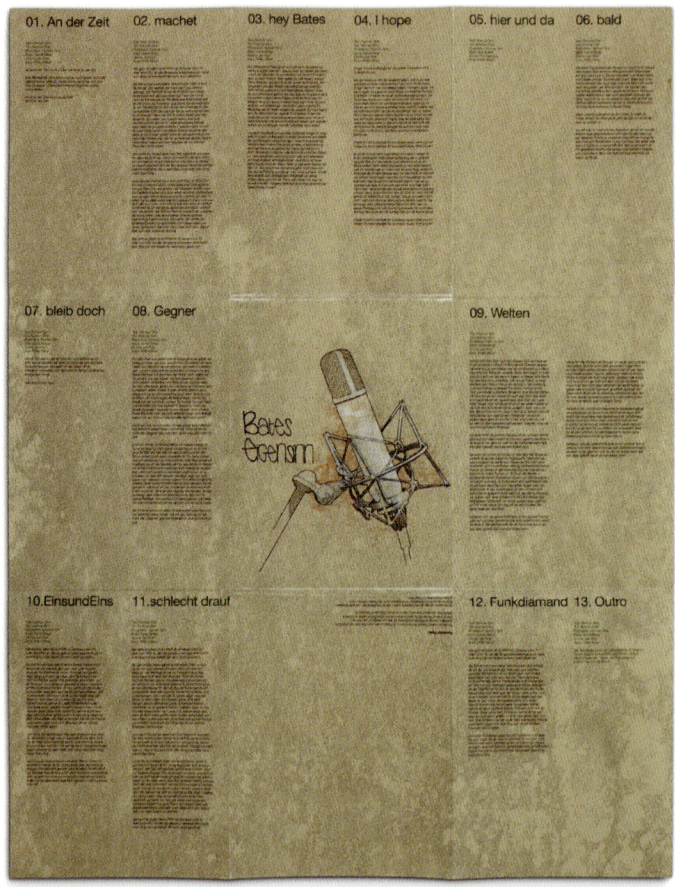

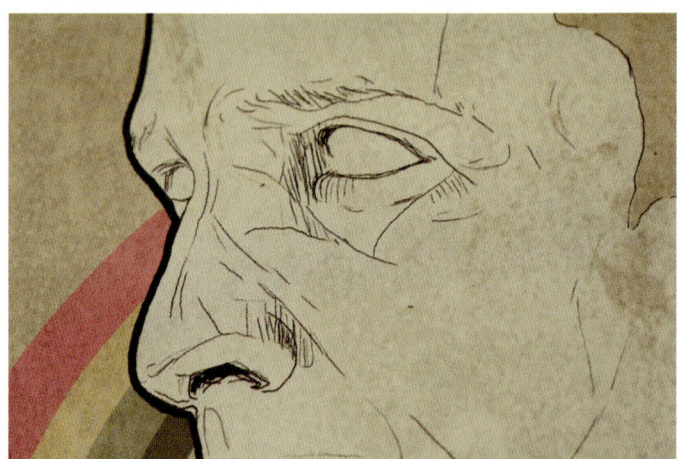

»Bates«

Student: Holger Jendrusch | Semester theme: Music | Semester: 7, Graphic design
Type/Scope: CD case | Mentoring: Prof. Johannes Graf | Free submission

Im Vordergrund der Gestaltung steht die illustratorische Arbeit. Diese spiegelt die handgemachte Musik des Künstlers Bates, der seine Anfänge in der urbanen Hip-Hop-Kultur hat, wider. Es geht um echte, kreative Musik, visualisiert durch den beflügelten Künstler. **In design, the illustrative work takes the most prominent place. This is reflected in the hand-made music of the artist Bates whose beginnings can be found in the urban Hip-Hop culture. This is real, creative music, visualised by an inspired artist.**

»tv-Kulturfernsehen« ist ein Konzept für eine Fernsehprogrammempfehlung, das die besten Beiträge aus den Genres Architektur [A], Design [D], Film [F], Kunst [K], Literatur [L], Musik [M] und Information [I] filtert und in einer dreiwöchigen Programmvorschau listet. Während sich auf der Innenseite des Plakats die Informationen zu den Sendebeiträgen befinden, befasst sich die Außenseite mit einem besonderen Sendebeitrag aus dem gesamten Zeitraum. Bei der Gestaltung nimmt die Arbeit Bezug auf die Lochmaske, welche in Röhrenfernsehern alle Bilder über einzelne Punkte [in meiner Arbeit wurden diese Löcher mit einer Nadel gestochen] darstellt. **»tv-cultural television«** is a concept for a television programme recommendation, which filters the best contributions from the genres architecture [A], design [D], film [F], Kunst [art] [K], literature [L], music [M] and information [I] and lists these in a three-week programme preview. While information on the inside of the poster provides information to the shows, the outside is dedicated to a special programme selected out of the whole period. For its design, the work refers to the shadow mask, which in CRT TV sets displays all pictures via individual dots [in my work these holes are punched with a needle].

»tv-Kulturfernsehen«
Student: Robert Börsting | Semester theme: Free subject | Semester: 8, Graphic design
Type/Scope: Fold-out poster | Mentoring: Prof. Xuyen Dam

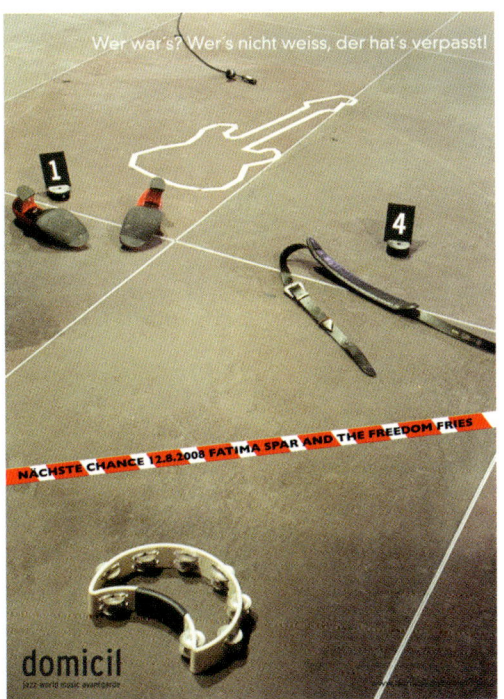

Uns geht es darum, die Konzertveranstaltungen des Dortmunder Jazzclubs Domicil mehr in den Vordergrund zu stellen und den ursprünglichen Charakter hervorzuheben. Wir wollen das Unmittelbare von Live-Musik zeigen. Um es schmackhaft zu machen und die Stimmung eines Konzerts oder einer Veranstaltung erlebbar zu machen, haben wir die Bühne als Tatort inszeniert. Die verschiedenen Accessoires – welche mit Unterstützung des Kriminalkommissariats Dortmund durchnummeriert wurden – lassen auf unterschiedliche musikalische Richtungen und Veranstaltungen schließen und verweisen auf das vielfältige Repertoire des Domicils. **Our aim is a more predominant positioning of the concert events of the Dortmund Jazz Club Domicil and to emphasise its down-to-earth character. We want to show the immediacy of live music. To whet the appetite a little and to allow the ambience of a concert or an event to be experienced, we have staged the backdrop as a crime scene. The various accessories – which were numbered with the help of the criminal detectives' office Dortmund – allow a conclusion of various musical styles and events and point out Domicil's multi-faceted repertoire.**

»Tatort Domicil«

Student: Elke Hübner, Ariane Tillmann | Semester theme: Sounds, images, places | Semester: Graphic design, Photo design
Type/Scope: Poster series | Mentoring: Prof. Sabine an Huef, Prof. Jörg Winde | Free submission

»exhibitiondesign«

Student: Marcel Paul Bleeck | Semester theme: Diploma | Semester: 8, Object and Interior design
Type/Scope: Showroom | Mentoring: Prof. Nora Fuchs

Die »Bright Tradeshow« ist eine Messe für Streetwear, Skateboarding, Sneaker und Fashion, die zweimal im Jahr in Frankfurt am Main im alten Polizeipräsidium, mit circa 300 Ausstellern statt findet. Marcel Bleeck gestaltete den Showroom der Firma Forvert/Köln als Diplomthema und gewinnt noch vor der Diplomprüfung mit der Realisation den 1. Platz. Dachlattenstrukturen, alles schwarzweiß, wehende Fäden im Raum, das Logo fliegt durch den Raum und wird zum Sitzmöbel erklärt, eine bewegte, aber zugleich auch strenge Rauminstallation. The »Bright Tradeshow« is a fair for street wear, skate boarding, sneakers and fashion, that takes place twice a year at Frankfurt am Main in the former police headquaters with about 300 exhibitors. Marcel Bleeck has designed a show room for the Forvert Company/Cologne as his diploma theme and by realizing his work is winning the first price even before having been examined. Structures of roof slats, all in black and white, blowing threads in the room, the logo moves through space and is declared a seat furniture, forming a moving, yet clearly regulatorily room installation.

»Domicil«

Student: Nico Schmitz | Semester theme: Sounds, images, places | Semester: 8, Photo design
Type/Scope: Poster series | Mentoring: Prof. Jörg Winde | Free submission

»Mythos Blond«

Student: Eva Baales | Semester theme: Fairy tales and myths | Semester: 10, Photo design
Type/Scope: 5 images | Mentoring: Prof. Jörg Winde | Free submission

In der Antike war das dem Gold entsprechende Blond die Haarfarbe der Göttinnen und Götter, der Heroen und der Herrscher. Der Haarfarbe Blond haftet ein Mythos an, der bis heute Vorurteile nährt und Ideale sät. Meine Arbeit ist eine Selbstportrait-Strecke. Hierbei stellt sich mir die Aufgabe, Selbst- und Außenwahrnehmung auszuloten, um dem Thema ICH auch nur ansatzweise gerecht zu werden. Mich auf die Haarfarbe zu beschränken erschien mir in vielerlei Hinsicht sinnvoll und sinnlos. Die Dialektik der Selbst- und Fremdwahrnehmung reizt mich besonders und gilt es am Objekt fotografisch zu ergründen. Weder möchte ich die typische Blondine als Männerphantasien stimulierendes Pin Up Poster-Girl geben, noch mein Gesicht unterschiedlichen Frisuren schenken. Die Herausforderung, insbesondere für meine Make-Up Artist und Stylistin, liegt darin, mich zu verfremden, ohne mir Prothesen wie falsche Nasen etc. aufzukleben. **In the Ancient World, the colour of the gods and goddesses, the heroes and rulers was blonde, analogous to gold. There is a myth associated with the hair colour blonde which, even today, nurtures prejudice and propagates ideals. My work is a self-portrait line. Hereby, I set myself the task of exploring self-perception and external perception so as to do justice to the subject »I«, albeit only rudimentarily. I felt that restricting myself to hair colour was, in many respects, meaningful and meaningless. The dialectic regarding self-perception and external perception was particularly alluring, and the purpose was to determine this photographically on an object. I would neither like to present the typical blonde as a pin-up stimulating men's fantasies, nor give my face up for different hairstyles. The challenge, in particular for my make-up artist and stylist, is to distort my appearance without the use of props such as false noses, etc.**

049 PETER WEIBEL, JAN HOET

IN KONTAKT MIT...
PETER WEIBEL, Vorstand des ZKM Karlsruhe, Kurator und Künstler

REFLEKTOR: Lieber Peter Weibel, für unsere zweite REFLEKTOR-Ausgabe nehme ich stellvertretend für das ganze Redaktionsteam heute per Internet mit Ihnen Kontakt auf. Ein E-Mail-Interview ersetzt inzwischen in den meisten Fällen eine direkte und persönliche Kontaktaufnahme und delegiert den Dialog in das Reich von Bits und Bytes. Wie können wir dabei sicher gehen, dass unsere Fragen von Ihnen, dem CEO des Zentrums für Kunst und Medientechnologie in Karlsruhe, beantwortet werden und nicht von irgendeiner künstlichen Intelligenz?

WEIBEL: Liebe Pamela Scorzin, wenn wir Glück haben, sehen wir uns morgen. Also Kontakt ON. Wenn wir Pech haben, bin ich in Stuttgart und wir sehen uns vielleicht nicht. Also Kontakt OFF. Ich mache in jedem Fall gerne bei Ihrem REFLEKTOR-Projekt mit... Wenn jemand klug ist, soll er zeigen, dass er klug ist? Gehört es zur Klugheit, zu verbergen, dass man klug ist? Wenn jemand künstlich klug ist, dann hat er allen Grund, zu verbergen, dass seine Klugheit nur künstlich ist bzw. auf künstlichen Hilfsmitteln basiert. Darüber hinaus gibt es den berühmten Turing-Test, der behauptet, dass zwischen natürlicher und künstlicher Intelligenz nicht mehr unterschieden werden kann, wenn ein Computer und ein Mensch hinter einem Vorhang Antworten auf die gleichen Fragen geben. Also ziehe ich es vor, hinter dem Vorhang zu bleiben.

REFLEKTOR: Welches Medium bevorzugen Sie persönlich für eine Kontaktaufnahme – insbesondere in Ihrer Funktion als künstlerischer Leiter, Kurator und Künstler?

WEIBEL: Wie das frivole Wort »Kontakthof« schon sagt, ist Nähe bzw. der Prozess, der zur Nähe führt, also die Kontaktaufnahme, etwas Anrüchiges. Einer meiner Helden, der Logiker Kurt Gödel, hat Gespräche mit seinen Kollegen am Institute for Advanced Studies in Princeton nur am Telefon geführt, stundenlang, auch wenn die Kollegen im Nebenzimmer saßen und die Kollegen ihn baten, das Gespräch doch persönlich zu führen, das heißt face to face – von Angesicht zu Angesicht. Auf die Frage, warum er dieses bescheidene Ansinnen ablehnte, antwortete Gödel: »If somebody is close to me, I feel him on top of me.« Für Gödel bedeutete also Nähe soviel wie Kontrolle. Nahe sein bedeutete für Gödel, unter jemandem zu sein. Nähe war also eine Form der ›Gouvernmentalität‹. »Rücken Sie näher!« ist weniger ein Ausdruck der Kameraderie als ein militärisches Kommando. Insofern bin ich ein Schüler Gödels. Ich ziehe in jeder Funktion die indirekte Kontaktaufnahme vor. Am liebsten in der Tat über E-Mail. Früher über Telefon. Alles, was darüber hinausgeht, scheint mir zu obszön oder zu militärisch bzw. unhygienisch. Kontaktaufnahme birgt die Gefahr von Infektionen. Nicht einmal telematische Kontaktaufnahme bannt die Gefahr von Viren, siehe die Computerviren!

REFLEKTOR: Können Sie sich noch erinnern, wann Sie zuletzt einen handgeschriebenen Brief verschickt haben?

WEIBEL: Ja, als Kind zum Geburtstag meiner Mutter.

REFLEKTOR: Im Foyer des ZKM Karlsruhe nimmt seit 2006 als erstes ein Spotlight mit Frauenstimme inquisitorisch Kontakt mit den Besuchern auf – noch bevor sie eigentlich an die Ticket-Theke treten [www.accessproject.net]. Was hat Sie dazu bewogen, gerade diese interaktive Medienkunstarbeit von Marie Sester im Eingangsbereich des ZKM Karlsruhe installieren zu lassen?

WEIBEL: Das Spotlight stellt der Besucher in ein Scheinwerferlicht. Das ZKM breitet gewissermaßen einen Teppich des Lichts aus und krönt den Besucher mit einem Lichtkegel zum Star. Dies ist gerade, was ich den Besuchern mitteilen möchte. Für das ZKM sind sie, die Besucher, das Wichtigste. Die Stars, die wir verehren. Die Arbeit von Marie Sester soll den Besuchern sagen: Hier im ZKM, dem Mekka der interaktiven Medien, zählt am meisten der Besucher. Und zwar nicht die Quantität, sondern der Besucher in seiner Einzigartigkeit als Individuum. Ohne ihn geht buchstäblich nichts in diesem Hause. Er wird mit Licht und Stimme auserkoren bzw. angesprochen, in eine Art profanen Heiligenschein gestellt, um ihn zu vereinzeln und auszuzeichnen. Der Besucher ist der Star. Wir, das Museum, sind Dienstleister. Wir dienen der Kunst und ihren Besuchern.

REFLEKTOR: Sie gelten seit Jahren als euphorischer Vertreter der neuen Medientechnologien und leiten nun bereits seit 1999 eine weltweit wirklich einzigartige Kulturinstitution, die weit über ihre Funktion als Museum hinaus, in ihrer Arbeit Forschung und Produktion, Ausstellung und Veranstaltungen, Vermittlung und Dokumentation in sich vereint. So wurden und werden am ZKM Karlsruhe viele netzbasierte Medienkunstwerke entwickelt und mit einem interessanten Interface ausgestattet – wie beispielsweise »CloudBrowsing« [2008/09] oder »T-Visionarium I und II« [seit 2005], die in der aktuellen Ausstellung »YOU_ser 2.0: Celebration of the Consumer« zu erfahren sind. Diese aktuelle Ausstellung macht sich im Grunde gesehen das enorme Kommunikationsbedürfnis und die Kontaktfreude der Menschen zu eigen. Würden Sie uns die Hintergründe und Ziele der »YOU_ser Art« etwas näher erläutern?

WEIBEL: Vollkommen richtig, Kommunikation ist mehr als eine anthropologische Konstante. Kommunikation und Informationsaustausch sind Bedürfnis und Notwendigkeit auch der Tiere und der Pflanzen. Jede Zelle lebt von Kommunikation. Was mich an der Kommunikation interessiert, kann durch einen kleinen anagrammatischen Rüttler bzw. Schüttler angezeigt werden: Tauschen Sie die Position von K mit A, dann lesen Sie das Wort Aktion. Mich interessiert der Übergang von der Kommunikation zur Aktion, zur Partizipation und Interaktion. User-Art stellt den Besucher in den Mittelpunkt, der aber nicht nur ein Betrachter ist, sondern auch ein Benutzer, ein User. Mit der Ausstellung »YOU_ser 2.0: Celebration of the Consumer« widmet sich das ZKM den Auswirkungen der netzbasierten, globalen Kreation auf

Kunst und Gesellschaft und zeigt erstmals in technisch avancierten Installationen den Zusammenhang zwischen »user generated content« und zeitgenössischer Kunst. Die in der Ausstellung präsentierten neuen Installationen übertragen das im Internet entwickelte Potenzial der Mitgestaltung durch den Benutzer in einen künstlerischen Kontext und ermöglichen den BesucherInnen, sich zu emanzipieren. Sie können als KünstlerInnen, KuratorInnen und ProduzentInnen agieren. Die AusstellungsbesucherInnen stehen als Nutzer, als emanzipierte Konsumenten im Zentrum. »DU [YOU] bist der Inhalt der Ausstellung!« »DU [YOU] bist der Inhalt der Welt!« Aber auch Nutzer [User] der Welt und Teil der Welt, somit Teilnehmer der Welt. Wer ein Teil der Welt ist, trägt klarerweise auch Verantwortung für die Welt, von der er ein Teil ist. Durch seine Teilnahme hast DU [YOU], der User [YOUser], die Chance, die Welt zu ändern. In technologisch avanciertesten Environments und Installationen werden der aktuellste Stand der Kunst der Teilnahme [The Art of Participation], the pARTicipation, gezeigt. Damit wird jene Tendenz unterstützt, die sich im Geiste der Aufklärung für Demokratie, für den schwellenlosen Zugang zur Bildung aller und für die Kreativität aller Menschen einsetzt.

REFLEKTOR: Inwieweit erleben Sie das ZKM Karlsruhe auch als Plattform für internationale Kontakte? Als wir im Januar 2009 mit unserem Dortmunder Seminar »Digital Art« bei Ihnen in Karlsruhe zu Gast waren, genossen wir vor allem die experimentelle Laborsituation, in der dort die Werke stehen, und registrierten die Vielzahl von internationalen Gästen, die sich auch schon im Foyer zu direkten Gesprächen begegneten!

WEIBEL: Oh ja, das ZKM ist eine enorme Plattform für internationale Kontakte. Gerade vorgestern, am Samstag den 27. Juni 2009, hatten wir im Vortragssaal ein Symposium mit der Columbia University, bei dem über 20 Diskutanten anwesend waren, u.a. Beat Wyss, Noam Elcott und Keith Moxey. Gleichzeitig hatten wir im Medientheater ein Seminar, geleitet von Hans Belting mit Ning Ding, Patrick D. Flores, Anthony Gardner, Elizabeth Harney, Agung Hujatnika, Carol Lu, Jesmael Mataga, Charles Merewether, Elizabeth Rogers, Samuel Sidibé und Adele Tan. Außerdem traf ich noch Freddy Paul Grunert, ein Künstler aus Italien, eine Doktorandin aus Kalifornien, Marina Hassapopoulou, dann zwei Professoren vom Clark Institute Massachussetts. Und das Schöne ist in der Tat, dass man mit all diesen Leuten im Foyer direkt Kontakt aufnehmen kann. So ist es nicht alle Tage, aber fast alle Tage!

REFLEKTOR: Wenn wir in 100 Jahren noch einmal Kontakt aufnehmen könnten, welches Medium stünde uns nach Ihren Prognosen dann wohl zur Verfügung? Werden die Menschen sich trotz allen telematischen Medien vielleicht wieder mehr nach direkten, persönlichen und physischen Kontakten sehnen?

WEIBEL: In 100 Jahren wird das dominieren, was heute als paranormale Phänomene marginalisiert wird, d.h. eine Wahrnehmung und Kommunikation scheinbar jenseits der natürlichen Sinnesorgane, genauer gesagt, scheinbar jenseits der Grenzen und Kanalkapazitäten und Funktionen der natürlichen Sinnesorgane. Wenn heute Nobelpreisträger Brian David Josephson [»Josephson junction«] öffentlich erzählt, er habe einen Test gemacht mit einem 18-jährigen chinesischen Mädchen, das ein von ihm mit dem Wort Wittgenstein beschriebenes Blatt Papier in den Mund nahm und kaute, also gewissermaßen mit der Zunge las und dann dieses Wort genauso, wie er es geschrieben hatte, nämlich in zwei Zeilen, ebenfalls auf ein Blatt Papier schrieb, ohne es aus dem Mund genommen zu haben, dann wird er belächelt und als pathologisch diffamiert. Mit Hilfe der Technologie wird es möglich sein, die Impulse vom Auge auf die Zunge zu lenken und das Gehirn wird lernen, die Signale der Zunge so zu interpretieren, dass es einem rudimentären Sehen gleich kommt. Der synästhetische Traum wird sich erfüllen: ein Sinnesorgan kann die Aufgabe des anderen Sinnesorgans übernehmen. Ebenso werden Fernempfindungen und Nahempfindungen austauschbar und übertragbar sein. Wenn heute schon Jugendliche im Kino sitzen und beim Anschauen eines Films ständig mit ihrem Handy beschäftigt sind und mailen, sehen wir, dass die Zukunft des physischen Kontaktes nicht allzu rosig ausschaut, sondern im Gegenteil die Macht der telematischen Medien zunimmt. In 100 Jahren werden die technischen Medien die Arbeit unserer natürlichen Sinnesorgane auf eine heute noch unvorstellbare Weise verändern. Kontakt wird dann weder ein Signal der Proximität, noch ein Signal für Außerirdische sein.

REFLEKTOR: Als Initiator, Herausgeber und Verfasser zahlreicher kulturwissenschaftlicher Abhandlungen, was bedeutet Ihnen persönlich heute im Zeitalter der Digitalisierung und globalen Vernetzung das doch bereits recht antiquarisch anmutende Medium Buch? Was ist für Sie eine gute Buchgestaltung?

WEIBEL: Es gibt das Gerücht, jeder Mensch habe eine Schwäche. Deswegen habe auch ich eine romantische, altmodische Seite. Ich bin ein ink addict und paper sniffer. Der Geruch von Papier, der Anblick von Buchstaben versetzt mich in Ekstase. Die Anmut eines Buches ist ein Versprechen des Glücks, nämlich ein Hafturlaub, aus den Nöten des Alltags und den vier Gitterstäben von Raum und Zeit befreit zu werden. Gute Buchgestaltung bedeutet für mich leicht lesbare Buchstaben, leichtes Papier und schwer verdaulicher Inhalt. Bücher sind Stollen in dem Berg des Wissens. Ich bin ein Arbeiter im Bergwerk der Bücher. Jeden Tag ein neues Buch ist meine Devise. Die Welt begann wie ein Buch: Am Anfang war das Wort.

REFLEKTOR: Peter Weibel, wir danken Ihnen herzlich für die gemeinsame Seminarsitzung am 17. Januar 2009 im ZKM Foyer und für die Beantwortung unserer REFFLEKTOR-Fragen.

[Das Interview mit Peter Weibel führte Pamela C. Scorzin für das REFLEKTOR2-Team, Juni 2009]

IN CONTACT WITH...
PETER WEIBEL, CEO of the ZKM Karlsruhe [Center for Art and Media Technology Karlsruhe], Curator and Poly-Artist

REFLEKTOR: Dear Peter Weibel, for the second edition of REFLEKTOR, I am contacting you on behalf of the entire editorial team via the internet. Meanwhile, an e-mail interview often replaces direct and personal contact and relegates the dialogue in the sphere of bits and bytes. How can we be sure that our questions are answered by you, the CEO of the Center for Art and Media Technology Karlsruhe, and not by some kind of artificial intelligence?

WEIBEL: Dear Pamela Scorzin, if we are lucky, we will see each other tomorrow. In this case, contact on. If we are unlucky, I will be in Stuttgart and we may not see each other. In this case, contact off. In any case, I happily take part in your REFLEKTOR project... If a person is intelligent shall he show that he is intelligent? Is hiding one's intelligence part of being intelligent? If a person is artificially intelligent, he has every reason to hide the fact that his intelligence is only artificial or that it is based on artificial aids. Furthermore, there is the famous Turing test which alleges that, if a computer and a person are positioned behind a curtain and asked to give an answer to an identical question, one can no longer distinguish between natural and artificial intelligence. So, I prefer to stay behind the curtain.

REFLEKTOR: Which means of communication do you actually prefer when making contact — in particular in your capacity as the artistic director, curator and artist?

WEIBEL: As implied in the frivolous words contact zone, closeness or the process leading to closeness, that is to say the initial contact, is somewhat loathsome. One of my heroes, the logician Kurt Gödel, only held conversations with his colleagues at the Institute for Advanced Studies in Princeton over the telephone, for endless hours, even if the colleagues were right next door and asked them to hold the conversation in person — that is, face to face. Asked why he rejected this modest request, Gödel answered: »If somebody is close to me, I feel him on top of me«. For Gödel, therefore, closeness implied control. For Gödel, being close meant being under somebody's control. Closeness thus became a form of governmental mentality. »Come closer!« is not so much an expression of comradeship as a military command. In this respect, I am a follower of Gödel. In any capacity, I prefer an initial indirect contact. Actually, the best is via e-mail. Previously this was the telephone. Anything above and beyond that, as far as I am concerned, feels too obscene or too military or unhygienic. Contact harbours the danger of infections. Not even telematic contact averts the danger of viruses — just look at computer viruses!

REFLEKTOR: Can you remember when you last sent a handwritten letter?

WEIBEL: Yes, as a child for my mother's birthday.

REFLEKTOR: Since 2006, there has been a spotlight in the foyer of the ZKM with a woman's voice inquisitively making contact with the visitors — even before they actually reach the ticket counter [www.accessproject.net]. What was your reason behind installing specifically this interactive media work of art by Marie Sester in the entrance area of the ZKM?

WEIBEL: The spotlight places the visitor in the limelight. The ZKM more or less lays out a carpet of light and crowns the visitor with a beam of light on a star. This is what I actually want to convey to the visitors. That they, the visitors, are the most important thing for ZKM. Stars that we revere. The message of Marie Sester's work is: Here, at the ZKM, the Mecca of interactive media, it is the visitor that counts the most. And this not in quantity, but rather in terms of the visitor's uniqueness as an individual. Literally, nothing at all works without visitors in this house. Each of them has been chosen with light and voice and has been spoken to, placed within a kind of profane halo, so as to single them out and honour them. The visitor is the star. We, the museum, are the service providers. We serve art and its visitors.

REFLEKTOR: For many years you have been considered as a euphoric advocate of new technologies for means of communication and, since 1999, have already been leading a worldwide, really unique cultural institution, which goes far beyond its function as a museum in uniting research and production, exhibition and events, procurement and documentation in its work. Many network-based means of communication were and are being developed at the ZKM Karlsruhe as works of art and equipped with an interesting interface — such as, for example, »CloudBrowsing« [2008/9], or »T-Visionarium I and II« [since 2005], which can be experienced in the current exhibition »YOU_ser 2.0: Celebration of the Consumer«. Basically, this current exhibition takes up the topic of the enormous need for communication and the sociability of people. Would you give us a more detailed explanation about the background and the aim of »YOU_ser Art«?

WEIBEL: Quite right, communication is more than just an anthropological constant factor. Communication and the exchange of information are desires and necessities, which also exist in the animal and plant kingdom. Each cell lives by communication. What interests me about communication can be demonstrated by a small anagram or shaker: Exchange the positions of C with A and then read the word »Action«. My interest lies in the transition from communication to action, to participation and interaction. User Art places the visitor in the centre; however, the visitor is not merely an observer but also a user. With the exhibition »YOU_ser 2.0: Celebration of the Consumer«, the ZKM dedicates itself to the effects on art and society of a network-based, global creation and, for the first time, in a technically advanced installation, shows the connection between the »user generated content« and contemporary art. The new installations presented in the exhibition transfer the user's co-designing potential developed in the internet in an artistic context. They can act as artists, curators and producers and thus actively participate. Visitors to the exhibition, in their part as users, as emancipated consumers, are at centre stage here. »YOU are the content of the exhibition!«, »YOU are the content of the world!« But they are also users of the world and part of the world, and therefore participants in the world. Somebody who is a part of the world naturally also takes responsibility for the world of which he or she is a part. Through this participation, YOU, the YOUser have the opportunity to change the world. The current status of The Art of Participation, the pARTicipation, is shown in highly sophisticated technological environments and installations. Thus, the very tendency that is applied in the spirit of enlightenment for democracy, for the barrierless access to education for all and for the creativity of all people, is supported.

REFLEKTOR: To what extent do you also experience the ZKM Karlsruhe as a platform for international contact? In January 2009, as your guest with our Dortmund Seminar »Digital Art«, we particularly enjoyed the experimental laboratory situation in which the works are positioned, and noticed that the majority of international guests had already started to engage in direct conversation in the foyer.

WEIBEL: Oh yes, the ZKM is a great platform for international contacts. Just the other day, on Saturday, 27 June 2009, we held a symposium with the Columbia University in the lecture hall. There were more than twenty guest speakers present, amongst others Beat Wyss, Noam Elcott and Keith Moxey. At the same time, we held a seminar in the Media Theatre led by Hans Belting with Ning Ding, Patrick D. Flores, Anthony Gardner, Elizabeth Harney, Agung Hujatnika, Carol Lu, Jesmael Mataga, Charles Merewether, Elizabeth Rogers, Samuel Sidibé and Adele Tan. In addition, I also met Freddy Paul Grunert, an artist from Italy, a doctorial candidate from California, Marina Hassapopoulou, as well as two professors from the Clark Institute in Massachusetts. And the beauty is, in fact, that one can make direct contact with all of these people in the foyer. It isn't like that every day, but almost every day!

REFLEKTOR: If we were to get in touch again in, say, 100 years time, which means of communication do you think would be available to us then? Despite all telematic media, won't people have the desire again for more direct, personal and physical contact?

WEIBEL: What today is marginalised as paranormal phenomenon will dominate in 100 years; that is to say, a perception and communication seemingly beyond natural sensory organs, or more precisely put, seemingly beyond the restrictions and channel capacities and functions of natural sensory organs. If Nobel Prize winner, Brian David Josephson, [»Josephson Junction«] today states in public that he did a test with an eighteen-year-old Chinese girl who put a piece of paper with the handwritten word »Wittgenstein« in her mouth, chewed on it – reading it with her tongue, so to speak – and then wrote this word in exactly the same way as he did, namely in two lines, also on a piece of paper without having taken the piece of paper out of her mouth, he is smiled at condescendingly and slandered as pathological. Through the help of technology, it will become possible to direct the impulses from the eye to the tongue and the brain will learn to interpret the tongue's signals so that it resembles a rudimentary type of sight. The synaesthetic dream will become reality: one sensory organ will take over the task of the other sensory organ. Equally, feelings of distance and closeness will be exchangeable and transferrable. If today's youth sit in the cinema and constantly busy themselves with their mobile phone during the film and send mails, we can see that the future of physical contact is not that bright – quite the opposite; the power of telematic

means of communication is increasing. Technical means of communication in 100 years time will change the work of our natural sensory organs in a way that we cannot imagine today. Contact will then neither be a signal of proximity nor a signal for the extraterrestrial.

REFLEKTOR: As the initiator, publisher and author of numerous cultural-scientific essays, what do the rather antiquated means of communication of a book mean to you personally, as seen today in the era of digitalisation and global networking? What do you consider a good book design?

WEIBEL: There is a rumour that every person has a weakness. And that is why I also have a romantic, old-fashioned side to me. I am an ink addict and paper sniffer. The smell of paper, the sight of letters transports me to seventh heaven. The charm of a book is a promise of joy, namely a holiday from prison, to be released from the plight of everyday life and the four bars of space and time. For me, good book design means readable letters, lightweight paper and hard to digest content. Books are underground passages of knowledge. I am a worker in the mine of books. Every day a new book – that's my motto. The world began like a book: In the Beginning was the Word.

REFLEKTOR: Peter Weibel, we thank you kindly for the joint seminar meeting on 17 January 2009 in the ZKM Foyer and for answering our REFKLETOR questions.

[The interview with Peter Weibel was conducted by Pamela C. Scorzin for the REFLEKTOR Team, June 2009]

IN KONTAKT MIT...
JAN HOET, Kurator, Kommunikator und Promotor

REFLEKTOR: Lieber Jan Hoet, um gleich mit einem Ende zu beginnen: Nun, nachdem Sie sich kürzlich vom MARTa Herford, dem neuen zeitgenössischen Museum für Kunst und Design, erbaut von Frank O. Gehry, als Gründungsdirektor verabschiedet haben, könnten Sie in einem Wort [oder einem Satz] diese achtjährige Liaison beschreiben?

HOET: Es war – in einem Wort – anachronistisch, und zwar hinsichtlich der lokalen politischen Situation.

REFLEKTOR: Als ein umtriebiger Kurator, großer Kommunikator und international renommierter Promotor der Künste stehen Sie mit vielen Leuten weltweit in Kontakt. Kann eine neu gegründete Institution wie das Museum für zeitgenössische Kunst und Design in Ostwestfalen-Lippe, das MARTa Herford, tatsächlich eine Plattform für Kontakte und Kreativität werden in einer Region, die zuvor nicht gerade als der Mittelpunkt der Kunstwelt und des spektakulären Designs galt? Wenn Sie als Belgier also auf Ihre Zeit in Herford zurückblicken, was war daran ein Gewinn und was war daran eher ein Verlust?

HOET: Als Gewinn sehe ich das wachsende Interesse an der peripheren Lage. Dazwischen gewannen wir mehr als 500 neue Mitglieder für die Vereinigung der Museumsfreunde. Einige davon begannen auch zeitgenössische Kunst zu sammeln und viele gehen nun in Museen zeitgenössischer Kunst und in die großen Kunstausstellungen anderer Länder und Städte. Viele international bekannte Künstler sind auf Besuch nach Herford gekommen. Die regionale Kunstszene bekam die Gelegenheit mit globalen Diskursen konfrontiert zu werden. Das Konzept eines Dreiklangs von Design – Kunst – Architektur hat sich sehr bewährt. 2008 zählten wir 72.500 Besucher – das bedeutet 10.000 mehr als Einwohner in Herford. Als einen Verlust sehe ich, dass ich es nicht schaffte, die politische Szene, nicht einmal den Großteil der Einwohner, wirklich für die Sache zu gewinnen. Die feindliche Haltung gegenüber der zeitgenössischen Kunst ist in Herford ein Fakt. Dort sieht man ein Museum lediglich als einen ökonomischen Faktor und die Politiker haben nur ihre nächste Wiederwahl im Blick.

REFLEKTOR: Sie haben sicherlich während Ihrer langen beruflichen Karriere über die Jahre hinweg viele Künstler, Architekten und Designer kennen gelernt. Wen mochten Sie am meisten, wen würden Sie gerne noch treffen, und mit wem gerne noch zusammen arbeiten? Mussten Sie jemals jemanden ausstellen, den Sie überhaupt nicht mochten? Und wer wird Ihrer Meinung nach der nächste Superstar der Kunstszene – nach Damien Hirst? Sollten wir etwa auch Casting Shows für Künstler und Designer betreiben wie im englischen Fernsehen?

HOET: Wir haben nur sehr wenige Museen, die Design und Kunst miteinander kombinieren, zwei unterschiedliche Disziplinen [funktional – afunktional], die in einer ambivalenten Haltung zueinander stehen. Für mich ist es sehr interessant zu entdecken, wie Design mit der Schaffung eines Kunstwerkes interferiert und was den Unterschied dabei ausmacht. Nach dieser Erfahrung würde ich sagen, ist es immer noch interessanter ein Kunstwerk zu sehen, in das Design hinein gewirkt hat, als Design, das sich mehr oder weniger als Kunst gebärdet. Meine Lieblingskünstler gegenwärtig? Aus einer nicht aufgeregten Sicht würde ich Ettore Spalletti nennen. Ich habe seine Ausstellung im Museum Kurhaus Kleve gesehen. Aus einer reflektierteren Perspektive würde ich dagegen Matthew Barney nennen. Die Medien sind sehr wichtig und könnten zur Entdeckung neuer, junger Künstler eine größere Rolle spielen. Kunst ist immer noch ein Motor für die Konstruktion unserer Identität. Kunstkritiker in der Medienszene könnten mehr von Sportjournalisten lernen, wie man sich durch Wiederholung auf ein Kunstwerk konzentriert und darauf, wie sich ein Künstler gibt und artikuliert.

REFLEKTOR: Sie selbst waren einst Kunststudent und Boxer – beides sind körperliche Aktivitäten, und beides benötigt viel Disziplin – viel Energie, was charakteristisch für Ihre Persönlichkeit ist. Was gibt Ihnen Energie für den Tag? Wie fanden Sie Ihren Weg in die Welt des Kuratierens? Uns erscheint Ihr fabelhaftes, legendäres Projekt »Chambres d'Amis«, 1986 in Gent, als ein Meilenstein in Ihrer Karriere – diese wundervolle Idee, Kunst in privaten Häusern öffentlich auszustellen und dabei neue Formen der Kontaktaufnahme zum Publikum zu finden. Könnten Sie uns bitte ein wenig mehr über die Idee erzählen, die aus Ihrer Sicht hinter »Chambres d'Amis« steckt?

HOET: »Chambres d'Amis« war zu allererst eine wichtige Angelegenheit. Es ging darum, ein soziales Netzwerk für die zeitgenössische Kunstszene aufzubauen. Zweitens betraf es das Problem des Privaten, das öffentlich wird, und des Öffentlichen, das mehr oder weniger privat wird. Es fand im gleichen Jahr wie Tschernobyl statt. Und es war auch eine Antwort auf den »White Cube« der Galerie. Diese Ausstellung hatte ebenfalls einen Dreiklang: den Betrachter – das Kunstwerk – den Lebensalltag, und ebenso das Psychologische hinter den Erscheinungen.

REFLEKTOR: Nach Ihrer Zeit am MARTa Herford in Ostwestfalen, was sind Ihre aktuellen Projekte und Pläne für die Zukunft? Werden Sie an Kunst und Design-Themen dranbleiben, oder gibt es noch andere Themenfelder aus der Kultur, die Sie uns gerne als nächstes zeigen möchten?

HOET: Im Augenblick kuratiere ich eine Ausstellung aus Anlass des Jubiläums der Varus-Schlacht im Jahre 9 nach Christus [www.colossal.de.com]. Zwanzig Künstler gaben dazu ihren persönlichen Kommentar [meist ironischer Art] ab, indem sie eigens eine Skulptur oder Installation zum Teil direkt auf dem Schlachtfeld oder auf den Ackerflächen um das Schlachtfeld herum anfertigten, zum Beispiel Dennis Oppenheim, Andreas Slominski, Fernando Sánchez Castillo, Massimo Bartolini,

Katinka Bock, Wim Delvoye, Yue Min-Jun, Fabrice Gygi, Bazon Brock und andere. Für Oktober 2009 bereite ich eine Ausstellung in einer renovierten Galerie in Stuttgart, ABTart Galerie, vor, die den Titel »[Z]Art« trägt, was schwierig ins Englische zu übersetzen ist und das Zärtliche, Fragile, Weiche bedeutet, aber »scharf« mit Künstlern wie Alberto Garutti, Ettore Spalletti, Katinka Bock, Ulrich Meister, Michael Budny, Adam Gillam und anderen besetzt ist. Und nächste Jahr werde ich eine völlig neue Version der »Chambres d'Amis« in einer anderen Stadt, Sint Niklaas, 35 Kilometer von Gent entfernt, auflegen. Ich werde sie mit der Literatur verknüpfen und sie wird wieder international angelegt sein.

REFLEKTOR: Am Ende eine Frage, die für unsere Schule hier in Dortmund von einiger Bedeutung ist: Was ist Ihrer ganz persönlichen Meinung nach »gutes Design«? Und bevor wir uns für das Interview bedanken, bitten wir Sie noch, an uns, die Redaktion des REFLEKTOR eine Frage zu richten — wir werden Ihnen die Antwort direkt in unserem REFLEKTOR-Band liefern, der im Herbst vor der nächsten Frankfurter Buchmesse erscheinen soll... Herzlichen Dank und viel Erfolg!

HOET: Ihnen zu antworten, wäre bereits »gutes Design«: Wie Sie wissen, starb vor einer Woche der Designer Pierre Paulin. Ich finde ihn großartig. Er war sich ästhetischer Regeln bewusst und er hatte auch keine Angst vor der Funktionalität. In allem, was er machte, gab es eine klare Stringenz. Sein Design basiert auf Materialexperimenten und geht über die funktionale anthropologische Form hinaus. Er hatte eine asketische Haltung gegenüber den Dingen und Objekten. Das ist eine mögliche Antwort. Sie können Sie aber auch als eine Frage nehmen — und zwar: Wie gelingt es, Design ohne Wiederholung und ohne die Funktion zu ignorieren herzustellen?

REFLEKTOR: Tja, leider hat Pierre Paulin nie in Westfalen gelehrt!

[Das Interview mit Jan Hoet führte Pamela C. Scorzin für das REFLEKTOR-Team, Juni 2009]

IN CONTACT WITH...
JAN HOET, curator, communicator, promoter

REFLEKTOR: To start with an end, Jan Hoet, now that you've just broken up with MARTa Herford, the new contemporary museum of art and design by Frank O. Gehry, could you please describe your 8-year ›affair‹ with MARTa in one single word [or maybe in one sentence] as its founding director?

HOET: Anachronistic [if one word] towards the local political constellation.

REFLEKTOR: As a prolific curator, great communicator and internationally renowned promoter of the arts, you stay in touch with many people from around the world all the time. Can a newly founded institution, a museum of art and design like the MARTa Herford in East Westphalia-Lippe, actually become a platform for contacts and creativity in a region that has formerly not been known as the centre of the art world and spectacular design? So if you, as Belgian, look back at the years at Herford, what has been a gain, what has been a loss?

HOET: As a gain, I see a growing interest towards a peripheric situation. Meanwhile we succeeded in gaining more than 500 members as museum friends. Some of them started to collect contemporary art and many are going to visit museums of contemporary art and the major exhibitions in other countries and cities. Many internationally known artists came to visit the city of Herford. The local artists got the opportunity to confront with a global discourse. The concept of a combination »design-art-architecture« has been firmly established. In 2008 we had 72,500 visitors. That means about 10,000 more than the population. As a loss, I still did not succeed in convincing the political constellation, not even the majority of the inhabitants. The hostility in Herford towards contemporary art is still a fact. They see a museum only as an economic factor and the politicians have only the election in view.

REFLEKTOR: You've surely met a lot of artists, architects and designersduring your long professional career over the years: Who has become your all-time favourite hero? Who would you still love to meet and work with? Have you ever had to show someone who you didn't like at all? And who will be, in your opinion, the next superstar of the art scene after Damien Hirst? Should we actually organise casting shows for artists and designers like they do on television in Great Britain?

HOET: We have very few museums that combine design and art, two different disciplines [function-dysfunction] in ambivalent relation to each other. It seems very interesting to me to discover how design interferes in the creation of an artwork and what makes the distinction. After such an experience, I would say that it is still more interesting to see an artwork in which design has fluctuated than design that tries to be more or less an artwork. My favourite artists today? I would prefer Ettore Spalletti [I saw his exhibition at the museum in Cleve] from a non-spectacular view, and Matthew Barney, from a more sophistic view. The media are very important and could play a more important role in discovering young artists. Art is still a motor in our construction of identity. Art critics in the media-scene could learn a lot from the sport journalists, how to focus by repetition on an artwork and on the way an artist expresses himself.

REFLEKTOR: You've been an art student and a boxing candidate; both are very physical activities, and both need a lot of discipline and a lot of energy, too, which actually seems to be a characteristic of your personality. What gives you energy for the day? How did you find your way into the world of curating? To us, that fabulous legendary project of yours in Ghent, »Chambres d'Amis«, back in 1986, seems to have become an important milestone in your career – the wonderful idea of showing art in private homes and finding new forms to make contact with the audience. Please could you tell us a little bit more about the idea behind ›Chambres d'Amis‹ in Ghent?

HOET: »Chambres d'Amis« for me was firstly an important issue in creating a social network for contemporary art. Secondly, it questioned the problem of the private which becomes public, and the public that becomes more or less private. It was the same year as Chernobyl. It was also an answer towards the »White Cube« of the gallery. This exhibition had a triangular construction: the viewer, the artwork, and the daily-life context, and also the psychological spirit behind the appearances.

REFLEKTOR: After MARTa Herford in East Westphalia, what are your current projects and future plans? Will you stick to art and design issues or are there any other fields of interest in culture you would like to show us next?

HOET: At the moment I am curating a show to mark the occasion of the anniversary of the VARUS-BATTLE of 9 AD [www.colossal.de.com]. Twenty artists gave their personal comment [mostly ironic] by making a sculpture or an installation, partly on the battlefield and partly in the domain of farms around the battlefield, for

example, Dennis Oppenheim, Andreas Slominski, Fernando Sánchez Castillo, Massimo Bartolini, Katinka Bock, Wim Delvoye, Yue Min-Jun, Fabrice Gygi, Bazon Brock and others. For October I am preparing an exhibition with artists, such as, Alberto Garutti, Ettore Spalletti, Katinka Bock, Ulrich Meister, Michael Budny, Adam Gillam and others in a renovated gallery in Stuttgart [ABTart Galerie], entitled «[Z]Art». It is difficult to translate into English but means tender, fragile, soft but sharp-edged. And next year I'm going to try a totally new version of »Chambres d'Amis« in another city, Sint Niklaas, 35 kilometres from Ghent. I will combine it with literature, which will also go international.

REFLEKTOR: To end, a question that is very important to our school here at Dortmund: What do you personally think is »good design«? And before we thank you very much for answering our REFLEKTOR questions, please ask us, the editorial team of REFLEKTOR, a question. We're going to give you the answer straight away in our volume, which is due out in autumn, shortly before the Frankfurt book fair... Thank you very much and good luck!

HOET: To answer what could be »good design«, as you know the French designer Pierre Paulin died a week ago. I think he is really great. He was aware of some aesthetic rules and he was not afraid of function. In everything he did there was a clear distinction. His design is based on experimenting with materials and is about functional anthropological form. He had an ascetic attitude towards things and objects. This is one possible answer. You can also put it as a question: How do you make design without recycling and without ignoring function?

REFLEKTOR: Well, but unfortunately Pierre Paulin has never taught at Westfalia!

[The Interview with Jan Hoet was conducted by Pamela C. Scorzin for the REFLEKTOR Team, June 2009]

061  WORKS TWO

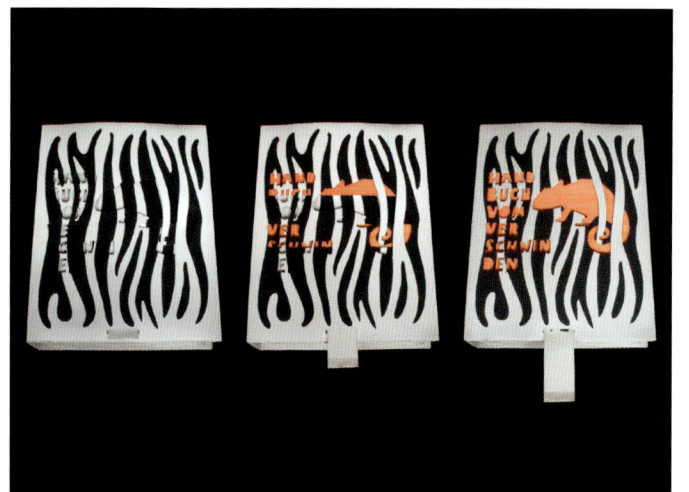
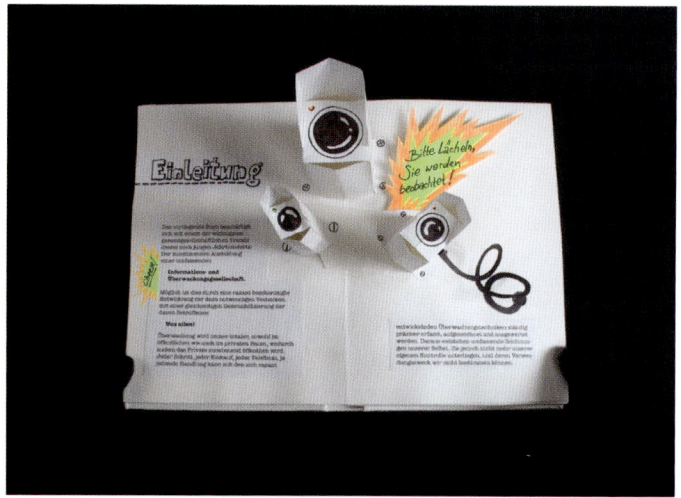
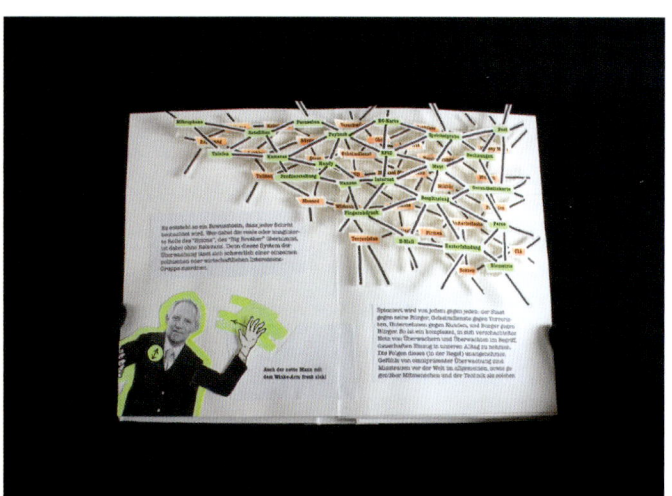
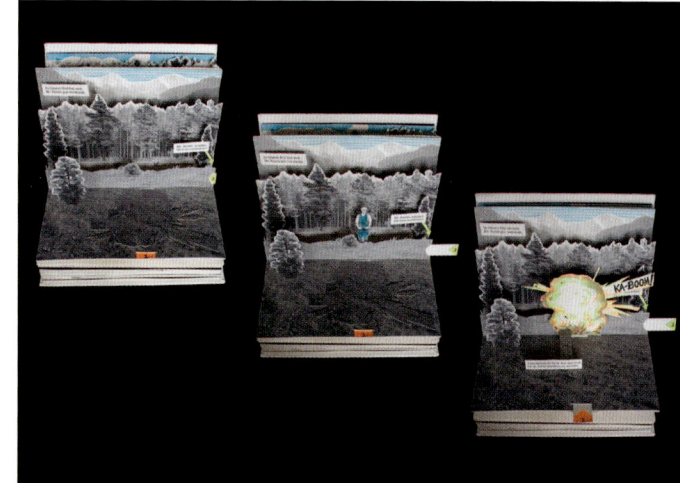

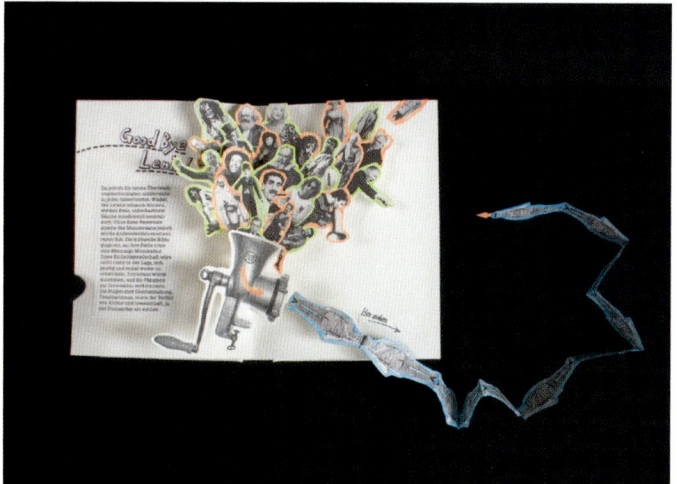

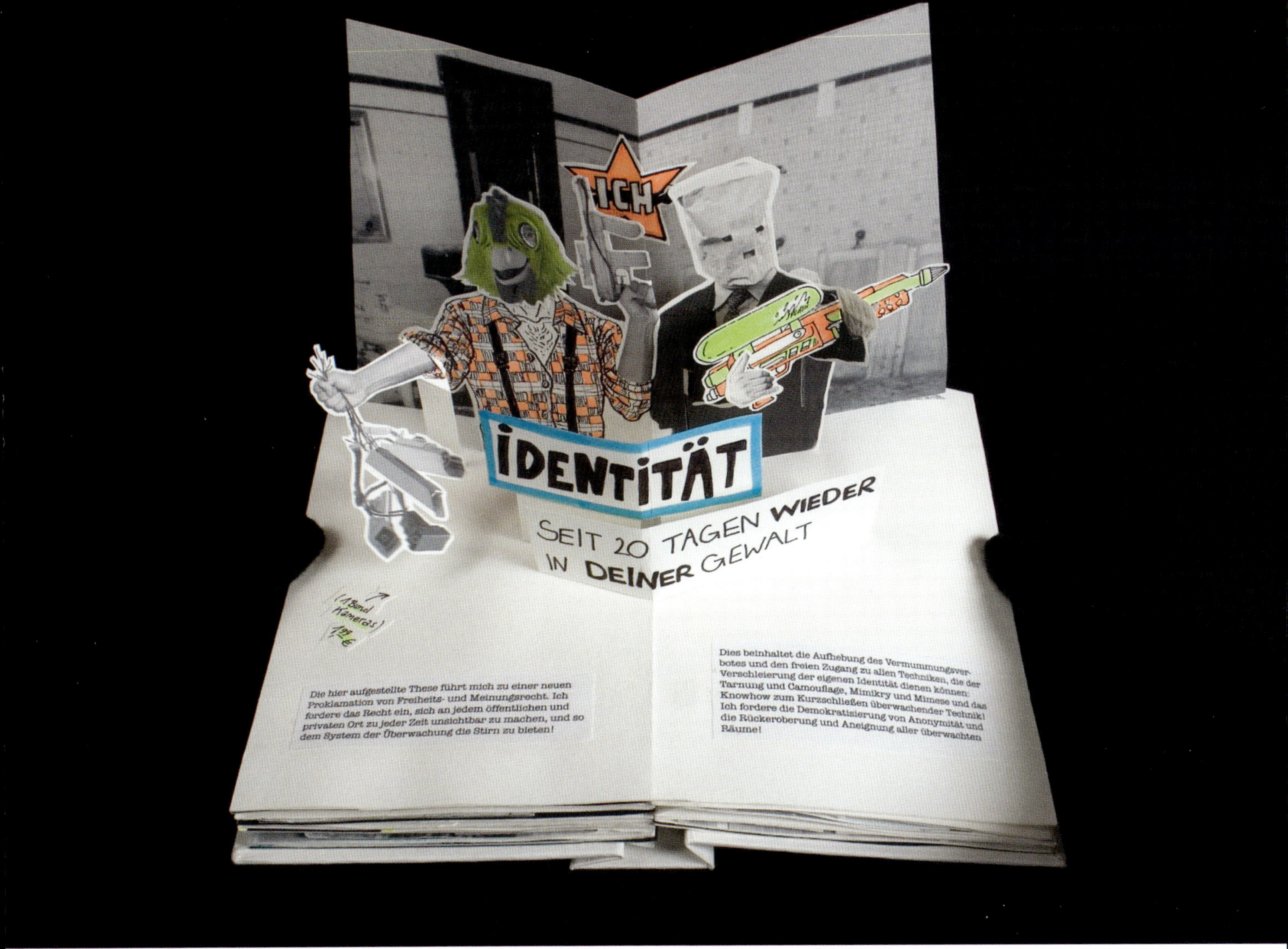

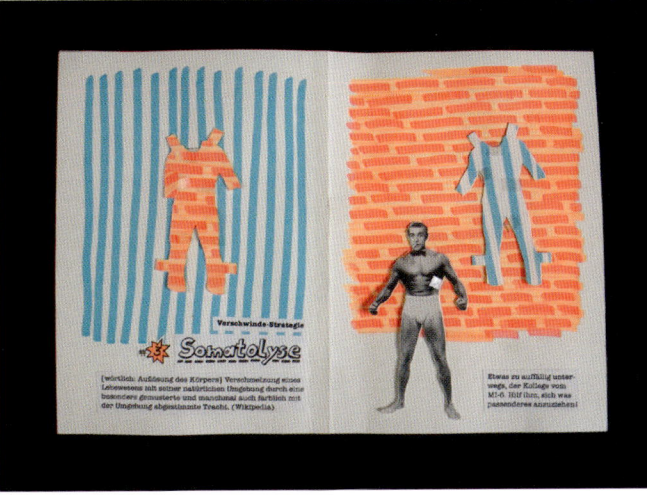

»Handbuch vom Verschwinden«

Student: Lil Nagel | Semester theme: Surveillance mafia | Semester: 8, Graphic design
Type/Scope: Pop-up book, 15 double pages | Mentoring: Prof. Dr. Heiner Wilharm

reddot design award
winner 2009

»On a night like this everybody's looking for somebody stranger. Turn the right corner and you can find anything«. In unserer Modestrecke »Nightstories« nehmen wir Bezug auf ein Zitat aus Frank Millers »Sin City« sowie auf dessen zwielichtige und düstere Atmosphäre. Die Serie erzählt verschiedene Kapitel einer fiktiven Stadt bei Nacht. Jedes Bild steht für sich, aber die zum Bildrand offenen Interaktionen, z.B. die Andeutung einer Begegnung, oder der nach Außen gerichtete Blick eines Protagonisten sollen die Möglichkeit einer zusammenhängenden Geschichte suggerieren. Ein roter Faden ist nicht vorgegeben, sondern bleibt der Imagination des Betrachters überlassen. Was die Bilder und die Charaktere jedoch verbindet, ist das Motiv der Suche und der Flucht. Angetrieben von Träumen, Begierde, Angst oder Trauer bewegen sich die Menschen rastlos durch die Stadt und sehen in der Nacht entweder ihren ewigen Freund oder Feind. »On a night like this everybody's looking for somebody stranger. Turn the right corner and you can find anything«. In our fashion shoot »Night Stories«, we refer to a quotation from Frank Miller's Sin City and to its shady and gloomy atmosphere. In various chapters, this series tells the story of a fictitious city by night. Each picture is autonomous but those half-interactions at the border of the picture, e.g. the suggestion of a meeting or the glance of one of the protagonists, are intended to suggest a continuous story. A storyline is not actually provided, but is rather left to the observer's imagination. The thing that connects the pictures and the characters, however, is the motif of search and flight. Driven by dreams, desire, fear or sorrow – people move restlessly through the streets and perceive the night to be their eternal friend or foe.

»Nightstories«

Student: Christian Breevaart, Eugen Litwinow, Nico Wöhrle | Semester theme: Fashion Editorial »Fantastique«
Semester: 3, Photo design Type/Scope: 9 images | Mentoring: Dietrich Halemayer | Free submission

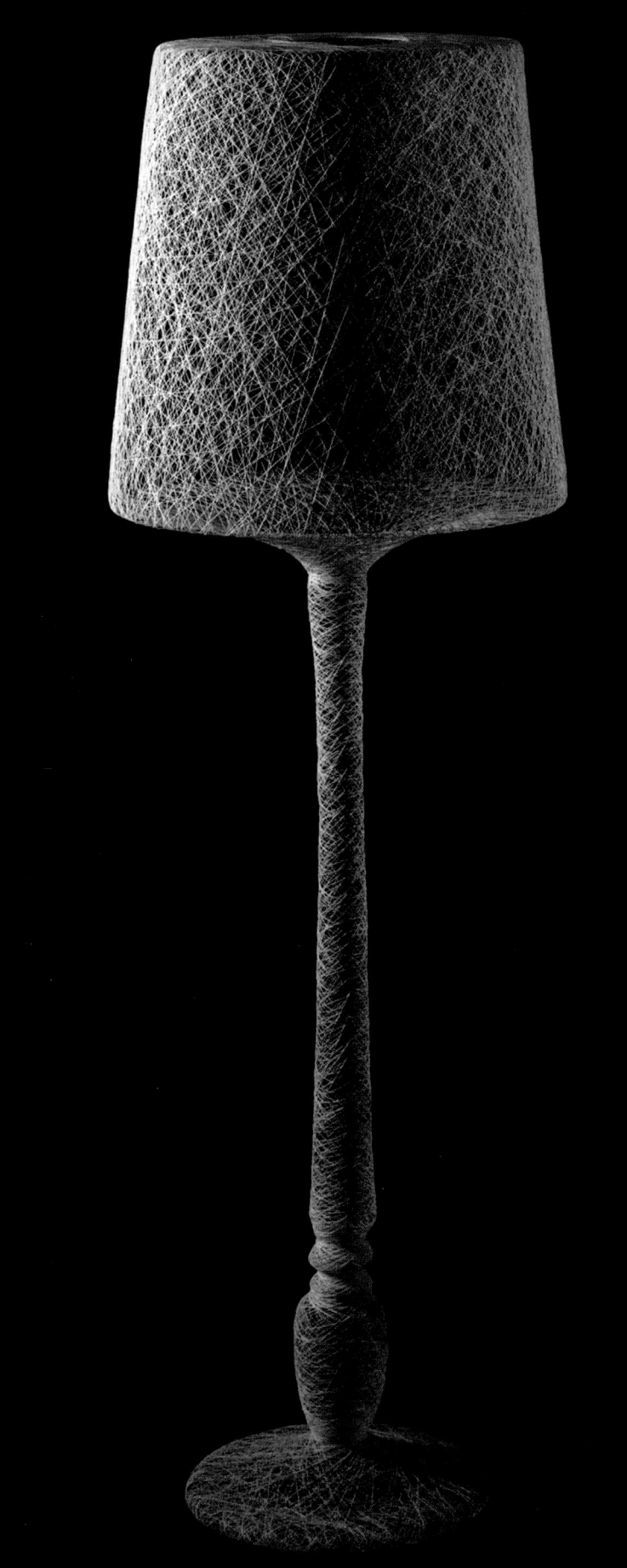

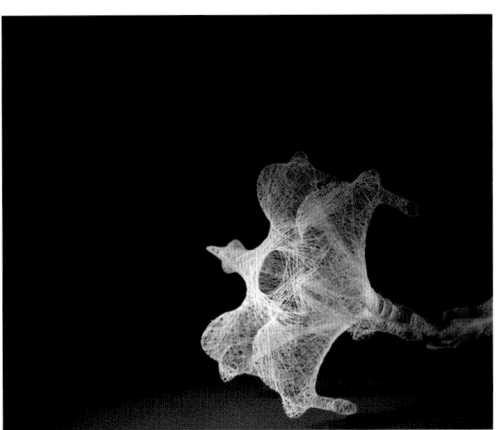

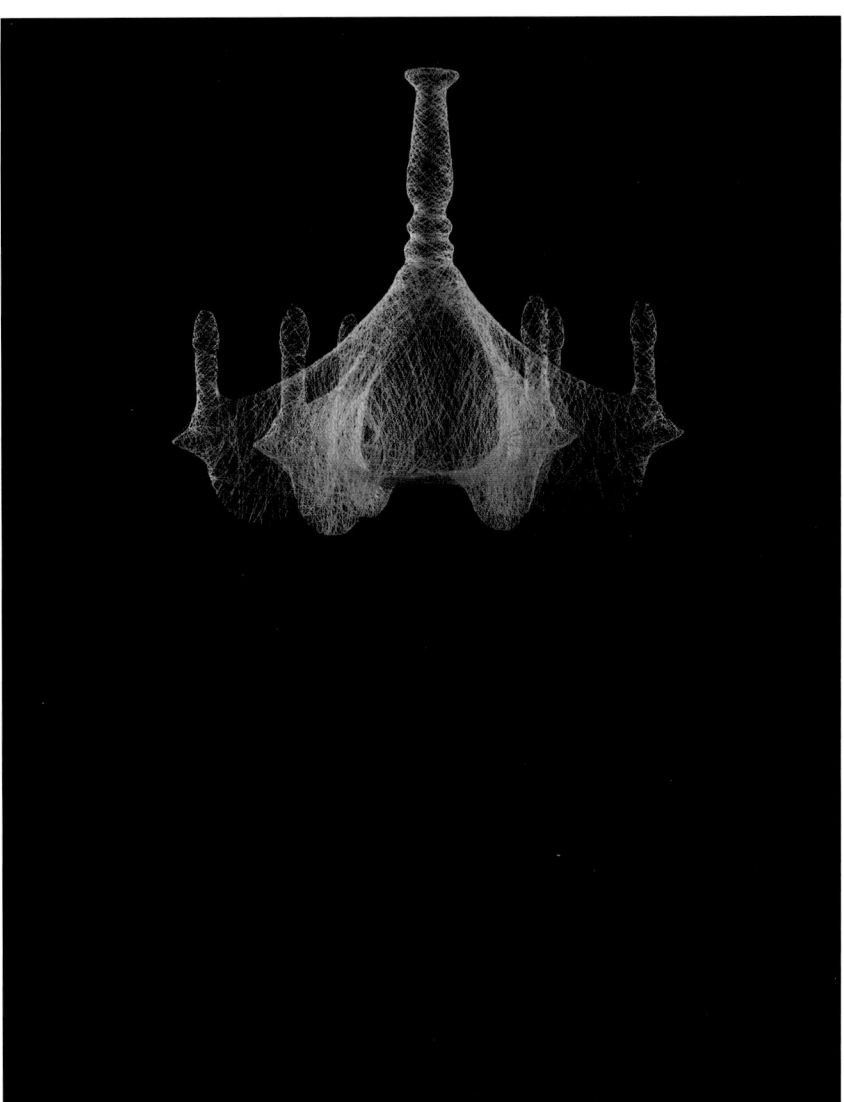

Ein Licht, nur ein Schatten, schöner Schein. Erinnerungen prägen unser Leben, doch sie verblassen mit der Zeit. Ob schön oder schmerzhaft, sie werden immer flüchtig sein. Wir unternehmen viel um sie festzuhalten, sie zu konservieren, um sie für die Zukunft zu sichern, doch dass kann auch immer nur ein Versuch sein, der wahre Inhalt bleibt vergänglich. Diese Objekte werden zu Zeugen ihrer Vergangenheit, indem ihr Körper wie ein Wirt funktioniert. Er wird mit dünnen Fäden umwickelt, um letztendlich aufgelöst zu werden, so bleibt lediglich die äußere Kontur wie ein Hauch im Raum bestehen. Diese nehmen weiterhin ihren gewohnten Platz im Raum ein, bilden dabei figürliche Skulpturen, die sich in ihrer Größe kaum von den ehemaligen Objekten unterscheiden. Hinterfragen und bestätigen dabei gleichzeitig durch ihr Fehlen ihren Sinn und ihre Funktion. **A light, a shadow, a deceptive appearance. Memories stamp our life, yet they fade away as time goes by. Whether pleasantly or hurting, they ever will be volatiley. »Wrapped« is a series of objects gone by. They've become testimonies of their own past, since their bodies function like a host. It will be wrapped into thin threads in order to loose its substance in the end, so that only the outer scheme remains in space like a ghostly impression. Like a left cacoon they take their right place in space again, forming figurative sculptures, which won't differ from their original objects' size. At the same time questioning and affirming their excistence by their holowness.**

»wrapped«

Student: Pierre Kracht | Semester theme: Diploma | Object and Interior design
Mentoring: Prof. Martin Middelhauve

Diese Arbeit ist im Rahmen des Themas »Haushaltsunfall« entstanden. Sie zeigt dem Betrachter einen surrealen Moment aus einer Reihe von Geschehnissen, ohne die Frage zu beantworten, wie dieser zustande kam. **This work was created under the subject »household accidents«. It shows the observer a surreal moment in a series of events without answering the question how this moment came about.**

»Verkopft«

Student: Felix Kahl | Semester theme: Household accident | Semester: 6, Graphic design
Type/Scope: Composite photograph | Mentoring: Reinhard Rosendahl | Free submission

Meine Intention war es, den klassischen Ballett-Tanz dem urbanen Breakdance dokumentarisch gegenüber zu stellen. Beide Tanzformen fordern von den Tänzern, über ein hohes Maß an Disziplin und athletische Fähigkeiten zu verfügen. Der moderne Breakdance unterscheidet sich vom Ballett insbesondere durch die »Battle-Kultur«, in der mehrere Kontrahenten wettkampfartig gegeneinander antreten. Ob im klassischen Ballett oder im modernen Breakdance besteht der Tanz selbst aus Körper-Bewegungen im Raum, Gestik und Mimik. Die dargebotenen Aufnahmen sollen sowohl die Analogien als auch die Unterschiede der Tanzstile zum Ausdruck bringen. **It was my intention to document classical ballet in contrast to urban break-dance. Both forms of dance demand a high degree of discipline and athletic abilities of the dancers. Modern break-dance differs from ballet particularly through its »battle culture« in which several opponents face each other in a contest. Whether in classical ballet or in modern break-dance, the dance itself consists of body movements, gestures and facial expressions. The purpose of the photographs presented is to express both the analogies as well as the differences in the styles of dance.**

»Ballet & Breakdance«

Student: André Chow | Semester theme: Dance | Semester: 1, Graphic design
Type/Scope: 26 images | Mentoring: Reinhard Rosendahl | Free submission

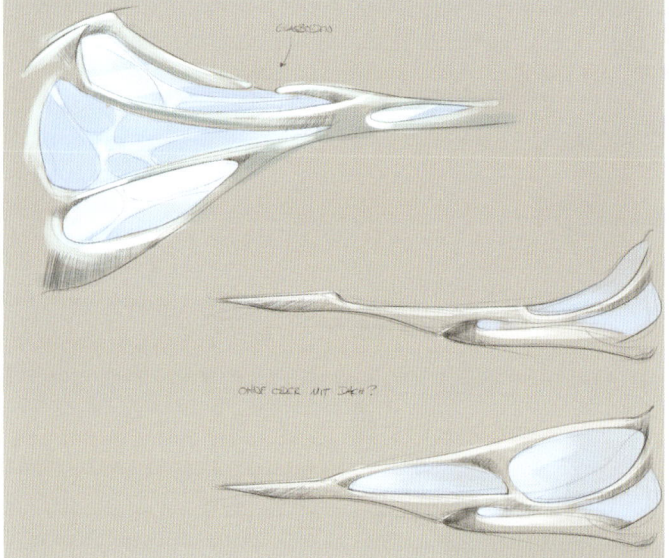

Es geht um einen Ort – um den Luftraum zwischen den Hochhäusern der großen Metropolen. Es geht um Kontraste – Raster und Aufbruch, Stress und Entspannung, Suche und Orientierung. Ausgehend von einer Farb- und Formanalyse, einer Sammlung von Impressionen und assoziativen Kreativtechniken entstanden zahlreiche Ideen und Konzepte zur Nutzung dieses Luftraums. Diese Ausstellung ist das Ergebnis der Vielfalt an Ideen. Sie präsentiert die Konzepte mit neun Modellen, fünf Bildtafeln, zwei Büchern und einer Raumgestaltung. Wir machen vor allem in den Büchern unseren Arbeitsprozess transparent und zeigen auf, wie man das Feld des räumlichen Designs begreifen kann. **This is about a place – the airspace between the skyscrapers of the large metropolises. This is about contrasts – resting and awakening, stress and relaxation, searching and orientation.** Starting off with a colour and form analysis, a collection of impressions and associative creative techniques, numerous ideas and concepts arose as to how to use this airspace. This exhibition is the result of the diversity of ideas. Nine models, five plates, two books and a room design present the concepts. Our work process is made transparent particularly in the books, and shows how one can grasp the field of interior design.

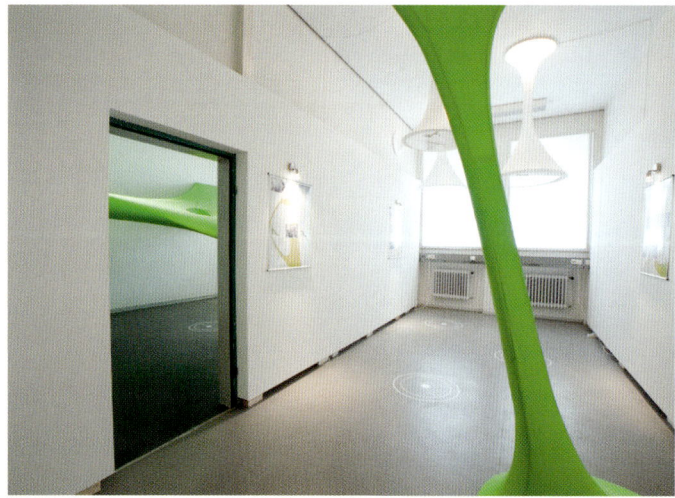

»Morphing Grid«
Student: Holger Nils Pohl, Björn Verch | Semester theme: Diploma | Semester: 7, Object and Interior design
Type/Scope: Installation, book, posters, animation | Mentoring: Prof. Martin Middelhauve

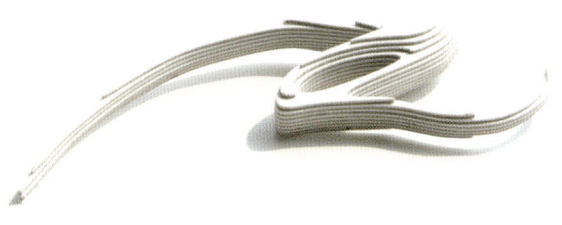

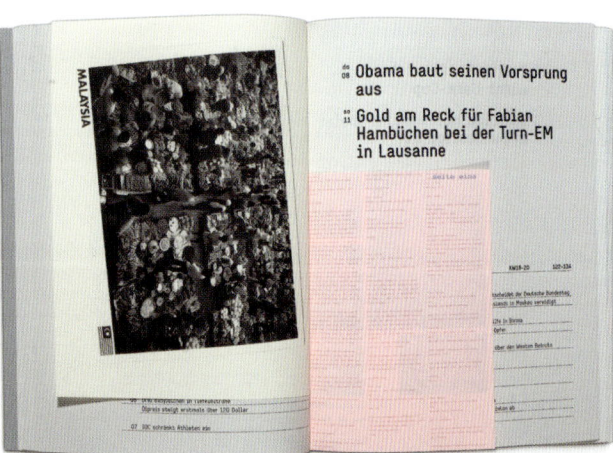
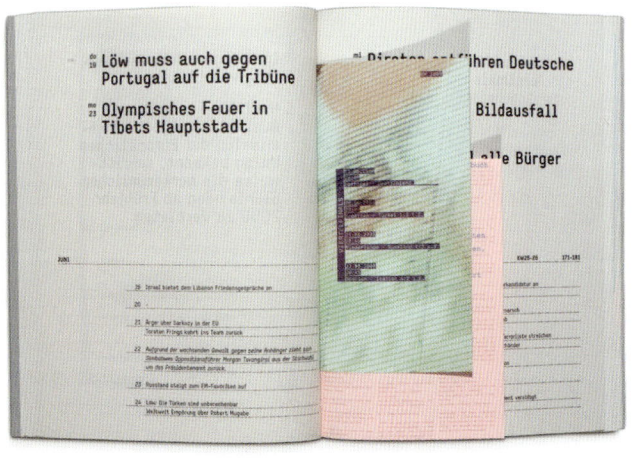

Ein persönlicher Rückblick des Jahres 2008. Die Arbeit bezieht sich auf das ständige Selektieren und Deselektieren von Informationen, Erfahrungen und Ereignissen in unserer Umwelt. Blickt man auf das persönliche Jahr zurück, so überlagern sich diverse Ereignisse, tauchen hier und dort mal wieder auf, und auch vermeintliche Nebensächlichkeiten drängen sonst so wichtige Nachrichten in den Hintergrund. »select/deselect« bietet einen Ansatz für solch einen persönlichen Rückblick. Headlines, die repräsentativ aus den Titelseiten dreier überregionaler Tageszeitungen ausgewählt wurden, bilden eine chronologische Orientierung; überlagert werden diese Headlines, von eigenen Kommentaren, aktuellen Erlebnissen, Fotos, Kommunikation. **A personal retrospect of 2008. The work refers to the constant selection and deselection of information, experience and events in our environment. In a personal retrospect on any given year, various events overlap, reappear every now and again, and even supposedly irrelevant issues force otherwise very important news into the background. »select/deselect« provides an approach for such a personal reflection. A chronological orientation, which was selected from the headlines of three national daily newspapers, portrays representative headlines for the relevant day; these are overlaid by personal comments, current experiences, photographs, communication.**

»select/deselect 2008«

Student: Tim Loffing | Semester theme: What do tomorrow's books look like? | Semester: 7, Graphic design
Type/Scope: Book | Mentoring: Prof. Sabine an Huef | Free submission

Entwicklung eines Erscheinungsbildes und eines Orientierungssystems für das PHOENIX-Areal in Dortmund Hörde. Gestalterische Grundidee ist hierbei, die Verbindung zwischen dem alten industriellen Standort und seinen neuen vielseitigen Funktionen zu visualisieren. Das zukünftige Areal teilt sich auf in drei verschiedene Nutzflächen: PHOENIX West wird ein hochmoderner Technologiepark, PHOENIX Park bietet ein stadtnahes Naturerlebnis und ist zugleich die Verbindung zum PHOENIX See mit seinen vielfältigen Freizeit- und Frholungsmöglichkeiten. Jedes der drei Areale ist ein eigenständiges Segment mit eigener Farb- und Bildsprache und kann sowohl einzeln als auch gemeinsam unter dem Dach PHOENIX kommuniziert werden. Die unterschiedlichen Farbkodierungen bekommen im Leitsystem eine besonders wichtige Rolle und dienen zur schnellen Orientierung vor Ort. Development of an appearance and signage system for the PHOENIX-Areal in Dortmund Hörde. From a design point of view, the basic idea is to visualise the association between the old industrial location and its new diverse functions. The future area is divided into three sections, each with a different purpose: PHOENIX West will become a cutting-edge technology park; PHOENIX Park offers a nature experience close to the city and at the same time connects to the PHOENIX Lake with its diverse leisure and recreation possibilities. Each of the three areas is an independent segment with its own colour and imagery and can be communicated both individually as well as jointly under the PHOENIX umbrella. The various colour codes take on a particularly important role within the guiding system and serve as a quick orientation on site.

»PHOENIX Areal Dortmund-Hörde«
Student: Sebastian Emmel | Semester theme: Free subject | Semester: 7, Graphic design
Type/Scope: Appearance, signage system | Mentoring: Prof. Xuyen Dam | Free submission

Die Farben »Orange/Rot« und »Blau« sollten innerhalb einer Beautystrecke in einem modernen Look realisiert werden. Die Kombination des modernen kühlen Looks und des ausgewählten Farbcodes wurde durch Reduktion und entsprechende Fokussierung herausgearbeitet. **The colours »orange/red« and »blue« were to be realised in a modern look within a beauty picture series. The combination of the modern, cool look and the selected colour code was defined through reduction and corresponding focusing.**

»Beauty-Editorial«

Student: Thomas Steuer, Chris Stock | Semester theme: Fashion Editorial »Fantastique« | Semester: 11, 9, Photo design
Type/Scope: 9-page editorial | Mentoring: Dietrich Halemeyer | Free submission

»Payback«

Student: Sebastian Michailidis | Semester theme: Surveillance mafia | Semester: 8, Graphic design
Type/Scope: Book | Mentoring: Carsten Strübbe | Free submission

Der technische Fortschritt des Informationszeitalters bedeutet einen Gewinn an Freiheit und Komfort. Er schafft ebenso Abhängigkeiten und die völlige Kontrollierbarkeit. Die Möglichkeit auf alles binnen Sekunden Zugriff zu haben, wird bezahlt durch den Verlust des Privaten. Der Versuch sich dieser Situation zu widersetzen kann als vergeblich betrachtet werden. Viel zu allgegenwärtig sind die zahlreichen, durch Staat und Wirtschaft ausgelegten Kontrollmechanismen. Dieser aussichtslosen Situation begegnet der Guerillaleitfaden auf die einzig mögliche Weise: mit fatalistischem Humor. Es werden absurde Strategien angeregt, die letztlich die Sinnlosigkeit aller Gegenwehr illustrieren. **Technological progress in the information age brings increasing freedom and comfort. It also creates dependencies and absolute controllability. The possibility of having access to everything within seconds is carried out at the cost of a loss of one's privacy. Any attempt to resist this situation can be regarded as futile. Too omnipresent are the many control mechanisms put in place by the Government and the economy. The guerrilla leitmotif confronts this desperate situation in the only possible way: with fatalistic humour. Absurd strategies are encouraged, which ultimately illustrate the pointlessness of all resistance.**

EINLEITUNG
PROBLEMATIK   SEITEN 6 & 7

Der technische Fortschritt
des Informationszeitalters
bedeutet einerseits einen
Gewinn an Freiheit und
Komfort, schafft anderer-
seits aber Abhängig-
keiten und die völlige
Kontrollierbarkeit der
Personen, die sich der
neuen Techniken bedienen.
Die Möglichkeit auf alles
binnen eines Augenblicks
informationstechnisch
Zugriff zu haben wird
bezahlt durch den Verlust
des Privaten. Alles ist
vernetzt und dadurch
überwachbar.

Gefangen im Netz

Frei wie Tarzan bewegt man sich durch den Datendschungel und ist sich dabei aber oft der Gefahren nicht bewusst.

Aufblasbares Badekroko unter die Burka und fertig ist die passende fundamentalistische Ehefrau.

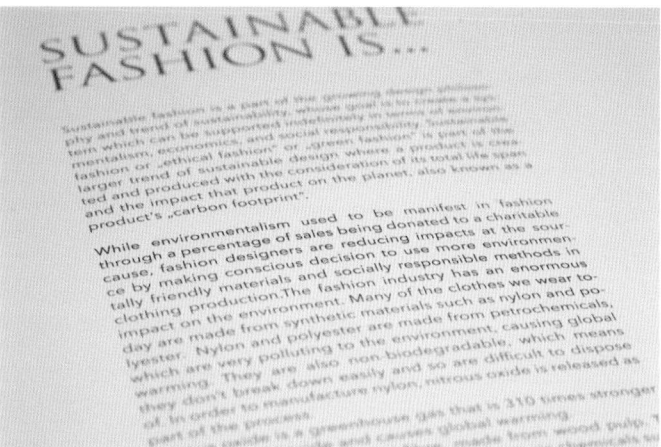

Bei der Überlegung, ein Skateboardmagazin bzw. Skateboards zu gestalten, wollten wir weg von dem Streetstyle, Graffiti und der Männerdomaine etc. Daher haben wir ein Modemagazin mit eigenen Fotos erstellt. Die Zielgruppe ist die modebewusste junge Frau auf dem Weg ins Businessleben. Sie legt Wert auf »organische Herstellung«. Daher auch die Motivwahl der Illustrationen auf den Skateboards: filigrane Motive aus der Natur, wie Paradiesvögel, Chamäleons und Kolibris. **When we thought about designing a skateboard magazine or skateboards, we wanted to move away from the street style, graffiti and the male domain, etc. And so we created a fashion magazine with our own photographs. The target group is the fashion-conscious young woman moving into the business world. She places a lot of value on »organic manufacture«. Hence, the choice of motifs for the illustrations on skateboards; filigree natural themes, such as birds of paradise, chameleons and humming birds.**

DECK BANDAROL
ART. 106 17 132
145,00 €

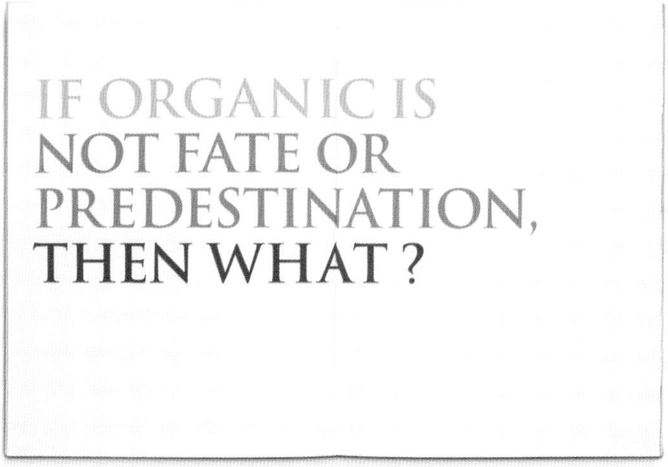

IF ORGANIC IS
NOT FATE OR
PREDESTINATION,
THEN WHAT ?

»Filligree«
Student: Anne Knobloch, Jana Durchleuchter | Semester theme: Skateboarding Semester: 8, Graphic design
Type/Scope: Magazine | Mentoring: Prof. Dieter Ziegenfeuter | Free submission

Das »Domicil«, ein international bekannter Jazzclub in Dortmund, wünscht sich mehr Präsenz in der Öffentlichkeit und will ein neues, junges Publikum für sich gewinnen. Auf den Plakaten sind unterschiedliche »Typen« zu sehen, an denen der Betrachter verschiedene Instrumente erkennen und so die Stimmung und die Beschaffenheit der verschiedenen Themenabende im Domizil erahnen kann. Ungewöhnliche Arrangements und bizarre Posen generieren Aufmerksamkeit. The »Domicil« is an internationally recognised Jazz Club in Dortmund and is seeking to gain more public presence and wants to win over a new, young audience. The posters depict different »types« on whom the observer recognises different instruments and in this way can imagine the atmosphere and the nature of Domicil's different themed evenings. Unusual arrangements and bizarre poses generate attention.

»Domicil«
Student: Stefan Becker | Semester theme: Sounds, images, places | Semester: 6, Graphic design
Type/Scope: Poster series | Mentoring: Prof. Sabine an Huef

Etwa vier Milliarden Jahre der Evolution haben auf unserem Planeten zur Entstehung einer Vielzahl beeindruckender, und in ihrer Erscheinung einmaliger, Arten geführt. Die besondere Einzigartigkeit eines Lebewesens wird jedoch oft erst durch eine Isolierung klar. Entnimmt man Tiere ihrer »natürlichen« Umgebung und setzt sie vor einen monochromen Hintergrund, so dass vom eigentlichen Motiv keinerlei Ablenkung mehr besteht, verändert sich plötzlich die Wirkung. Meine Arbeit zeigt bekannte Tiere verschiedenster Gattungen in einem für sie untypischen Kontext. Die Loslösung von bekannten Formen, Farben und Hintergründen führt zu einer visuellen Neuentdeckung der charakteristischen Merkmale der Tiere. **About four billion years of evolution have led to the development of a variety of impressive and, in their appearance, unique species on our planet. The particular uniqueness of a living being, however, often only becomes apparent through isolation. If you remove animals from their »natural« habitat and place them in front of a monochrome background, so that there is no distraction from the actual motif, the effect will suddenly change. My work shows well-known animals of various species in an atypical context. The removal of familiar forms, colour and backgrounds leads to a visual rediscovery of the animals' typical features.**

»Animal Portaits«
Student: Steffi Müller | Semester theme: Free subject | Semester: 7, Photo design
Type/Scope: 26 images | Mentoring: Prof. Caroline Dlugos | Free submission

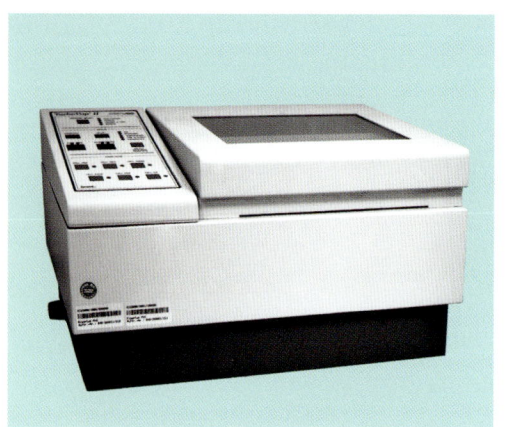

»Die Ausschaltung des Zufalls« ist ein Versuch der Remystifizierung der Maschinen. Die elf Analysegeräte sind in der Lage, jede beliebige Substanz in fünf Schritten bis auf die molekulare Ebene zu untersuchen, sie könnten also eine vollständige Erfassung der Welt vornehmen und den Menschen dabei weit hinter sich lassen. **»Deactivating coincidence«** is the attempt of a remystification of machines. The eleven analysis devices are able to examine any random substance in five steps right down to the molecular level; they can therefore carry out a complete understanding of the world and at the same time leave the people far behind them.

»Die Ausschaltung des Zufalls«
Student: Joscha Bruckert | Semester theme: Coincidence | Semester: 2, Photo design
Type/Scope: 11 images | Mentoring: Prof. Susanne Brügger | Free submission

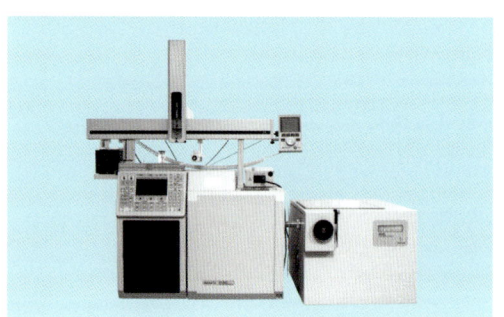

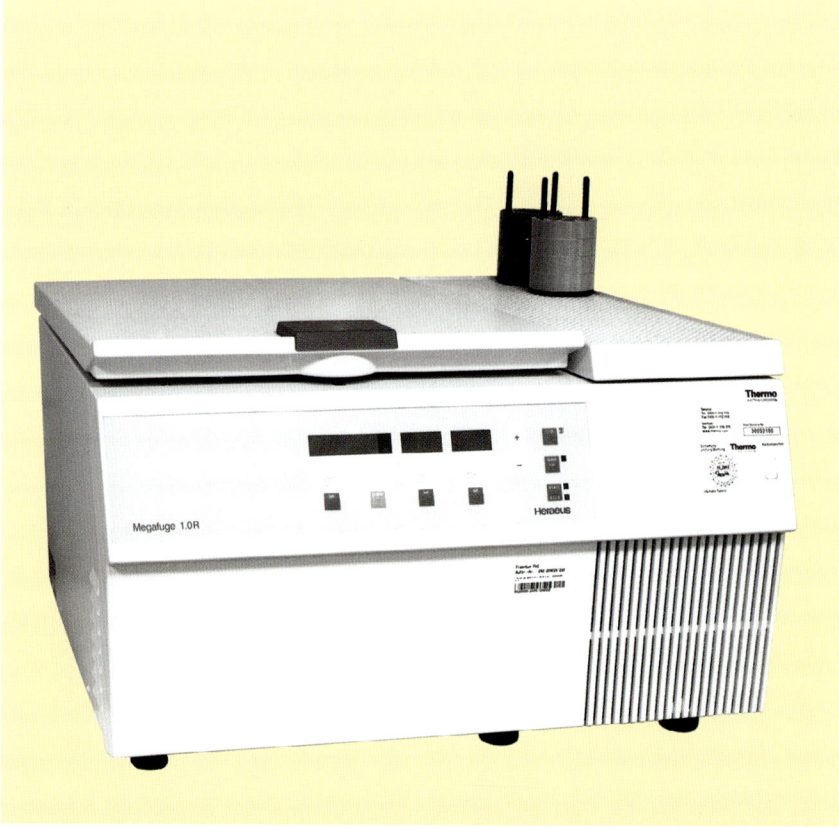

Sri Lankas Regierung konzentriert sich seit 1983 stark auf den herrschenden Bürgerkrieg zwischen radikalen Tamilen und Singhalesen. Den ärmlichen Verhältnissen in den Dörfern und in den Vororten der Großstädte wird seitens der Regierung kaum Beachtung geschenkt. Seit 2009 ist der Bürgerkrieg beendet und es ist nun abzuwarten, ob die Regierung sich mit den Problemen und Sorgen der einfachen Bewohner beschäftigen wird. Nilanthe lebt zusammen mit seiner Familie in einer für die Lebensverhältnisse in Sri Lanka typischen Holzhütte. Er ist Gelegenheitsarbeiter auf dem Fischmarkt von Beruwela und verdient gerade so viel Geld, um seine Familie zu ernähren. In der Hütte staut sich die Hitze auf mehr als 40 Grad Celsius. Vor allem zur Monsunzeit dringt der Regen durch das undichte Dach in den Wohnbereich ein. Strom und Gas gibt es nicht. **Since 1983, the Sri Lankan government has been concentrating to a large degree on the prevailing civil war between radical Tamils and Singhalese. The government hardly pays any attention to the poor conditions in the villages and suburbs of the large cities. The civil war ended in 2009, and it remains to be seen whether the government will take up the issue of the problems and concerns of the ordinary inhabitants. Nilanthe and his family live in a wooden hut, which is typical for the living conditions in Sri Lanka. He is a casual labourer at the fish market of Beruwela and earns just enough money to support his family. The heat in the hut reaches temperatures of more than 40 °C. Particularly during the monsoon, rain seeps into living area through the leaking roof. There is no gas or electricity.**

»A Family in Sri Lanka«
Student: Yannik Willing | Semester theme: Free subject | Semester: 4, Photo design
Type/Scope: 12 images | Mentoring: Dirk Gebhardt | Free submission

Der Titel der Arbeit Pughatory setzt sich aus Gareth Pugh und purgatory [Hölle] zusammen. In meiner Arbeit beschäftige ich mich mit Dingen, die uns in unserem Alltag begegnen. Meist kennen wir sie als unspektakuläre Objekte und schenken ihnen kaum Beachtung. Diese Gegenstände werden in meiner Arbeit aus ihrer gewöhnlichen Umgebung herausgenommen, ihrer ursprünglichen Funktion entzogen und in einen anderen Kontext gesetzt. In dieser neu erschaffenen, bizarren Welt, in der Mensch und Objekt verschmelzen und zu einer dantesquen Gestalt komponiert werden, steht die auf diese Art und Weise entstandene Magie durchaus im Mittelpunkt. **The work's title Pughatory is a combination of the name Gareth Pugh and purgatory. In my work, I deal with those things we encounter in our everyday life. Usually, we regard them as unspectacular objects and hardly take any notice of them. In my work, these objects are removed from both their usual surroundings and their original function and placed in a different context. In this newly created bizarre world in which man and object amalgamate and are composed into a dantesque figure, the thus emerging magic absolutely becomes the point of focus.**

»Pughatory«

Student: Sylwana Zybura | Semester theme: Transversale – The Magic of Objects | Semester: 3, Photo design
Type/Scope: Photography | Mentoring: Prof. Caroline Dlugos

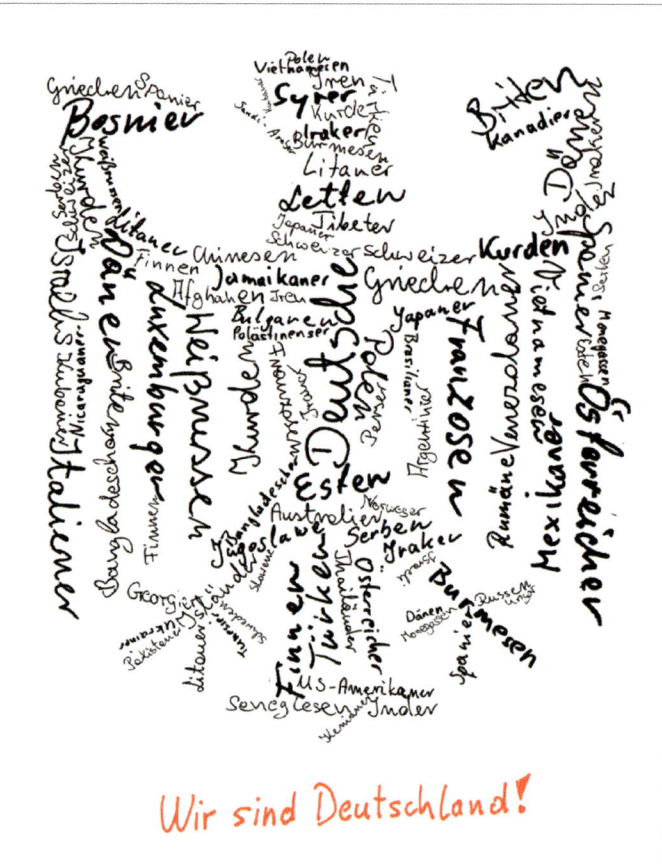

Wir sind Deutschland!

Sigrid S. zieht mit ihren märchenhaften Theaterstücken Kinder in ihren Bann.

Annett M. kümmert sich sehr fürsorglich um Menschen in einem Seniorenheim.

»artikeleins.de«
Semester theme: posters against right-wing radicalism | Graphic design
Type/Scope: Postcards | Mentoring: Prof. Johannes Graf

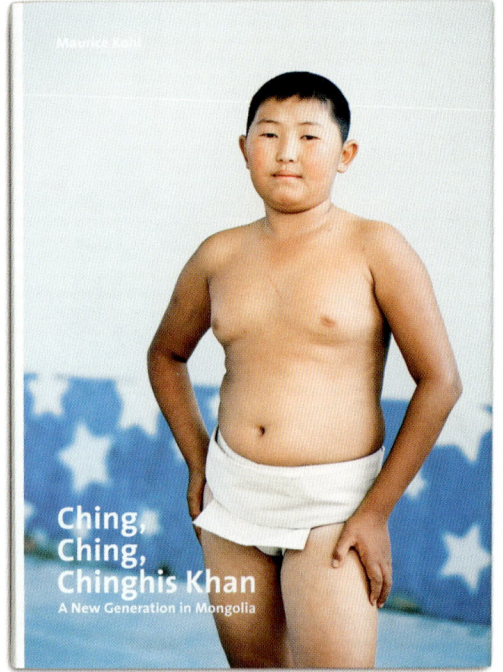

Maurice Kohl widmet seine fotografische Arbeit Jugendlichen, die mit ihren 12 bis 18 Jahren an der Schwelle zwischen Kindheit und Erwachsensein stehen. Das Stadium des Heranwachsens entspricht sinnfällig der Transformation der Mongolei von einer kommunistischen Diktatur zur kapitalistischen Demokratie seit 1992. Diese Wandlung ist — wie der Prozess der Adoleszenz — widersprüchlich: der Bruch mit Traditionen gehört ebenso dazu wie die folkloristische oder spirituelle Rückbesinnung auf eigene Kulturmerkmale. Die Absicht besteht darin, gegen romantische Klischees von friedlichen Trachtenträgern in idyllischer Landschaft dokumentarische Bilder eines Bevölkerungsquerschnitts zu setzen. Wir begegnen in den Portraits der jungen Mongolen zunächst uns selbst, schließlich erkennen wir die Portraitierten als vielversprechende Zeitgenossen in einer Welt scheinbar aufgehobener Grenzen. **Maurice Kohl** dedicates his photographic work to the youths who, between the ages of twelve and eighteen, are on the threshold between childhood and adulthood. Metaphorically speaking, the period of adolescence corresponds to Mongolia's transformation from a communist dictatorship to a capitalist democracy; a transformation, which started in 1992 and still continues. Just like the period of adolescence, this transformation is contradictory: breaking away from tradition is as much a part of this as the folkloric or spiritual return to one's own cultural elements. The intention is to juxtapose documentary pictures of a cross-section of a population on the one hand, and romantic clichés of peaceful wearers of national costumes in an idyllic landscape on the other hand. In these portraits of young Mongolians, we first discover ourselves; finally we recognise the person portrayed as promising contemporaries in a world of seemingly abolished borders.

»Ching, Ching, Chinghis Khan«
Student: Maurice Kohl | Semester theme: Diploma | Semester: 7, Photo design
Type/Scope: Book | Mentoring: Prof. Xuyen Dam, Wolfgang Flamisch | Free submission

Die alte Zechensiedlung im Stadtteil »Unser Fritz« gehört zu den Gebieten, die auf Grund von Bergbau im Revier abgesunken sind. Da sie unter dem Niveau der Emscher liegen, schützt ein Pumpwerk vor Überflutung. Ich habe mich gefragt, wie wohl die Gärten aussehen würden, wenn sie unter Wasser stünden? Meine Serie zeigt daher ein spielerisches und skurriles Unterwasserszenario, in dem Kinder zum Mittelpunkt einer Märchenwelt werden. **The old mining settlement in the district »Unser Fritz« [Our Fritz] is one of the areas whose elevation sank as a result of mining activity. As this area is below the level of the Emscher, a pump protects against flooding. I asked myself what the gardens would look like if they were submerged under water? My series therefore depicts a playful and bizarre underwater scenario where children are the centre of a fairy-tale world.**

»Unter Wasser«

Student: Hanna Witte | Semester theme: Our Fritz | Semester: 8, Photo design
Type/Scope: 5 images | Mentoring: Prof. Jörg Winde | Free submission

»Molecular Food«
Student: Thorsten Kleine Holthaus | Semester theme: Advanced studies | Semester: 9, Photo design
Type/Scope: 12 advertisements, 12 backlit advertisements in two phases | Mentoring: Prof. Susanne Brügger

Der Begriff Molekularküche bezeichnet die einflussreichste Entwicklung in der Haute Cuisine der letzten 15 Jahre. In der von naturwissenschaftlichen Erkenntnissen inspirierten Avantgarde-Küche werden Texturen und Formen einzelner Produkte verändert. Die Kampagne folgt der Idee der Molekularküche. Durch Irritationen und eine ungewöhnliche Bildsprache wird die innovative Küche des 65° Restaurants beworben. Die Gerichte werden nicht auf Tellern, sondern in einem minimalistischen Umfeld fotografiert. Die weißen Objekte lassen keinen eindeutigen Schluss über Perspektive und Schwerkraft zu. Die Kampagne gliedert sich in Anzeigen und Außenwerbung in Form von Citylights. Die Anzeigen und die Citylightkampagne sind in zwei aufeinander folgende Phasen gegliedert, die nacheinander geschaltet werden. **The term molecular food describes the most influential development in haute cuisine of the last fifteen years. In the avant-garde cuisine, inspired by scientific knowledge, textures and forms of individual products are changed. The campaign follows the concept of a molecular cuisine. The innovative cuisine of the 65°C restaurant is promoted through irritations and an unusual design vocabulary. The dishes are photographed in a minimalist environment, not on plates. The white objects do not allow accurate conclusions on perspective and gravity. The campaign is divided into print advertisements and backlit outdoor advertising. The print and outdoor advertising campaigns represent two sequential phases, which are run one after the other.**

SHANKS – selbst gemachte Waffen der Insassen in Gefängnissen – so nannte ich meine Seife. Das Hauptprodukt meiner Arbeit bildet die Kernseife, die in einer Prägung den Markennamen »SHANKS« zeigt. Das Element der Prägung wurde ebenfalls bei der Verpackung der Kern- und der Flüssigseife wieder aufgegriffen. Es sollte ein rauer und handgefertigter Charakter erzielt werden. Eine Broschüre klärt über den Alltag von Gefängnisinsassen und das Projekt auf und zeigt die gefertigten Produkte im Gefängnisalltag. SHANKS – self-made weapons made by prison inmates – is what I have called my soap. The main product of my work is curd soap, which shows the embossed brand name »SHANKS«. The element of embossing was again used on the packaging of the curd soap and the liquid soap. The aim was to achieve a rough and self-made character. A brochure gives an explanation on the daily life of prisoners, and the project shows the finished products in everyday prison life.

»SHANKS – Die Knastseife«

Student: Mailin Lemke | Semester theme: Soap | Semester: 4, Graphic design
Type/Scope: Soap, fluid, packaging | Mentoring: Prof. Dieter Ziegenfeuter | Free submission

Bei »MotherEarth« geht es um gezielte Aktionen der fiktiven Umweltschutzorganisation MotherEarth. Diese Organisation platziert ihr Signet in überdimensionaler Größe an ausgewählten Orten, um auf sich aufmerksam zu machen. Sie will damit einen Denkanstoß zum Umweltbewusstsein geben, um klar zu machen, dass es sich nicht allein um Naturschutz handelt, sondern die Folgen unserer massiven Umweltverschmutzung sich maßgeblich auf unsere Gesundheit und unser Leben auswirken. Bei diesen real durchgeführten Aktionen wurden Passanten angesprochen und Flugblätter verteilt. Auf den fiktiven Inhalt dieser Kampagne wurde stets hingewiesen. Die Embryonen bestehen aus 36 Bettlaken, die von meiner Oma Sonja Jablonski zusammengenäht wurden. Zu den Gestaltungsaufgaben gehörten die Fotografie der Plakatmotive und die Entwicklung des Logos und der Plakatkampagne. »MotherEarth« is a targeted campaign of the fictitious environmental protection organization MotherEarth. This organisation places its signet in larger-than-life size at selected locations to draw attention. It wants to give food for thought on the issue of environmental awareness; to make it clear that this not only refers to the protection of nature, but that the consequences of our massive environmental pollution has a decisive effect on our health and our life. People passing by were approached and given leaflets during this real campaign. The fictitious nature of the campaign is always mentioned. The embryos are made from thirty-six sheets and are sewn together by my grandmother Sonja Jablonski. The design assignment also included photographing the poster motifs and the development of logos and the poster campaign.

»Mother Earth«

Student: Sascha Dörger | Semester theme: Campaign for a fictitious protection organisation | Semester: 7, Graphic design
Type/Scope: Photograph, poster series | Mentoring: Prof. HD Schrader, Thomas Linke

DIE LUFTVERSCHMUTZUNG DURCH ABGASE
TÖTET WELTWEIT JÄHRLICH ÜBER DREI MILLIONEN MENSCHEN.
DAS SOLLTEN WIR ÄNDERN.

MOTHER-EARTH.COM

JEDE SEKUNDE STIRBT WELTWEIT EIN MENSCH
AN DEN FOLGEN VON WASSER- UND BODENVERSCHMUTZUNG.
DAS SOLLTEN WIR ÄNDERN.

MOTHER-EARTH.COM

»Format³«

Student: Clemens Müller, Marvin Boiko | Semester theme: Reception culture Grugapark | Semester: 4, 6, Object and Interior design, Graphic design
Type/Scope: Three-dimensional concrete objects | Mentoring: Prof. Martin Middelhauve

»Les Animaux de la Forêt«

Student: Juliane Herrmann | Semester theme: Light | Semester: 1, Photo design
Type/Scope: Installation | Mentoring: Prof. Magareta Hesse

Die Arbeit »Les Animaux de la Forêt« ist eine Anlehnung an die Installationsserie »Theâtre des Ombres« von Christian Boltanski aus den 1980er Jahren. Meine Installation soll die Erinnerungen der Kindheit mit aktuellen Bezügen zu Tierversuchen, Genmanipulation und Umweltverschmutzung verknüpfen. Bei genauerem Hinsehen fällt auf, dass sich die zuerst banal wirkenden Spielfiguren zu Monstern entwickeln, deren Schatten an Wesen aus der griechischen Mythologie erinnern. Insgesamt 10 Tiere bilden eine Art Mobilé, welches sich langsam um die eigene Achse dreht. Durch die Bewegung kommt es zu Interaktionen der Wesen untereinander und mit dem Raum. Verstärkt wird die unheimliche Atmosphäre von Geräuschen wilder Waldtiere. **The work »Les Animaux de la Forêt« is designed to hark back to the installation series »Theâtre des Ombres« by Christian Boltanski from the 1980s. My installation intends to associate childhood memories with current references to experiments on animals, genetic engineering and environmental pollution. On careful examination, it becomes apparent that what at first glance seem to be ordinary toy figures develop into monsters, whose shadows recall Greek mythological beasts. A total of ten animals form a kind of mobilé, which slowly revolves around its own axis. The movement causes the beasts to interact with each other and with the room. The eerie atmosphere is enhanced by the sounds of wild woodland animals.**

out put

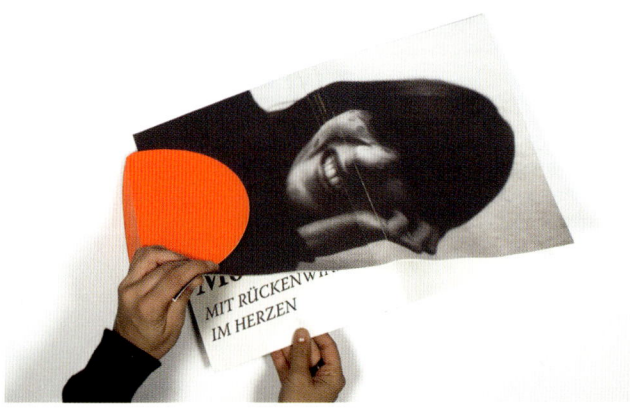

Konzept und Realisation einer Designzeitschrift. Die Zeitschrift besteht aus vier Zeitungen, jede Zeitung beinhaltet ein Thema. Die Themen sind, Illustration, Fotografie, Typografie und Mode. In der jeweiligen Zeitung wird ein »Künstler« aus der Szene mit seinen Werken vorgestellt. Die Zeitung besteht aus einzelnen A2 Plakaten. Der Umschlag ist ein A1 Plakat und gleichzeitig das Inhaltsverzeichnis und hält die Zeitungen zu einer Zeitschrift zusammen. Der neon-farbige Aufkleber fungiert gleichzeitig als Verschluss und als Werbeträger. Wie in drei kleinen Promotionvideos oder auch als Flyer. **Concept and realisation of a design magazine. The magazine is made up of four newspapers; each newspaper covers one subject. The subjects are: illustration, photography, typography, and fashion. An »artist« from the respective scene is introduced in the relevant newspaper with his or her works. The newspaper consists of individual A2-size posters. The envelope is an A1-size poster and also serves as a table of contents and keeps the newspapers together to make up a single magazine. The neon-coloured sticker simultaneously acts as a seal and as an advertisement. Just as three small promotional videos or also as a flyer.**

»Vormarsch-Designmagazin«
Student: Marle Koerdt | Semester theme: Design magazine | Semester: 8, Graphic design
Type/Scope: Magazine – 4 newspapers | Mentoring: Prof. HD Schrader | Free submission

»Was mich bewegt«

Student: Bettina Gross, Caroline Hentschel | Semester theme: Free subject | Semester: 5, Graphic design
Type/Scope: 32 images/book | Mentoring: Thomas Linke | Free submission

In unserer Arbeit beschäftigen wir uns mit dem Phänomen, dass Schuhe viel über einen Menschen aussagen können. So können Schuhe einerseits eine bestimmte Gruppenzugehörigkeit symbolisieren [z.B. Springerstiefel, Birkenstocksandalen etc.], andererseits, je nach Zustand, Aufschluss über den sozialen Status geben. Wir haben unterschiedliche Charaktere und ihre individuellen Schuhe porträtiert und auf 32 Tafeln zusammengestellt. Wie bei Memory, ist es hier die Aufgabe des Betrachters, die Schuhe, den jeweiligen Trägern zuzuordnen. So kann der Betrachter selbst entscheiden, welche Zugehörigkeit ihm am stimmigsten erscheint. In our work, we concern ourselves with the phenomenon that shoes can say a lot about a particular person. On the one hand, shoes can symbolise a certain group membership [e.g. combat boots, Birkenstock sandals, etc.] and on the other hand, their condition can give an insight into social status. We have put together different personalities and portrayed their individual shoes on thirty-two boards. Similar to playing ›Memory‹, the observer is asked to match the shoes and their wearer. That way, the observers can decide for themselves which pairing appears to be the best match.

Die Fotografieserie »Schopf« umfasst vier inszenierte Portraits junger Frauen, die durch ihre Haare optisch mit der Natur verschmelzen. Struktur und Farbe des Frauenhaars greifen Charakteristika von natürlichen Materialien wie beispielsweise Blättern auf. Die Arbeit ist 2008 im Fredenbaumpark in Dortmund entstanden. **The photo series »mop of hair« comprises four staged portraits of young women who optically blend in with nature through their hair. Structure and colour of the women's hair pick up on the characteristics of natural materials such as leaves. The work was realised in 2008 in the Fredenbaumpark in Dortmund.**

»Schopf«
Student: Vera Drebusch | Semester theme: Dortmund parks | Semester: 6, Photo design
Type/Scope: 4 images | Mentoring: Prof. Caroline Dlugos | Free submission

Was passiert, wenn man den Modestil Haute Couture [Licht und Pose] mit [extrem] sexy Klischeekostümen kombiniert? Ziel ist es, ein neues Frauenbild zu schaffen, das an der Oberfläche [Kleidung] verführerisch und sexy wirkt, darunter zugleich stark ist und dadurch mit seiner Gestik kühle Eleganz und Erhabenheit ausdrückt. Diesen Spannungsbogen möchte ich in meiner Arbeit Fantasy-Beauties aufnehmen und ausreizen. **What happens when you combine the fashion style of haute couture [light and posture] with [extremely] sexy cliché costumes? The aim is to create a new perception of women; one which appears sexy on the surface [clothes], and, at the same time, is strong underneath, thus expressing a cool elegance and dignity through its gestures. It is this arc of suspense that I would like to capture and thrash out in my work Fantasy Beauties.**

»Fantasy Beauties«
Student: Marco Deling | Semester theme: Fashion Editorial »Fantastique« | Semester: 5, Photo design
Type/Scope: Magazine | Mentoring: Dietrich Halemeyer | Free submission

Für ein Editorial Shooting des Moskauer Institute of Modern Art wurde in Zusammenarbeit mit einer Newcomer Fashion Designerin das Thema »Moscow Girl« vorgeschlagen. Als unbeeinflusster Europäer machte ich mich selber auf die Suche nach einem Model. Anja lernte ich in der Metro nach Strogino, dem letzten, weit entfernten Vorort von Moskau kennen, welchen wir auch als Location nutzten. Sie sagte sofort zu. Sie verkörpert auf eine besondere Art den schönen, aber auch rohen und ungeschminkten Flair der Zehnmillionenstadt. **For an editorial shooting by the Moscow Institute of Modern Art in collaboration with a newcomer fashion designer, the theme »Moscow Girl« was suggested. As an unbiased European, I went looking for the model myself. I met Anja in the Metro [underground] on the way to Strogino, the last, furthest suburb of Moscow, which we also used as a location. She agreed immediately. In a very special way, she is the embodiment of the beautiful, but also natural and straightforward flair of this city with its ten million inhabitants.**

»Moscow Girl«
Student: Claudio Oliverio | Semester theme: Editorial for a fashion range | Semester: 8, Photo design
Type/Scope: 5 images | Mentoring: Konstantin Vladimirovich | Free submission

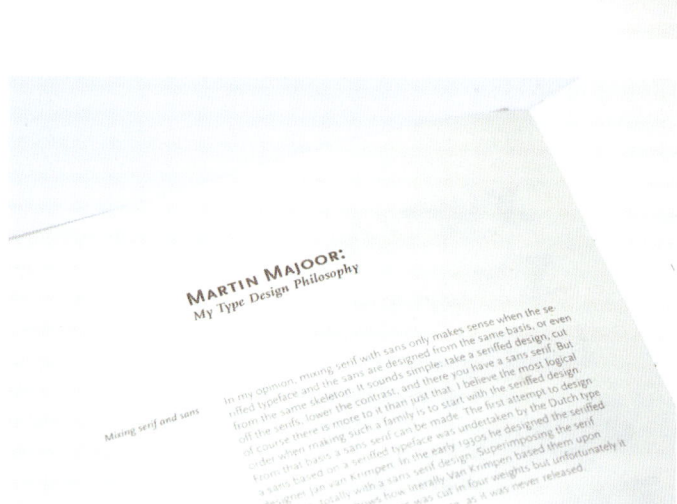

Ich entschied mich, ein Buch über die Schrift-Familie Scala von Martin Majoor anzufertigen, da sie moderne und traditionelle Ansätze der Typografie vereint. Um den typografischen Ansatz Majoors auch in meiner Publikation deutlich werden zu lassen, habe ich einige Elemente von Hand gestaltet: Die Linie, die unten am Seitenrand entlangführt, wurde mit Feder und Tinte geschrieben. Die Farbe Orange steht dabei zum einen für die Niederlande, zum anderen sollte sie meiner im Wesentlichen eher traditionell gehaltenen Veröffentlichung Modernität verleihen. Den Schriftzug auf Vorder- und Rückseite habe ich mit Linolschnitt gedruckt. Die Publikation enthält Texte über Martin Majoor und die Entwicklung der Scala.

I decided to create a book on the font family Scala by Martin Majoor, as this family unites modern and traditional aspects of typography. In an effort to make Majoors' typographical approach visible in my publication as well, I have designed certain elements by hand: the line leading down the side margin was written in ink. The colour orange stands for the Netherlands, but it was also used to give a modern touch to my otherwise rather traditional publication. I printed the lettering on the front side and reverse side with linocut. The publication includes texts on Martin Majoor and the development of Scala.

»Scala«

Student: Beke Rodewald | Semester theme: Typography | Semester: 1, Graphic design
Type/Scope: Book | Mentoring: Prof. Sabine an Huef | Free submission

»Bauhelvetica«

Student: Matthias Smukal | Semester theme: Helvetica – the best font of all time | Semester: 3, Graphic design | Type/Scope: Letters in 15 mm steel | Mentoring: Jörg Hemker | Free submission

Da ich Helvetica für eine der besten Grotesk Schriften halte, die es je gab, wollte ich sie unscheinbar und zugleich offensichtlich darstellen. Ich zerlegte die Schrift in ihre Konstrukte und schuf daraus ein Baukastenset, bestehend aus 98 Teilen. Manche Elemente des Systems sind gleich, andere wiederum sehr speziell. Somit kann die Schrift auf spielerische Weise neu erfahren werden. Um den unverwüstlichen Charakter der Schrift zu unterstreichen, ließ ich den Bausatz aus 1 cm dickem Stahl herauslasern. Zur Orientierung liegt ein Bauplan bei, der als Plakat genutzt werden kann sowie zwei Aufkleber zum Gestalten der Metallbox. **As I consider Helvetica one of the best Grotesque Fonts that ever existed, I wanted to present it as unobtrusive and simultaneously obvious. I broke down the font into its constituents, and from this I created a construction kit consisting of 98 parts. Some of the system's components are identical, whilst others are very unique. In this way, the font can be playfully re-experienced. In order to emphasise the indestructible character of the font, I had the construction kit lasered out of 1-cm-thick steel. A construction plan, which can be used as a poster, is attached as a guideline, as well as two stickers to decorate the metal box.**

Ausgehend von einer Mode, die traditionelle und moderne Elemente kombiniert, verknüpfe ich Auszüge des Heimatfilms mit moderner Modefotografie. Das Hauptmerkmal des Heimatfilms ist die übertriebene Idylle. Diese Eigenschaft greife ich durch meine künstliche Kulisse auf und übertreibe den Aspekt des Unwirklichen. With a fashion that merges traditional and modern elements as a starting point, I combine extracts from the Heimatfilm [sentimental films in idealised regional settings] with modern fashion photography. The characteristic feature of the Heimatfilm is an exaggerated idyll. I pick up on this characteristic through the use of my artistic scenery and exaggerate the aspect of the unreal.

»Heimat«
Student: Vera Schäper | Semester theme: Fashion | Semester: 6, Graphic design
Type/Scope: 9 composite photographs | Mentoring: Jörg Winde | Free submission

109 JOCHEN GERZ, KARL-HEINZ PETZINKA

IN KONTAKT MIT...
JOCHEN GERZ, Konzept- und Installationskünstler

REFLEKTOR: Lieber Jochen Gerz, Sie leben zur Zeit im Norden Europas, in Irland, und realisieren nach »Das Zwanzigste Jahrhundert« [Oberhausen 1996], »Das Geschenk« [Dortmund 2000] und »Tausch der Tabus« [Duisburg 2006] gerade zwei weitere Arbeiten für das Ruhrgebiet. Sie entstehen für das Kunstprogramm der RUHR.2010 derzeit als work[s]-in-progress unter direkter Beteiligung der Menschen vor Ort: Seit 2007 der »Platz des europäischen Versprechens« in Bochum und seit 2009 die »2-3 Straßen« in Dortmund, Duisburg und Mülheim. All diese Projekte sind jeweils auch mit einer kurzen Beschreibung auf Ihrer Website im Internet dokumentiert: www.jochengerz.eu. Wie kam es eigentlich zu diesem anhaltenden intensiven Kontakt zur Metropolregion Ruhr – einem postindustriellen Verdichtungsraum, dessen Transformationsgesellschaft im Zusammenhang mit der Auslobung zur Europäischen Kulturhauptstadt 2010 gerade als ein europäischer Modellfall diskutiert wird? Gibt es für Sie als Künstler und Kosmopolit persönlich besondere Gründe, sich für das Ruhrgebiet zu interessieren und zu engagieren? Im Jahr 2000 hatten Sie ja auch schon einmal hier am Fachbereich Design der Fachhochschule Dortmund unterrichtet...

GERZ: Ich habe einen Teil der Schulzeit im Rheinland verbracht und kenne das Ruhrgebiet seither. Seit Anfang der siebziger Jahre war ich immer wieder hier wegen Ausstellungen, Preisen, Vorträgen, Workshops, Performances und Arbeiten im öffentlichen Raum. Es gibt keine andere Region, die so viele kulturelle Institutionen hat wie das Ruhrgebiet. Trotzdem ist die Metropole, wie man hier jetzt sagt, keine Metropole. Man merkt komischerweise der Region ihre Kultur bisher nicht an... Ist das vielleicht ein Grund dafür, dass so viele Leute hier von der Zukunft sprechen?

REFLEKTOR: Haben Sie selbst, der schon sehr früh auch im Ausland studiert hat, heute international arbeitet und dabei nicht mehr in Deutschland lebt, je kulturelle Unterschiede in der Kontaktfreudigkeit der Europäer erfahren?

GERZ: Zuerst bedeutete in der Nachkriegszeit für einen Deutschen, von Nichtdeutschen als eine Art Besonderheit angesehen zu werden, etwas zwischen Dracula und einem Verstörten. Man lebte mit dem Blick der Anderen, und Kontakte waren oft für beide Seiten keine Routine. Es war nicht der gewöhnliche, kleine Rassismus, wie er ja auch heute noch zwischen den Menschen Europas zu finden ist, sondern der fast kulturelle Rassismus, der in den Verbrechen der Nazidiktatur eine fast ultimative Bestätigung und ein Alibi gefunden hatte. Diese »Bedingung« im Ausland führt immer wieder zu ganz intensiven Beziehungen und zu einer großen Neugier auf die kulturellen Unterschiede in Europa oder anders gesagt, für die Vielfalt im immer wieder ganz Ähnlichen. Europa ist zu viel für ein Leben.

REFLEKTOR: Mit Ihren verschiedenen Aktionen und partizipativen Arbeiten suchen Sie im öffentlichen Raum Kontakt zu Ihrem Publikum. Wird es heute zunehmend schwieriger, fremde Menschen zur Teilnahme an Ihren Arbeiten zu aktivieren? Und wie vermeiden Sie das Risiko, vielleicht dabei gerade auch nicht Ihr »ideales« Publikum zu adressieren? Was bedeutet Ihnen persönlich dieser mittelbare Kontakt über Ihre interaktiven Installationen zu den Ruhrgebiet-Bewohnern?

GERZ: Ich habe kein Publikum. Der Betrachter ist eigentlich eine enttäuschende Erfahrung für die Kunst [und auch für die Demokratie]. Ich suche Teilnehmer, Autoren wie ich sie nenne. Ich habe mich vor 2000 entschieden, keine Arbeit mehr zu machen, die ich alleine realisieren kann. Seither spielt die Öffentlichkeit eine große Rolle in meiner Arbeit. Wir haben gelernt, die Werke Anderer zu schätzen. Jetzt ist es an der Zeit, die eigenen Vorstellungen von der Welt an sich selbst zu messen.

REFLEKTOR: In zahlreichen Arbeiten scheinen Sie Austausch und Kontakt auch ganz entschieden als Tausch, als ein Geschenk oder als eine Gabe zu definieren. Damit wäre vielleicht auch symbolisch der Stellenwert von Kommunikation und Interaktion in Ihrem Werk markiert: Kontakt ist demnach wertvoll, kostbar und immer ein Gewinn für die Gesellschaft. Kann Ihrer Meinung nach dabei aus Kontakt[en] auch Kreativität entstehen?

GERZ: Die Wörter wechseln, doch die Sehnsucht nach Kontakt ist immer schon vor den Wörtern da. Es gibt viele Gründe und viele Formen der Sehnsucht, auch die Grausamkeit und der Krieg oder auch Spiel, Sport, Liebe und Frieden sind Formen der Sehnsucht nach Kontakt. Und die Kunst? Jeder sagt es auf seine Art und anders: ohne Kommunikation macht nichts Sinn. »Auf seine Art und anders« zu sprechen bedeutet kreativ sein. Ich glaube nicht, dass Kreativität nur in der Kunst zu finden ist, im Gegenteil. Man sollte beim Künstler nicht suchen, was man in der Gesellschaft und bei sich selbst nicht finden kann.

REFLEKTOR: Ihre Arbeiten werden immer auch von Büchern und Katalogen und neuerdings auch von Websites im Internet [wie aktuell unter www.pev2010.eu] dokumentiert. Wie lässt sich Ihrer Meinung nach aus dem mittlerweile etwas antiquierten Format Buch ein gutes, originelles und zeitgemäßes Kommunikationsmedium herstellen? Ein Vehikel für geistige Kontakte über die Zeiten hinweg?

GERZ: Jahre dauernde ästhetische Prozesse, die oft kein materielles Objekt zeitigen, brauchen eine Stütze in konventioneller Form. Wir leben hier und unsere Kultur hat uns gelehrt, allem nur nicht unserer Zeitlichkeit zu trauen. Wir investieren in Objekte. Ein Buch ist wie ein Andenken. Es hilft erinnern, wenn man alleine ist. In der Arbeit, die ich mit vielen Menschen mache, ist man eigentlich nicht alleine, doch mit dem Buch ist man alleine, nachher, und denkt an die Anderen.

REFLEKTOR: Zum Schluss bitte noch Ihre Antwort auf eine Frage, die wir, das Redaktionsteam vom REFLEKTOR, in unserer Kontaktaufnahme per E-Mail an Sie NICHT gestellt haben? Herzlichen Dank!

GERZ: Kontakt hin oder her. Was gefällt Ihnen denn besser: ohne Antwort zu bleiben oder ohne Fragen?

[Das Interview mit Jochen Gerz führte Pamela C. Scorzin für das REFLEKTOR-Team, Juni 2009]

IN CONTACT WITH...
JOCHEN GERZ, Concept and Installation Artist

REFLEKTOR: Dear Jochen Gerz, you are presently living in northern Europe, in Ireland to be exact. After completing projects like »Das Zwanzigste Jahrhundert« [The Twentieth Century] [Oberhausen, 1996], »Das Geschenk« [The Gift] [Dortmund 2000] and »Tausch der Tabus« [Exchanging Taboos] [Duisburg, 2006], you are currently realising two further works for the Ruhr Area. At the moment they are being created for RUHR.2010's arts programme as work[s]-in-progress with the direct participation of the local people: since 2007, the »Platz des Europäischen Versprechens« [Square of the European Promise] in Bochum, and since 2009, the »2-3 Straßen« [2-3 Streets] in Dortmund, Duisburg and Mülheim. There is a brief documentation and description of these projects on your website: www.jochengerz.eu. What actually brought about this continuous intense contact to the Ruhr metropolitan region – a post-industrial conurbation whose society's transformation is currently being talked about as a European model case in connection with its having been offered the European Capital of Culture 2010? Are there special reasons for you personally, as an artist and cosmopolitan, to take an interest and become involved in the Ruhr area? You were already a teacher here once in 2000 in the design department at the University of Applied Sciences and Arts Dortmund.

GERZ: Part of my schooling was spent in the Rhineland and I have known the Ruhr area since then. At the beginning of the 1970s I was often here for exhibitions, prize-giving, lectures, workshops, performances and to work in public places. No other region has so many cultural institutions as the Ruhr area. Nevertheless, the metropolis, as it is referred to now, is not a metropolis. Funnily enough, so far, you can't really notice the region's culture... Is this possibly the reason that so many people here speak about the future?

REFLEKTOR: Having also studied overseas very early on and now working internationally without living in Germany, have you personally experienced cultural differences in the sociability of Europeans?

GERZ: Initially, in the post-war period, Germans were often perceived by non-Germans as a kind of anomaly; something between Dracula and a mental patient. You lived with the other person's glances, and contacts were often not commonplace for either person. It wasn't the general, minor racism as can be found today between people in Europe, but rather a cultural racism, which found an almost ultimate confirmation and alibi in the crimes committed during the Nazi dictatorship. This »condition« abroad, often led to very intense relationships and a large degree of curiosity with regard to cultural differences in Europe or, to put it another way, for the diversity of repeated total similarities. Europe is too much for one lifetime.

REFLEKTOR: Through your various events and participatory works, you seek contact with your audience in public places. Is it becoming increasingly difficult nowadays to motivate strangers to participate in your works? And how do you avoid the risk of possibly not addressing your »ideal« audience? What does this indirect contact to the inhabitants of the Ruhr area via your interactive installations mean to you personally?

GERZ: I do not have an audience. The viewer is actually a disappointing experience for art [and also for democracy]. I look for participants; authors as I call them. I decided before 2000 not to do any more work, which I can realise by myself. Since then, the public plays a big role in my works. We have learnt to appreciate the work of others. It is now time to measure one's own perceptions of the world against oneself.

REFLEKTOR: In numerous works, you seem to define exchange and contact – even quite uncompromisingly – as an exchange, as a gift or as a talent. This would possibly symbolically mark the significance that communication and interaction has in your work: consequently, contact is valuable, precious and always a benefit to society. In your opinion, can contact[s] also bring about creativity?

GERZ: Words change, but the longing for contact is always here before the words. There are many reasons for longing and many types of longing; even cruelty and war or games, sport, love and peace are forms of a desire for contact. And art? Each person has their own different way of expressing himself: nothing is meaningful without communication. Expression »in its own way and differently« means being creative. I do not believe that creativity can only be found in art, quite the contrary. One should not look to artists to find something that one cannot find within oneself or in society.

REFLEKTOR: Your works are always being documented in books and catalogues and now also in the Internet [such as currently under www.pev2010.eu]. In your opinion, how can one create a good, original and modern communication medium from a, meanwhile, somewhat antiquated book format? A vehicle for mental contacts beyond all time?

GERZ: Aesthetic processes lasting many years, which often do not produce any material object, require conventional support. We are living here and our culture has taught us to trust everything except our temporality. We invest in objects. A book is like a memento. It helps to remember when one is alone. In the work that I do with many people, one is actually not alone, but with a book one is alone, and afterwards thinks of the others.

REFLEKTOR: Finally, please could you answer one question which we, the editorial team of REFLEKTOR, did not ask in our e-mail when first making contact? Many thanks!

GERZ: Contact or not. What would you prefer: to be without an answer or without a question?

[The interview with Jochen Gerz was conducted by Pamela C. Scorzin for the REFLEKTOR Team, June 2009]

IN KONTAKT MIT...
KARL-HEINZ PETZINKA, Architekt, Professor für Baukunst, Vorstand und Künstlerischer Programmdirektor der RUHR.2010 GmbH

REFLEKTOR: Lieber Karl-Heinz Petzinka, seit Jahren übernehmen Sie neben Ihrer Arbeit als profilierter Architekt [u.a. des mit dem MIPIM-Award ausgezeichneten Düsseldorfer Stadttors am Rheinufertunnel] und Professor für Baukunst an der renommierten Akademie in Düsseldorf immer wieder unterschiedliche Preisrichtertätigkeiten auf nationaler wie internationaler Ebene. Bitte zu Beginn ein Statement zum Geschäft des Jurors – Last oder Lust? Und wie erfahren Sie als etablierter Profi mit vielen Kompetenzen die Kreativität des studentischen Nachwuchses? Worauf achten Sie?

PETZINKA: Die zeitliche Inanspruchnahme durch meine Preisrichtertätigkeit ist eine angenehme Last. Ich müsste lügen, würde ich etwas anderes behaupten. Inhaltlich und unterm Strich überwiegt ganz klar die Lust; die Lust, – wenn auch indirekt – Gebäude, Städte und Landschaften nach strengen Qualitätsmaßstäben mit zu gestalten, und zwar über das hinaus, was ich selbst als Architekt entwerfe. Es gibt einen guten Grund dafür, dass ich meine Lehrtätigkeit nach der Übernahme der Vorstandsfunktion bei der THS nicht aufgegeben habe. Dass ich sie beibehalten kann, war für mich eine nicht verhandelbare Bedingung, als ich vor der Entscheidung stand, die verantwortungs- und anspruchsvolle Tätigkeit bei dieser Immobiliengesellschaft anzunehmen. Die frische Herangehensweise und Unverbrauchtheit der Studenten schätze ich. Ich bin zwar der Dozent, aber es gibt keinen Jahrgang, aus dem ich nicht auch etwas mitnehme. Gutes Handwerk setze ich voraus. Was mich bei den Studenten immer wieder beeindruckt, ist, wenn sie neue und unkonventionelle Lösungsansätze finden für Herausforderungen, die wir aus den Erfahrungen des Lebens anders, vielleicht auch pragmatisch gelöst hätten. Diese Frische ist bemerkenswert. Sie erinnert mich immer an mein Ziel, selbst so vorbildlich unvoreingenommen wie die jungen Leute zu bleiben.

REFLEKTOR: Ihnen eilt schon lange der Ruf als kreativer Vordenker der Architekturszene voraus – neben Ihrer persönlichen Verbundenheit zum Ruhrgebiet ist das vermutlich auch ein Grund dafür, dass Sie 2007 von der RUHR.2010 GmbH, der Trägergesellschaft für das Europäische Kulturhauptstadtjahr 2010, zu einem der vier künstlerischen Direktoren berufen wurden, und in dieser Funktion seitdem das Programm für das Themenfeld »Stadt der Möglichkeiten« verantworten. Die Metropole Ruhr darf 2010 auf viele Veranstaltungen und Szenografien gespannt sein. Welche Rolle wird neben der Architektur und der Kunst darin das Design spielen?

PETZINKA: Mit Ihrer Erlaubnis möchte ich die Frage nach der Rolle des Designs in Bezug auf Architektur und Kunst so nicht beantworten. Design ist letztlich eine Frage der Oberflächengestaltung, des Gefallens, des Missfallens, des Zeitgeistes usw. Die Fragen, die uns im Rahmen der Kulturhauptstadt wirklich beschäftigen, behandeln eher inhaltliche und perspektivische Aspekte. Hier sind insbesondere metropolitane Ideen Thema – Veränderungspotentiale, Transformationspotentiale und die große Frage der Nachhaltigkeit. Die Kulturhauptstadt hat sich das Motto »Wandel durch Kultur, Kultur durch Wandel« gegeben. Daran sehen Sie, wie umfassend wir Kultur begreifen. Sie lässt sich nicht auf einzelne Facetten wie Architektur und/oder Kunst reduzieren. Wir arbeiten mit einem erweiterten Kulturbegriff – im Übrigen schon seit IBA Emscher Park. Provokant formuliert könnte ich feststellen, dass immer dann, wenn es darum geht, Wagnisse einzugehen, ein Großteil der Menschen aufgrund ihrer über Jahre antrainierten Sehgewohnheiten dem ablehnend gegenüber steht. Je allgemein verständlicher jedoch im jeweiligen Kontext Anspruch und Aufgabe sind, umso höher die Akzeptanz. Nehmen wir zum Beispiel den Begriff der »Urbanen Kulturlandschaft«. Er ist eine Wortneuschöpfung im besten Sinne: Es geht in der Metropolendiskussion des Ruhrgebiets einerseits um Fragen des Urbanen, es geht aber auch um Fragen der Kultur und des Landschaftsraums – das vereint der Begriff »Urbane Kulturlandschaft«. Es geht nicht um die Frage von Design und Oberflächengestaltung im Sinne eines zu entwerfenden Erscheinungsbildes. Vielmehr müssen sich neue und konsensfähige Bilder für diese neue Metropolregion aus den Zielsetzungen des erweiterten Kulturbegriffes quasi organisch entwickeln. Nicht umsonst steht bei uns die Transformationsidee im Mittelpunkt. Auf der einen Seite werden die Emotionen und der geschichtliche Kontext damit eingefangen, auf der anderen Seite wird über die Transformation und das Impuls gebende Neue in der Regel das Übermorgen bezeichnet, und hier ist der Erfolg der Projekte auch bei den Bewohnern des Ruhrgebiets am größten. Sie verstehen ihre Herkunft, sie akzeptieren ihre Vergangenheit und sie streben nach Aufbruch und Zukunft. Nichts ist geeigneter als die Transformation der großen Monumente, um eine solche neue Welt widerzuspiegeln. Sie sind wichtige Gesichter und bildgebende Bauten für die Herausforderungen von übermorgen.

REFLEKTOR: Der kreative Imperativ scheint derzeit für die Metropolregion RUHR allgegenwärtig. Der Slogan »Wandel durch Kultur – Kultur durch Wandel« bestimmte bereits die Bewerbung des Ruhrgebiets um den Titel und Austragungsort »Europäische Kulturhauptstadt 2010«. Auch Sie scheinen dabei ganz auf die Kreativität als Motor zu vertrauen. Lässt sich eine postindustrielle Region wie das Ruhrgebiet durch Bildende Künste revitalisieren? Schaffen Inszenierungen und Szenografien hier neue Wirklichkeiten, indem sie die Entwicklungen in einer Region in Transformation beschleunigen?

PETZINKA: Nehmen wir ein zentrales Kulturhauptstadt-Projekt, »Die Emscher-Kunst-Insel«, eingerahmt durch den Rhein-Herne-Kanal und die Emscher. Es wäre ein Leichtes gewesen, international anerkannte Künstler aufzufordern, ihre bildende Kunst in den Kontext eines Landschaftsraumes zu implantieren. Wir haben uns aber für einen anderen Weg entschieden. Über eine Strecke von 35 km haben wir auf der Emscher-Insel sogenannte Suchräume definiert. Es waren letztlich sieben an der Zahl. Diese Suchräume ihrerseits markieren und bezeichnen ganz besondere Landschafts- und Industriegebäudekonstellationen: kreuzende Kanäle, aufgelassene Klärwerke, von der Autobahn zerschnittene Parkanlagen usw. Beim Projekt »Emscher-Kunst-Insel« war nicht der Künstler allein konzeptgebend. Vielmehr fungierte die vorgefundene Ausgangssituation als Motor der Kreativität. Wir haben jeweils zwei Künstler unterschiedlicher Denkrichtung zu einem Duo zusammengespannt, mit ihnen die Suchräume ausgekundschaftet und nach Ideen und Lösungen geforscht. Nicht überraschend war, dass die Künstler erst durch das, was sie vorfanden, den eigentlichen Einstieg in das Projekt gefunden haben. Es sind dabei unglaubliche Kunstwerke entstanden, von denen wir alle das Gefühl haben, dass sie dauerhaft an diesen neuen Ort gehören. Daraus ist die Idee entstanden, auf der Emscher-Insel biennale Kunst zu etablieren. So wurde die Umgestaltung des »Neuen Emschertals«, die mit der Renaturierung der Emscher einhergeht, fest eingebunden in eine Mehrwert schaffende Idee – nämlich Kunst, Landschaftskunst, schlichtweg das ganze Spektrum gestaltender Künste in den neuen Emscherraum einzubeziehen. Hier wird es am Ende kein starres Kunstfeld als Vermächtnis von 2010 geben, sondern einen fortgesetzten integrativen Prozess, innerhalb dessen Künstler und Geldgeber mit großer Experimentierfreudigkeit agieren und Neues wagen können. Jetzt schon ist dies eines der Projekte, die mit besonderer Aufmerksamkeit in den einschlägigen anspruchsvollen Medien verfolgt werden. Gleichermaßen spielt die Lichtkunst eine bedeutende Rolle. Bereits jetzt ist das Ruhrgebiet die bedeutendste Lichtkunstregion der Welt überhaupt. Bisher sind 148 Lichtkunstwerke der berühmtesten Lichtkünstler aus allen Teilen der Erde in diesen großen urbanen Kulturraum integriert worden. Nicht nur festivalartig, sondern auch im Biennale- und Triennale-Turnus werden hier ständig neue Impulse gesetzt. An diesen beiden Beispielen können Sie schnell erkennen, dass die Metropole auf den Kulturtourismus setzt. Mit Superlativen lässt sich nicht nur gut werben, sondern es gibt auch anspruchsvolles touristisches Publikum, das mit Neugierde einen solchen neuen Metropolenbereich durchstreift, entdeckt und möglicherweise – und das ist das Ziel – wiederkehrt. Insofern ist Ihre Frage sicher in dem Sinne zu beantworten, dass wir eigentlich vitalisieren und nicht revitalisieren, dass wir Inszenierungen und Szenografien im Sinne eines künstlerischen Wertes schaffen und dass wir nicht neue, sondern andere Wirklichkeiten entwickeln, die die Region in der Tat in die Zukunft tragen sollen. Eine elementare Botschaft unserer Projekte ist auch, dass wir eine unkonventionelle Metropole sein wollen. Wir lassen Dinge zu, die es woanders weder zu denken noch zu realisieren gibt.

Wir stellen Räume, Flächen und Möglichkeiten zur Verfügung, die Sie so schnell in keiner anderen Region finden. Uns kommt hier gerade der kritische Zeitpunkt des Wandels von der industriellen zu einer postindustriellen bzw. zu einer von Kultur getragenen Zukunft begünstigend entgegen.

REFLEKTOR: Das Ruhrgebiet ein Europa im Kleinen? Die Region wurde durch eine Einwanderung aus allen europäischen Ländern geprägt. Gibt es für Sie überhaupt so etwas wie eine seit der Industrialisierung gewachsene Identität des Ruhrgebiets? Wir erleben jedoch gerade hier seit einigen Jahren auch einen massiven Strukturwandel: Das Ruhrgebiet scheint gerade durch die Vergabe des »Europäischen Kulturhauptstadt 2010«-Titels, ähnlich wie Linz 2009, zum europäischen Modellfall erkoren, der zeigt, wie eine postindustrielle Transformationsgesellschaft neue Bilder für ihre noch unbestimmte Identität im Zeitalter der Glocalization sucht. Welches Potential eröffnet sich für Sie als maßgeblicher Verantwortlicher hinter dem Ereignis RUHR.2010, einem mehr als bloßen Marketing- und Tourismusevent?

PETZINKA: Es mag paradox klingen, aber die neue Identität des Ruhrgebiets ist für mich eben diese Wandlungsfähigkeit. Hier kann man doch heute schon an jeder zweiten Ecke staunen. Und die Bevölkerung trägt das mit. Das hat sicher damit zu tun, dass wir hier keine Tabula rasa machen und einen radikalen Neustart auf den Weg bringen, sondern transformieren. Wir heben die ursprüngliche Identität und die Geschichte der Menschen mit auf, in dem, was wir tun. Modell für Europa – das ist der Anspruch, den alle Projekte, die wir in unser Programm mit aufgenommen haben, erfüllen mussten. Natürlich wollen wir auch Bilder schaffen, die faszinieren und um die Welt gehen. Aber würde ich RUHR.2010 als reines Marketing- und Tourismusevent betrachten, hätten wir gerade in meinem Verantwortungsbereich »Stadt der Möglichkeiten« nicht so viele Projekte, die im kommenden Jahr zwangsweise Baustellencharakter haben werden, weil sie sich in einer größeren städtebaulichen Dimension bewegen. Für ein einjähriges Feuerwerk sind die knappen finanziellen Ressourcen des Reviers zu kostbar. RUHR.2010 kann im besten Fall Initialzündung und Katalysator sein für eine perspektivische, längerfristige Entwicklung. Im Ansatz ist das vergleichbar mit der IBA oder eine Fortschreibung der IBA – allerdings sind wir weniger gut ausgestattet mit Fördermitteln und Sponsorengeldern.

REFLEKTOR: Sehen Sie Bestrebungen im Gange, um über 2010 hinaus, Nachhaltigkeit für das Vertrauen in den kreativen Wandel bzw. für die Kreativität des Wandels im Ruhrgebiet zu schaffen? Es wird ja in jüngster Zeit, insbesondere in Dortmund mit dem ambitionierten »U-Projekt« immer wieder von einer umfassenden »Kreativwirtschaft« geschwärmt. Wo und wie könnte Ihrer persönlichen Meinung nach gerade der Nachwuchs, etwa die Studierenden hier des Fachbereichs Design der Fachhochschule Dortmund, mit seinen profilierten Schwerpunkten auf Kommunikation und Visueller Kultur, daran heute schon partizipieren?

PETZINKA: Ich sagte es bereits: Nachhaltigkeit ist eine Grundvoraussetzung für die Kulturhauptstadtprojekte von RUHR.2010. Aber es ist ja nicht so, als wäre jetzt bereits alles gelaufen und fest zementiert. Stichwort »Dortmunder U«: Bringen Sie sich doch ein, melden Sie Bedarf und Interesse an.

Darauf warten wir förmlich. RUHR.2010 ist in diesem Sinne keine gemachte, zeitlich begrenzte Sache, sondern ein Anfang – eher wie eine Schneise. Viele der neuen kreativen Quartiere, von denen wir reden, müssen im Übrigen gar nicht neu gebaut, sondern vielmehr nur erobert werden.

REFLEKTOR: Heute schon ein weiterer kleiner Ausblick auf die Zeit nach RUHR.2010 – zum Abschluss bitte kein offizieller, sondern eher ein persönlicher! Es heißt, Sie planen zusammen mit dem »Malerfürsten« Markus Lüpertz die Gründung einer neuen privaten Akademie in Potsdam. Uns, das REFLEKTOR-Team, interessiert natürlich nur eins: Planen Sie die Akademie mit oder ohne Design als kreativer Disziplin?

PETZINKA [lacht]: Wer hat Ihnen denn das erzählt? Es ist sicherlich eine interessante Idee, aber lassen Sie sich bitte nicht in die Irre führen. Ich plane keine Gründung einer neuen und privaten Akademie in Potsdam mit Markus Lüpertz. Richtig ist, dass ich mit ihm an einer Monumentalplastik arbeite, die ich auf den Turm unserer THS Hauptverwaltung Nordstern und auf ein Stück von mir entwickelter Architektur stellen möchte. Damit habe ich mich natürlich in einen kommunikativen Prozess begeben, der – das können Sie sich gut vorstellen – nicht immer von Zustimmung geprägt ist. Ich habe bewusst einen der größten Ikonografen der Kunstszene gewählt, um mit ihm eine solch zeichenhafte Figur – in diesem Falle wird es der Herkules sein – zu entwickeln. Lüpertz' Pläne, in Potsdam eine Architekturschule zu gründen, haben möglicherweise ganz andere Zielsetzungen als wir zunächst glauben. Lüpertz war über 20 Jahre Rektor der Kunstakademie in Düsseldorf und ist weit entfernt vom Ruhestand. Dass er sich jetzt für eine Zeit lang nach Berlin bzw. Potsdam gezogen fühlt, das mag ihm Grundlage für neue Höhenflüge sein. Das, was ich schätze, sind der Wunsch und der Wille zu immer wieder neuem Anfang, zu immer wieder neuen Ideen. In Lüpertz' Fall ist das eben eine neue und private Malerschule. Ich käme nicht auf die Idee, Herrn Lüpertz die Designdisziplin anzutragen. Er würde es nicht nur nicht machen, er hat mit Design tatsächlich nichts zu tun. Er ist Künstler, ungerichtet und quer denkend. Wenn Sie mich umgekehrt fragen, inwieweit Design als kreative Disziplin in Zukunft eine Rolle spielen wird, da bin ich überzeugt, dass im »Dortmunder U« genau der richtige Ort sein wird – durch das Implementieren neuer Kreativgruppen, durch die Kommunikationswelt, den Chanel 2010, das kreative Umfeld, das die Stadt Dortmund dort ansiedeln will, und viele Dinge mehr. Das wird auch einer Kreativdisziplin wie dem Design andere und weiter reichende Impulse geben. Ich bin gespannt, was aus solchen Chancen wird. Ich bin gespannt, ob der Hinweis »Beteiligt Euch an der Diskussion, bringt Euch ein in diese Diskussion« aufgenommen wird. Das wäre ein Zeichen dafür, dass wir mit den Ideen der Kulturhauptstadt tatsächlich fruchten und Impulse setzen.

[Das Interview mit Karl-Heinz Petzinka führte Pamela C. Scorzin für REFLEKTOR, Juli 2009]

IN CONTACT WITH...
KARL-HEINZ PETZINKA, Architect, Professor of Art and Architecture, Member of the Board of Directors and Artistic Programme Director for RUHR.2010 GmbH

REFLEKTOR: Dear Karl-Heinz Petzinka, for several years already, in addition to your work as a renowned architect [amongst other things receiving the MIPIM Award for the Düsseldorf City Gate on the banks of the Rhine] and as Professor for Architecture at the prestigious Academy in Düsseldorf, you have always taken part in varying judging activities on a national as well as an international level. Please can you just give a statement as to the judging business – burden or pleasure? And how do you, as an established professional with numerous competences, experience up-and-coming students? What do you pay attention to?

PETZINKA: The time taken up by my judging activities is more of a pleasure than a burden. I would be lying if I said anything else. When it comes to content, the bottom line clearly has to be pleasure; the pleasure – albeit indirectly – to design buildings, cities and landscapes according to strict quality standards, in fact over and beyond that, which I myself, as an architect, design. There is a good reason why I did not give up my teaching activity after I took on the function as a member of the board of directors at THS. To continue teaching was for me a non-negotiable condition when faced with the decision to accept the responsible and demanding position at this real-estate company. I appreciate the students' fresh and unspent approach. Even though I am the lecturer, I get something out of each year. I take good craft for granted. What never ceases to impress me with the students is how they find new and unconventional approaches to a solution for challenges, which we, based on our life experience, would have solved differently, possibly even pragmatically. Such freshness is remarkable. It always reminds me of my goal: to constantly stay as exemplarily unbiased as the young people.

REFLEKTOR: The reputation as a creative pioneer in the architectural scene has preceded you for a long time already. Besides your personal solidarity with the Ruhr area, this is most likely one of the reasons why in 2007 you were called by RUHR.2010 GmbH, the sponsoring company for the »European Capital of Culture Year 2010«, to be one of the four artistic directors. Since then, you are, in this capacity, responsible for the programme »City of Possibilities«. The metropolitan area Ruhr can certainly look forward in anticipation to the many events and scenographies. What role will design play in addition to architecture and art?

PETZINKA: With your permission, I would prefer not to answer the question as to the role of design in relation to architecture and art in this way. In the final analysis, design is a question of surface configuration, appeal, dislike and Zeitgeist. The questions which really occupy us within the framework of the cultural capital rather concern aspects related to content and perspective. Here, the issue is more of a metropolitan nature – potential for change, potential for transformation and the important question of sustainability. The cultural capital has adopted the slogan: »Change through Culture – Culture through Change«. You can see how comprehensively we perceive culture. It cannot be reduced to individual aspects such as architecture and/or art. We are working with an expanded concept for culture – and, by the way, have been doing so since the IBA Emscher Park. Provocatively expressed, I was able to notice that whenever one is about to take a risk, one is faced with opposition by the majority of people based on their longstanding ingrained viewing habits. The more generally understandable, although demanding in the relevant context and task, the higher the acceptance. As an example, let us use the term »urban cultural landscape«. This is a typical new word creation: on the one hand, when discussing the metropolis of the Ruhr Area, the issue is about urbanism, but it is also about issues related to culture and the landscape – this then combines the term: »urban cultural landscape«. The question is not about design and surface design within the context of an image that requires design. Rather, new images as well as those images able to produce a broad consensus must develop for these new metropolitan regions, quasi organically, out of goals for an expanded concept of culture. It is not without reason that our focus is on transformation. On the one hand emotions and historical concepts are thus captured, and on the other hand, via the transformation and the new creation, which provides the impulse, defines the day after tomorrow. And it is here that the projects' success is the greatest – also with the inhabitants of the Ruhr area. They understand their origin; they accept their past and strive towards an awakening and the future. Nothing is more appropriate than the transformation of the large monuments in order to reflect such a new world. These are important faces and image-providing buildings for the challenges of the day after tomorrow.

REFLEKTOR: The creative imperative appears to be omnipresent for the Ruhr metropolitan region. The slogan: »Change through Culture – Culture through Change« already determined the Ruhr area's application for the title and locality for »European Capital of Culture 2010«. You, too, appear to fully trust creativity as the driving force. Can a post-industrial region, such as the Ruhr area, be revitalised through visual arts? Will productions and scenography be able to bring about new realities here by speeding up the developments within a region, which is in transformation?

PETZINKA: Let us look at a central cultural capital project »The Emscher Art Island«, enclosed by the Rhine-Herne-Channel and the Emscher. It would have been very easy to ask internationally recognised artists to implant their visual art in the context of a landscape. We decided, however, to go another route. Over a distance of thirty-five kilometers, we identified so-called »search areas« on the Emscher Island. In the end there were seven. These search areas individually represent and define very special constellations in terms of landscape and industrial buildings, intersecting canals, abandoned wastewater treatment plants, parks cut across by the motorway, etc. Not only the artist provided the concept for the project »Emscher-Art-Island«. Rather, the existing initial condition acted as the driving force for creativity. We created teams of two artists with differing schools of thought, scouted out the search areas with them and searched for ideas and solutions. It was not a surprise that the artists could only identify with the project once they had actually seen the location. Incredible works of art came about, which we all feel belong in this new location for all times. This is where the idea to establish biennial art on the Emscher Island originated. In this way, the redesign of the »New Emschertal«, a consequence of the renaturation of the Emscher, is firmly integrated in a concept of added value, namely to include art, landscape art, simply the whole spectrum of formative arts in the new Escher area. Instead of a stark art field as a legacy of 2010, there will be a continued integration process. This process will allow artists and sponsors to daringly create something new and be enthusiastic whilst proactively trying out original ideas. This is already now one of the projects being followed in pertinent, discerning media and being given particular attention. Equally, light art also plays an important role. Already now, the Ruhr area is actually the most important light art region in the world. So far 148 light art works of the most famous light artists worldwide have been integrated in this large urban cultural area. New impulses are constantly being established not only for festivals, but also on a bi-annual and tri-annual rotation. You can quickly see by these two examples that the metropolis is counting on cultural tourism. Not only do superlatives make for good self-advertising, but there is also a demanding touristic public, which combs though, discovers and possibly – and this is the actual goal – returns to such new metropolitan areas with curiosity. In this respect, your question must be answered against the background that we actually vitalise and not revitalise; that we create productions and scenographies according to an artistic value and that we do not develop new but other realities, which should effectively carry the region into the future. Our projects' basic message is also that we want to be an unconventional metropolis. We permit things to happen, which are neither considered nor realised elsewhere. We provide rooms, space and opportunities, which would be hard to find in another region. It is particularly this critical period of change from an industrial to a post-industrial or a culture-based future that works in our favour.

REFLEKTOR: The Ruhr area – Europe on a small scale? The region was influenced by immigration from all European countries. Do you feel that the Ruhr area actually has an identity, which emerged from the period of industrialisation? For a few years already, we have been also been experiencing a massive structural change here. Since it was

awarded the title of »European Capital of Culture 2010« – similar to Linz in 2009, the Ruhr area seems to be have been selected as a European model case, which shows just how a post-industrial transformation society is seeking new images for its still undetermined identity in an area of »glocalization«. What potential do you personally, as someone with decisive responsibility, feel about the event RUHR.2010, besides a mere marketing and tourism event?

PETZINKA: It might sound paradoxical, but for me the Ruhr area's new identity is actually all about this kind of flexibility. Even today, there is something amazing taking place at every street corner – with the backing of the population. This is certainly partly due to the fact that we are not making a clean sweep and introducing a radical new start, but transforming. We incorporate the original identity and the history of the people in all that we do. Model for Europe – that is the claim that we had to fulfill for all projects, which we included in our programme. Naturally, we also wanted to create images that fascinate and are of global appeal. But if I were to see RUHR.2010 as being a mere marketing and tourism event, we would not have so many projects – particularly in my field of responsibility »City of Possibilities« – which in years to come would have the characteristics of a building site as these projects move in dimensions involved in larger town planning. The tight financial resources are much too precious for a one-off firework. At best, RUHR.2010 can be the initial spark and catalyst for a perspective long-term development. In essence, this can be compared with the IBA or an update of the IBA, however, with less plentiful subsidies and sponsorships at our disposal.

REFLEKTOR: Do you see any attempts being made to create sustainability beyond 2010 in terms of trust in the creative change, or for the creativity of change in the Ruhr area? Recently, the rave is all about a comprehensive »creative economy«, in particular with regards to Dortmund with its ambitious »U-Project«. In your personal opinion, where and how could the students participate in this today, particularly the upcoming generation such as, in this example, the students in the design department at the University for Applied Sciences and Arts Dortmund with its profiled main emphasis on communication and visual arts?

PETZINKA: As I have already mentioned: Sustainability is the basic precondition for projects related to the cultural capital of RUHR.2010. But it isn't as though everything has already happened and is written in stone. Look at Dortmund's »U-Project«: Participate! Tell us about your needs and interests. We are anxiously waiting for this kind of response. In this respect, RUHR.2010 is not a completed, time-restricted thing but more of a beginning – like paving the way. As a matter of fact, many of the new creative districts, which we will be talking about, do not even have to be built from scratch, but rather only conquered.

REFLEKTOR: In conclusion, can you give us a further outlook for the time after RUHR.2010 – but please not from an official but rather from a personal point of view! There is talk that you are planning to establish a new, private academy in Potsdam together with the »Painting Prince«, Markus Lüpertz. We, the REFLEKTOR Team, are naturally only interested in one thing: Are you planning an academy with or without design as a creative discipline?

PETZINKA [laughs]: Who told you that? It is certainly an interesting idea; but don't let yourself be misled. I am not planning to establish a new and private academy in Potsdam with Markus Lüpertz. It is true, however, that we are currently working together on a monumental sculpture, which I plan to place on the tower of our THS Headquarters Nordstern and on an architectural object that I created. This naturally meant that I became involved in a communicative process which – as you can well imagine – is not always met with approval. I have purposely chosen one of the greatest iconographs in the art scene to develop such a symbolic figure – in this case it will be Hercules. Lüpertz's plans to establish a school for architecture in Potsdam could possibly have completely different objectives than we initially believe. Lüpertz was the rector of the art academy in Düsseldorf for more than twenty years and is a long way off retirement. The fact that he feels attracted to Berlin, or rather Potsdam, for a while, may be the reason for wanting to climb new heights. What I appreciate is the desire and the will for repeated new beginnings and repeated new ideas. In Lüpertz's case this happens to be a new and private school for painters. It would not cross my mind to suggest that Mr. Lüpertz adopt design as a discipline. Not only would he not do so, but he actually has nothing to do with design. He is an artist; undirected and thinks outside the box. If you were to ask me the other way round in how far design will play a role as a creative discipline in the future, I am convinced that the »Dortmunder U« will be exactly the right place – through implementation of new creative groups; through the world of communication; Chanel 2010, the creative environment that the City of Dortmund wants to establish there; and many other things. This will also provide a creative discipline, such as design, with other and far-reaching impulses. I am quite curious what will become of such opportunities. I am curious whether the remark »Take part in the discussion, include yourself in these discussions« will be accepted. This would be an indication that our ideas for the cultural capital are actually bearing fruit and providing impetus.

[The interview with Karl-Heinz Petzinka was conducted by Pamela C. Scorzin for the REFLEKTOR Team, July 2009]

WORKS THREE 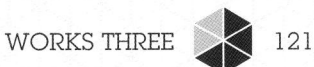 121

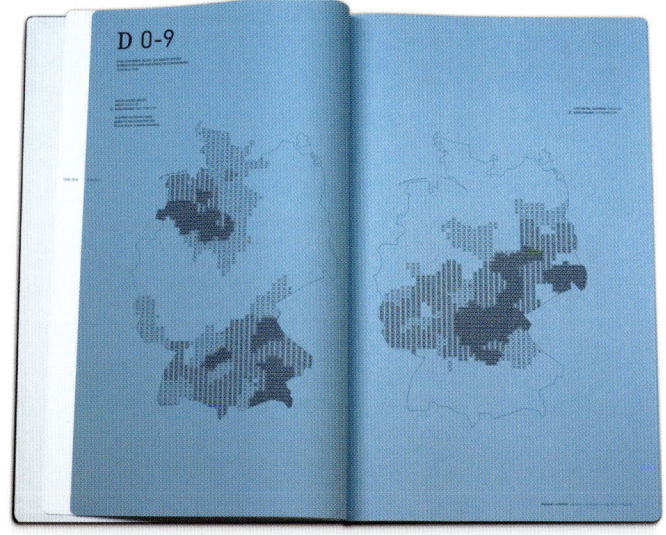
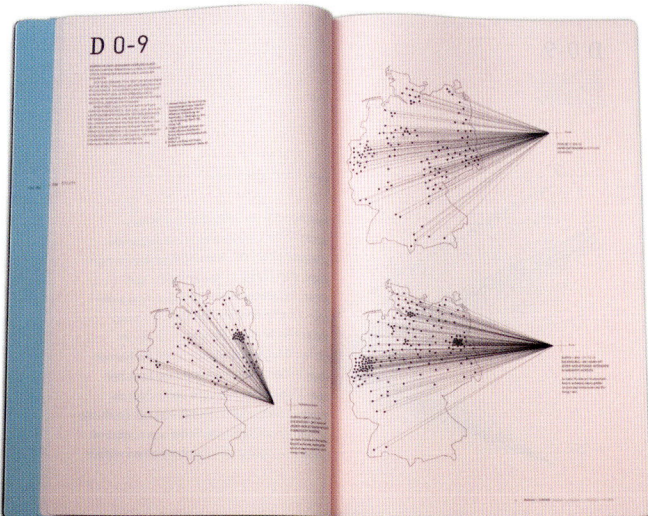

64 Karten, 10 Postleitzahl-Bezirke. Familiennamen haben in Deutschland einen hohen kulturellen Stellenwert. Wissenschaftler vermuten, dass es hierzulande an die 500.000 verschiedenen Familiennamen gibt. In diesen Namen sind viele Informationen konserviert, die sich im Spannungsfeld der unterschiedlichsten wissenschaftlichen Disziplinen bewegen. Eine visuell spannende Schnittmenge bot mir die geografische Verbreitung von Familiennamen, deren Kartierung Volkswanderungen, Dialektgrenzen, Sippennester und andere Phänomene offen legte. Neben dem Buch ist eine Rauminstallation konzipiert, die sich mit der Bewegung von Namen im dreidimensionalen Raum beschäftigt. **64 cards; 10 postal code districts.** Family names have a strong cultural significance in Germany. Scientists assume that there are some 500,000 different family names. In these names, so much information is preserved, which touches the boundaries of the most diverse scientific disciplines. The geographical distribution of family names seemed to me to be an exciting visual convergence because their mapping revealed migrations of peoples, dialect borders, family clans and other phenomena. In addition to the book, a room installation has been conceived, which deals with the movement of names in three-dimensional space.

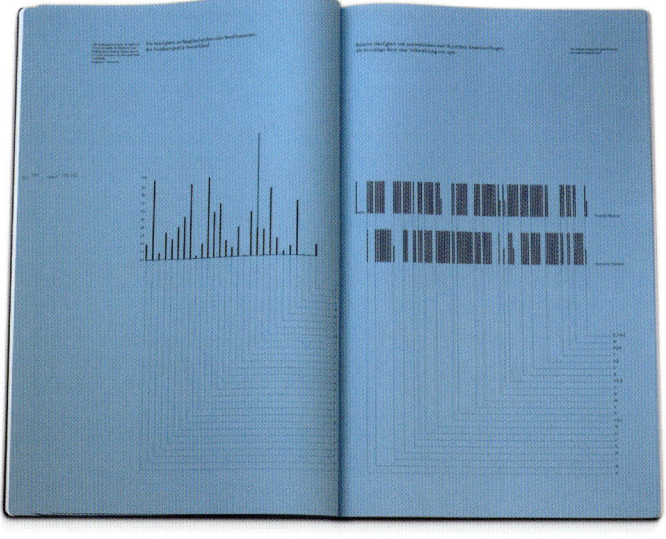

»D 09-64«
Student: Katharina Monkemöller | Semester theme: Diploma | Semester: 11, Graphic design
Type/Scope: Book and model for the room installation | Mentoring: Prof. Sabine an Huef, Prof. Xuyen Dam

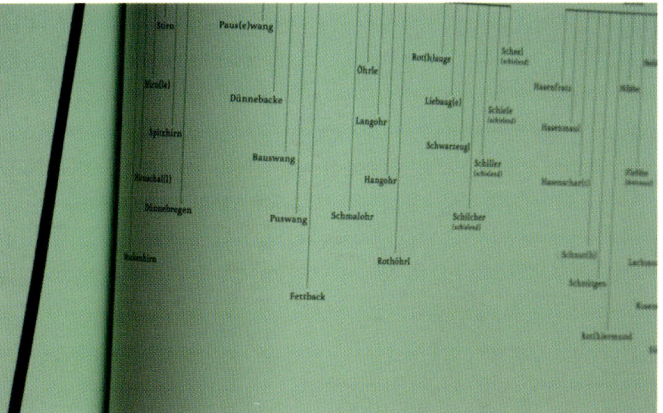

Wenn es dunkel wird... Im Winter, trifft man zur Dämmerung nur wenige Menschen auf den Straßen des Dortmunder Vororts Deusen. Allerdings gibt es dort gerade abends eine Vielzahl von Sport- und Freizeitangeboten, vor allem für Kinder und Jugendliche. Schummrig beleuchtete Eingänge weisen den Weg zu Sportvereinen, Turnhallen, Schwimmbädern und Umkleidekabinen. Beim Vereinssport können die Kinder Selbstvertrauen und Annerkennung erfahren, Teil einer Gruppe werden und sich mit ihrer Sportart identifizieren. Meine Arbeit zeigt Kombinationen aus Portrait, Raum und Stillleben. In den Aufnahmen überwiegt der sehr persönliche Eindruck der geheimnisvollen Atmosphäre dieses abendlichen Sporttreibens. Durch die Lichtführung und die inszenierten Posen wird die mystische, traumhafte und fast schon surreale Atmosphäre der Orte, Gegenstände und Personen noch verstärkt. **When darkness falls...** Nightfall in winter is not a place where you encounter many people on the streets of the Dortmund suburb of Deusen. But this is precisely the place offering numerous sports and leisure activities – particularly for children and youths. Dimly-lit entrances show the way to sports clubs, gyms, swimming pools and changing rooms. Children gain self-confidence and recognition at sports clubs; they become part of a group and identify with their sport. My work shows combinations of portrait, space and still life. The very personal impression of the mysterious atmosphere of nightly sporting activities is predominant in these photographs. The mystical, dreamlike and almost surreal atmosphere of the places, objects and people is further increased by the lighting management and staged poses.

»Nachts«
Student: Hanna Witte | Semester theme: Grid Project | Semester: 8, Photo design
Type/Scope: 5 images | Mentoring: Dirk Gephart | Free submission

»Octanorm«
Student: Johanna Bähner, Veronika Grunst | Semester theme: Micro trade-show stand for the University of Applied Sciences and Arts Dortmund
Semester: 7, Object and Interior design Type/Scope: Computer slide show, 3-D | Mentoring: Prof. Martin Middelhauve

Die Fachhochschule Dortmund möchte sich mit einem Mikromessestand, der aus dem Messebausystem Octanorm gefertigt wird, präsentieren. Der von uns gestaltete Messestand, der sowohl im Gebäude der Fachhochschule, als auch auf externen Veranstaltungen zum Einsatz kommen soll, besteht aus zwei rechtwinklig zueinander stehenden Rahmen mit hochformatigen Paneelen. Auf diesen Stehlen werden großformatige, sympathische Bilder aus dem Fachhochschul-Alltag gezeigt, die mit Texten zum Studium und aktuellen Ausstellungen versehen sind. **The University of Applied Science and Arts in Dortmund would like to present itself with a micro exhibition stand, which is made up of the exhibition system Octanorm. The exhibition stand we designed consists of two right-angled frames respectively positioned with panels in portrait format. This exhibition stand will be used in our building as well as at external events. Large format, sympathetic photographs on pillar-like sections, which will be complemented by study texts and current exhibitions, will depict daily life at the University.**

Rebornsammler mit ihren nahezu lebensechten Puppenbabys. Reborn Babys sind Puppen, die einem echten Kind so genau wie möglich ähneln sollen. Sie werden von sogenannten. »Puppenkünstlern« modelliert, gegossen, bemalt und mit Echthaar bestückt. Es gibt vor allem in den USA eine große Fangemeinde – aber auch in Deutschland boomt der Markt mit den kleinen Puppen. Sie werden gesammelt, bemuttert und verkauft. Ein paar dieser Sammler habe ich mit ihren Lieblingsstücken inszeniert. Die Posen und Gesichtsaudrücke der Sammler geben Rückschlüsse auf die doch sehr emotionale Beziehung zu den täuschend echt aussehenden Plastikpuppen. **Collectors of the Reborn range with their almost lifelike baby dolls. A Reborn baby is a doll designed to resemble a real child as closely as possible. They are modelled, moulded, painted and decorated with real hair by »doll artists«. The number of fans is huge, particularly in the USA; but there is also a booming market for the little dolls in Europe. The dolls are collected, mothered and sold. I have staged a few of these collectors with their favourite showpieces. By looking at the collectors' poses and facial expressions, one can surmise just how emotional the relationship is between the collector and the deceptively lifelike plastic dolls.**

»Reborn«

Student: Hanna Witte | Semester theme: Oddballs | Semester: 8, Photo design
Type/Scope: 5 images | Mentoring: Norbert Hüttermann | Free submission

»Sei doch nicht so«
Student: Alexander Hagmann | Semester theme: Photography in context | Semester: 2, Photo design
Type/Scope: 24 images | Mentoring: Prof. Susanne Brügger | Free submission

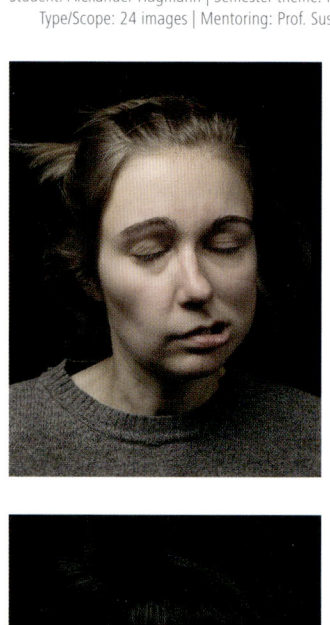

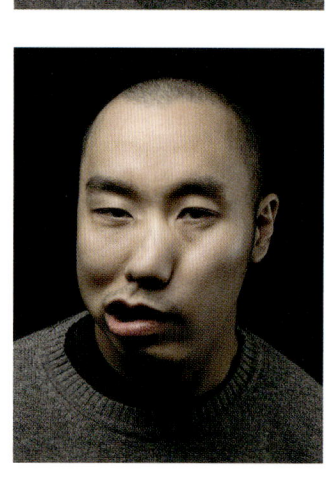
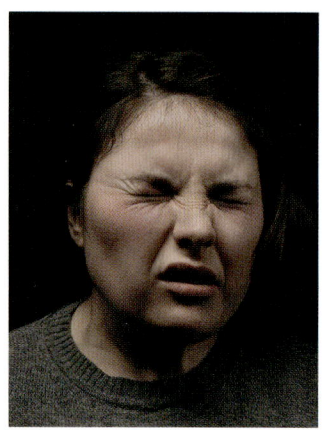
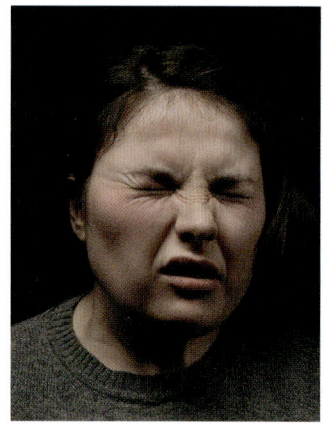

»Schüttel Deinen Kopf solange bis es blitzt! Danach ist alles wieder vorbei.« Das war die Anweisung, welche die Personen vor der Kamera von mir bekamen. Entstanden aus einem Partyspaß mit Freunden machte ich von 24 Kommilitonen Fotos, auf denen sie das bereits bekannte Bild ihrer selbst ablegen mussten und durch die Momentaufnahme in einer Bewegungsausübung einen Gesichtsausdruck bekamen, den man eigentlich so nie zu Gesicht bekommt. Um keine Ablenkung zu erzeugen, waren alle Modelle mit einem neutralen grauen Pullover bekleidet.

»Shake your head until you see the flash! Then it's all over.« That was the instruction I gave the people in front of my camera. Created out of a party-fun mood with friends, I took twenty-four photographs of fellow students in which they were asked to present the image of themselves already known. As a result of the snapshot while they were in motion, they were given a facial expression one would otherwise never get to see. To cause a small distraction, all models were dressed in a neutral, grey sweater.

Die Kleidung in dieser Reihe wurde eigens für diesen Zweck entworfen und aus Haushaltsmüll zusammen gebaut. In diesem Kontext ist Müll ein sehr ursprünglich menschliches Erzeugnis, welches sich der Rationalisierung und Ästhetisierung im Regelfall entzieht. Auch die Studio-Umgebung, in der die Bilder aufgenommen wurden, verweigert sich ihrer gewohnten Aufgabe und entblößt den menschlichen Eingriff. Das ausgewählte Model entspricht zwar in vielerlei Hinsicht den von der Modefotografie geforderten Normen, meidet diese aber auch gezielt an anderer Stelle. **The clothes in this series were especially designed for this purpose and put together from household refuse. In this context, rubbish is a very natural human product that normally is removed from rationalisation and aesthetisisation. Even the studio environment where the photos were taken denied its usual duty and lays bare the human intrusion. In many ways, the chosen model corresponds to those standards required by fashion photographers, however, intentionally also avoids these elsewhere.**

»Mode«

Student: Marina Weigl | Semester theme: Fashion Editorial | Semester: 3, Photo design
Type/Scope: 9 images | Mentoring: Kai Jünnemann | Free submission

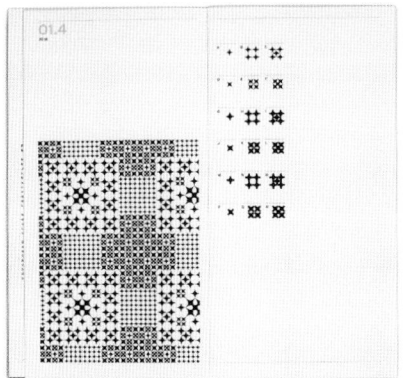

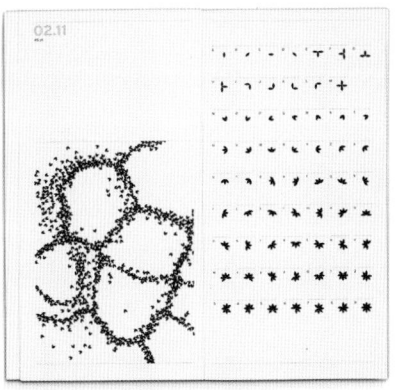

Mit diesem Katalog ist es möglich, sein eigenes, individuelles Muster in jedem Schriftbearbeitungsprogramm zu generieren. Das Muster wird – wie jede andere Schrift – installiert und mit der möglichen Textbearbeitung verändert. Variation entsteht beispielsweise durch Veränderung der Punktgröße des Grundelementes. Der Benutzer kann so spielerisch weitere Muster aus dem gleichen Grundelement entstehen lassen und sich ohne ein Layoutprogramm kreativ betätigen. Durch dieses Medium ist der Benutzer nicht auf die Muster angewiesen, die ihm von anderen Designern vorgegeben werden. Auf der beiliegenden CD sind alle Grundelemente als Open Type vorhanden, die wie jede andere Schrift nur installiert werden müssen. **This catalogue makes it possible to generate one's own personal pattern in any font-processing programme. The pattern is installed – just like any other font – and altered with available word processing. To give you an example, the variation would then come about through changing the basic component's point size. In this way, the user can playfully develop further patterns out of the same basic component and be creative without a layout programme. By using this medium, the user is not dependent on patterns prescribed to him by other designers. All basic components are on the enclosed CD as Open Type which, just like any other font, only requires installation.**

»01_02_03_04_05«
Student: Marek Kowalewski | Semester theme: Free subject | Semester: 5, Graphic design
Type/Scope: Catalogue design Open Type sample | Mentoring: Prof. Xuyen Dam

Die Idee, altertümliche Charaktere in die imaginäre Zukunft oder gar parallele Welt zu holen, beruht auf der Erkenntnis, dass viele Geschichten zeitlos sind. Ich will antike Gestalten aus der altertümlichen Welt in die Science-Fiction Welt bringen und in eigener Bildsprache darstellen. Prometheus, Herkules, Narziss, Ikarus und Pandora sollen in den für sie typischen Situationen dargestellt aber gleichzeitig aus dem Altertümlichen ins Sci-Fi transferiert werden. **The idea to include ancient characters in an imaginary future, or even a parallel world, is based on the recognition that many stories are timeless. I will introduce ancient figures from the Ancient World into a world of science fiction and present them in their own picture language. Prometheus, Hercules, Narcissus, Icarus and Pandora will be presented in a typical situation but, at the same time, transported from the ancient into sci-fi.**

»Neo Olympia«

Student: Dimitri Zaitsev | Semester theme: Fairy tales and myths | Semester: 4, Photo design
Type/Scope: Composite photographs, 4 images | Mentoring: Prof. Jörg Winde

»Ein Mongolenschamane sagte mir, dass ein Stein, der aus dem Boden gegraben werde, sich darüber jahrelang nicht beruhigen könne. Ich halte das für wahrscheinlich.« [Martin Mosebach] Für mich klingt der Satz stimmig und ist ein Teil meines Puzzles, in das Hesses »Siddhartha« ebenso hinein gehört wie Schriften über Morphogenetische Felder, anthropologische Ansätze ebenso wie die Theorie über ein kollektives Bewusstsein. Ich stellte mir die Frage, ob es eine objektive Realität gibt oder wir Gefangene unseres Geistes sind. Dabei sehe ich die Ausdehnung nicht unbedingt darin, sich überschwänglich und pathetisch ins Unermessliche und Metaphorische zu steigern, sondern auch aufs Kleine zu zielen. Um, wie Richard David Precht sagt: »...der Unruhe des Steins das Gehör zu verschaffen, das sie verdient.« Mit meinem Leporello wollte ich die Tür zu ›meinem Zimmer‹ einen kleinen Spalt öffnen.

»A Mongolian shaman told me that a stone which is dug out of the earth is uneasy for many years. I think this is probable.« [Martin Mosebach] I think this sentence is consistent and is a part of my puzzle, which equally includes Hesse's »Siddhartha«, as well as literature about morphogenetic fields, anthropological approaches, in the same way as the theory of a collective consciousness. I ask myself the question whether an objective reality actually exists, or whether we are prisoners of our mind. Hereby, I do not see expansion to effusively and emotively increase into the immeasurable and the metaphoric, but rather to target the small. So as, according to Richard David Precht: »...to give the stone's unease the attention it deserves.« Through my concertina folder, I wanted to leave the door to »my room« ajar – just a little bit...

»Ausdehnung ist alles«
Student: Regine Jentzsch | Semester theme: Adaptation, representation, etchings | Semester: 3, Graphic design
Type/Scope: Book | Mentoring: Gerd Erdmann-Wittmaack, Bernd Dicke | Free submission

»Hundefutter«
Semester theme: Packaging | Graphic design
Mentoring: Prof. Johannes Graf

Zahnwehpaste, Schlankmacher, Wohlfühlwasser oder zahnpflegende Hundekuchen für »Kräftige Beisser«: »Dr. Dog« hat alles, was Hunden gut tut. Die Erste-Hilfe-Marke für den Hund ist eine von mehr als 100 Verpackungen, die Grafikdesign-Studierende gestaltet haben. Unter Leitung von Professor Johannes Graf sollten sie für fiktive Hundefutter-Produkte Markennamen, Logo und mindestens fünf unterschiedliche Verpackungen entwickeln. »Alpha« heißt zum Beispiel eine bewusst billig aussehende russische Hundefutter-Serie, die Deftiges enthält: Echte Rinderohren und Schweinepfötchen, getrocknete Scholle oder Hering – Leckerbissen, die zum Glück für die Nase fest eingeschweisst sind. Ganz anders präsentiert sich die Marke »Tinkerbell« von Heike Becker, die mit ihrer Diätfutter-Linie Modepüppchen-Hunde wie den von Paris Hilton »auf die Schippe« nimmt: Knochen am Stil, damit Frauchen sich die Hände nicht schmutzig macht, charming chocolate oder Ruhigsteller-Pralinen sollen Hundehalter kaufen, bei denen das Tier zum Accessoire verkommt. Für Kampfhamster, Tretminenleger und Teppichporsche gedacht ist die Marke »Rebell«, bei der alles 100-prozentig ist: 100% Knochig, 100% Parma, 100% Beef Flavour und vieles mehr hat die Serie zu bieten. Die Zielgruppe für »Hansen« ist da schon ein ganz anderes Kaliber: Die Spezialnahrung für ausgebildete Wachhunde überzeugt durch edles Aluminium-Design und stählende Inhalte. »Frechdachs« heißt die Marke für den kleinen Hund, der nur Unsinn im Kopf hat. Das Gesundfutter »Methusalem« verspricht ein langes Leben für den älteren Hund. Und »Dogma« vertreibt nur »gesegnetes« Hundefutter. Toothache paste, slim maker, feel good water, toothcaring dog biscuit for a powerful bite: »Dr. Dog« has everything dogs need to feel good! The first aid – brand for dogs is just one of more than one hundred packagings that have been designed by students of graphic design. Supported by Professor Johannes Graf, they had to design brands, logo and at least five different packages for ficticious dog food. »Alpha« for example is the title of an especially cheap looking Russian dog food series that contains hearty meal: real beef ears and pig paws, dried plaice or herring – delicatessen, fortunately looked up away from our noses. A completely different offer comes from the brand »Tinkerbell« by Heike Becker, who takes the mickey out of lapdogs such as the ones owned by IT girls like Paris Hilton with her slim line product. Bones on sticks, so that the Mistress won't get dirty fingers, charming and sedative chocolate, are to be bought by those owners who consider their dog a nice accessory. Developed for battle hamsters, mines rugs or carpet porsches is the brand »Rebell« that offers everything the heart wants on 100 percent: 100% bony, 100% Parma, 100% beef flavour, and much more… Of a completely different kind is the target group of »Hansen«: The special food for trained watchdogs is convincing by its noble aluminum design and strengthening. »Rascal« is the title of a brand for small dogs that have only making nonsense on their mind. The healthy food »Methuselah« promises a long living to elder dogs. And »Dogma« sells blessed food only.

Unsere Wahrnehmung für das Design eines Gegenstandes geht bei gewöhnlichen Dingen des alltäglichen Lebens schnell verloren und es steht nur noch seine Funktionalität im Vordergrund. Um so überraschender und bereichernder kann der Moment sein, den der Betrachter beim genauen Hinsehen erlebt, wenn sich ihm unerwartete Facetten eines Gegenstandes offenbaren und die Dinge plötzlich ein Eigenleben entwickeln. Der Blick für das Gewöhnliche verändert sich, das Wissen um den Gegenstand erweitert sich. Die Fotografie sorgt hier nicht nur für die Abbildung der Dinge, sondern für die Abbildung der Wahrnehmung der Dinge, die sich in einem bestimmten Arrangement ergibt. **Our perception for an object's design is quickly lost when it comes to ordinary daily things and only the object's functionality remains. Therefore, the moment experienced by the observer when taking a closer look, when the unexpected aspects of an object are revealed to him and the things suddenly develop an independent existence, can become all the more surprising and enriching. The eye for the mundane changes, the knowledge of the object expands. Here, photography not only ensures a portrayal of objects, but a portrayal of the perception of the objects, which arises from a certain arrangement.**

»Niemalswelken«
Student: Anneke Dunkhase | Semester theme: Transversale – The Magic of Objects
Semester: 7, Photo design | Type/Scope: 9-11 images | Mentoring: Prof. Caroline Dlugos

Die Beschleunigung in der Arbeitswelt und die stetig schneller werdende Kommunikation durch E-Mail und Mobiltelefon wecken die Sehnsucht nach Entschleunigung. Die Entwicklungen in Mode und Technik schreiten in rasender Geschwindigkeit voran, so dass die beständige Sorge geweckt wird, nicht »zeitgemäß« zu sein. So wird Zeit zum Grundbedürfnis und Luxus. Als durchgängiges Gestaltungselement zieht sich eine waagerecht verlaufende Linie durch das Buch. Sie ist angelehnt an einen Zeitstrahl und zeigt den Fortlauf bzw. eine Bewegung. Durch ihre Position teilt sie das Format. Es entsteht ein waagerechtes Format, das der Ausdehnung von Zeit entspricht. Die reduzierten, stilisierten Illustrationen arbeiten mit einer Doppellinie, die sich auf die Bewegung bezieht. Es wird Dynamik erzeugt. In dem Buch geht es um den Wert der Zeit und darum, wie kostbar Zeit ist – deswegen die Farben Schwarz und Gold. **The acceleration in the professional world and the constantly increasing speed of communication via e-mail and mobile phones stir a desire for deceleration. The developments in fashion and technology are racing forward to such an extent that one cannot help but fear not being »up-to-date«. So time becomes a basic need and a luxury. A horizontal line is drawn through the book as a consistent design element. It recalls a timeline and shows the flow or a movement. Its position divides the format. A horizontal format is created, which corresponds to the expansion of time. The reduced, stylised illustrations work with a double line, which refers to the movement. A dynamic force is created. The book deals with the value of time and with the fact of just how precious time is; hence the colours black and gold.**

»Zeitgemäß«

Student: Katharina Bucheld | Semester theme: Movement and stasis | Semester: 7, Graphic design
Type/Scope: Book | Mentoring: Ben Santo | Free submission

»Was bleibt«

Student: Anja Plonka | Semester theme: Light | Semester: 1, Photo design
Type/Scope: Installation | Mentoring: Prof. Magareta Hesse

Die Arbeit »was bleibt« besteht aus fünf fluoreszierenden Flächen [100 cm x 70 cm], die in einem völlig dunklen Raum installiert sind. Der Blick in den Sternenhimmel weist bekanntlich Leuchtkörper auf, die vermutlich nicht mehr existieren. Das Wahrgenommene ist lediglich das Nachleuchten dieser Körper. Die Arbeit greift diese Thematik auf. Es werden fünf Diaprojektoren – einer für jede Fläche – im Raum verteilt, sie zeigen abwechselnd Fund-Dias aus verschiedensten Nachlässen. Die Dias zeigen ganz intensive, persönliche Momente der Personen aus verschiedenen Zeiten [60er - 80er Jahre]. Das technische Prinzip: Die Projektoren wurden mit Zeitschaltuhren gesteuert. Projektor 1 geht an – dann wieder aus. Projektor 2 geht an. Auf der Projektionsfläche des ersten Projektors sieht man nun das Nachleuchten und das langsame Verschwinden des Dias. So verhält es sich mit den fünf weiteren Projektoren. **The work »what remains« consists of five fluorescent surfaces [100 cm x 70 cm], which are installed in a pitch-black room. As is widely known, looking at the night sky shows light sources, which in all probability no longer exist. That which is perceived is merely the after-glow of these bodies. The work picks up on this subject. Five slide projectors – one for each surface – are distributed in the room; they alternate in showing slides of objects found in various estates. The slides show quite intense, personal moments of the people from various decades [1960s - 1980s]. The technical details: the projectors are controlled by time switches. Projector 1 is switched on – then off again. Project 2 is switched on. On the projection area of the first projector, the previous slide's afterglow and its slow disappearance can be seen. And this is how it works with the five other projectors.**

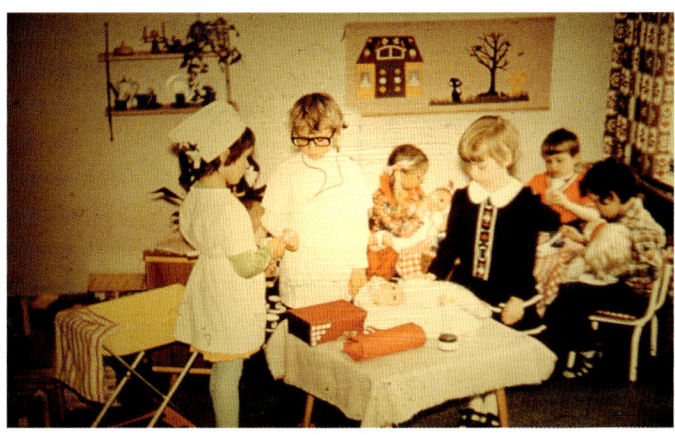

»Lokinique«
Student: Britta Rosing | Semester theme: Diploma | Semester: 12, Graphic design
Type/Scope: 3 packages, posters | Mentoring: Prof. Sabine an Huef | Free submission

Kein Geld, um in den Urlaub zu fahren? Kein Problem! Die Lokinique-Urlaubspakete enthalten alle Informationen und Utensilien, die Sie benötigen, um mit Ihrem Traumurlaub auf Lokinique, in dem Sie angeblich waren, aufzutrumpfen – eine Satire auf unsere »höher-schneller-weiter«-Gesellschaft. Inhalte der Pakete sind: Reiseführer, grundlegende Informationen über die Insel, inklusive Angeber-Tipps, Lernkarten, persönliche Erlebnisse, Aktivitäten etc. zur jeweiligen Urlaubsart, eine Anleitung zur richtigen Nutzung des Paketes und für das richtige Verhalten während des »Urlaubs«, Souvenirs, Postkarten, Flugtickets, Hin- und Rückflug, benutzt, inklusive abgerissener Boardkarten, Selbstbräuner, Blondierungsspray, Autoaufkleber in Inselform, Zusätzlicher Service, Urlaubsfotos vor verschiedenen Kulissen. **No money for a holiday? No problem!** Lokinique holiday packages include all information and utensils, which you need to brag about your dream holiday that you supposedly spent on Lokinique – a satire on our »faster-higher-stronger« society. The package contains: travel guides, basic information on the island, including bragging tips, learning cards, personal experiences, activities, etc. for the relevant type of holiday, instructions for the proper use of the package and for the correct behaviour during the »holiday«, souvenirs, post cards, used airline tickets for the return journey, including torn-off boarding cards, self-tanning lotions, bleaching spray, island-shaped car stickers, additional service, and holiday photographs against different backgrounds.

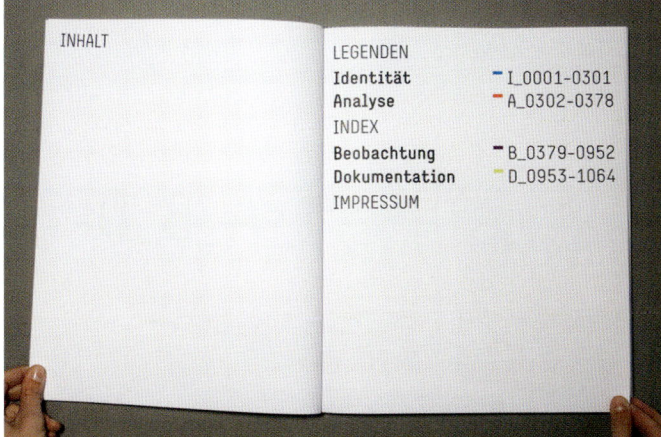

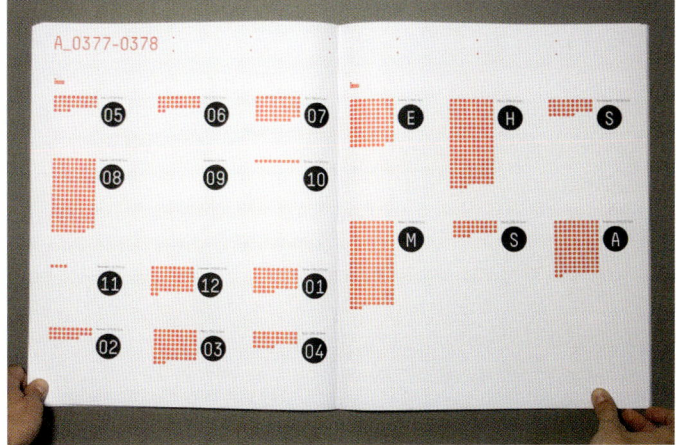

»I_A_B_D«
Student: Marle Koerdt | Semester theme: Diploma | Semester: 9, Graphic design
Type/Scope: Book | Mentoring: Prof. Xuyen Dam

Eine Untersuchung zum Thema Ordnung. Das Buch zeigt eine visuelle Auseinandersetzung mit dem Thema Ordnung, veranschaulicht durch Spuren aus meinem Leben, die mich in die Gesellschaft einordnen. Es zeigt, wie man verschiedenste Informationen ordnet und in einen logischen Zusammenhang bringt. Die Kapitel sind in Zeitabstände gegliedert. Eine Zeitleiste, die sich durch das ganze Buch zieht, zeigt Zeitpunkte bzw. Zeitandauern. Zusätzlich enthält jedes Dokument eine Nummer. In der Mitte des Buches befindet sich ein Index, indem man weitere Informationen zum Dokument findet. Zwei Legenden helfen dem Betrachter, sich mit den Zeichen im Buch zurechtzufinden. **An exploration of the concept of order. The book shows a visual analysis of the concept of order, exemplified by elements from my life, which classify me within society. It shows how one can sort the most varied types of information and combine them into a logical context. The chapters are divided into intervals. A timeline, which is followed throughout the entire book, shows points in time as well as intervals of time. In addition, each document is given a number. There is an index in the middle of the book providing additional information on the document. Two legends help the observer to get to grips with the symbols in the book.**

»HotelHotel – Szenografie in der Hotellerie«

Student: Falko Wübbecke | Semester theme: Master | Semester: 4, Scenography
Type/Scope: Installations, 6 Books, Movie | Mentoring: Prof. Heiner Willharm

Mit sieben Studenten aus dem Fachbereich Design entwickelte Falko Wübbecke für das Pullman Hotel Dortmund das Konzept »Die Stadt im Hotel - Das Hotel in der Stadt« und stellte im Team szenografische Umsetzungsmöglichkeiten der Hoteldirektion vor. Ziel dabei war es, die Stadt Dortmund in den Hotelalltag zu integrieren und dem zukünftigen Gast einen berichtenswerten Eindruck der Stadt zu vermitteln. Schon vor dem Hotel sowie in der Tiefgarage wird der Gast mit einer Klanginstallation von Vogelstimmen begrüßt. Sie stellt »Dortmund« als eine der grünsten Städte des Ruhrgebietes vor. **Together with seven students from the Design Department, Falko Wübbecke developed the concept »The city within a hotel – A hotel within the city« for the Pullman Hotel Dortmund. They presented the scenographic possibilities for its implementation to the hotel management. Their target was to create a direct connection between the city of Dortmund and daily hotel business and thus provide future guests with a worthy memory of the city to be recounted. In the reception area, the guest is welcomed with the theme »Arrive and Decelerate«. The atmosphere has just the right degree of peace for a regular day of work. The particularity of the new fountain installation is the oversized shower head on the fifth floor. Thanks to the open structure, drops of water quietly enter the pool in the reception area in calm sequences. The circles that are created on the surface of the water are projected onto the ceiling by using a halogen spotlight.**

»Der Gast weiß nicht, in welcher Stadt er sich gerade befindet. Unser Ziel ist es, dies durch die Zusammenarbeit mit dem Fachbereich Design der Fachhochschule Dortmund zu ändern.« Uwe Schlünsen, Hoteldirektor Mercure Hotel Dortmund«. **»Currently the guest does not recognise what city he or she is in when staying at the hotel. It is our goal to change that by working together with the design department of the University of Applied Sciences and Art Dortmund«.**

Im Eingang offenbart sich dem Gast eine Lichtskulptur, die einzelne »Schichten« der Stadt darstellt. **In the entrance area, the guest has the chance to observe a light sculpture showing the city in its single »layers«.**

Die Kohle: Arbeitsplatz der Vergangenheit und Dortmunds Grundstein. Die Parks: Die Grünflächen der Stadt – eine der grünsten Städte im Ruhrgebiet. Der BVB: Dortmunds Fußballmannschaft. Die Stadt: It- und Messestadt. Das Bier: Dortmunds wirtschaftliche Vergangenheit, aber auch Gegenwart und Zukunft. Im Foyer wird der Gast unter dem Stichwort »Ankommen und Entschleunigen« mit der nötigen Ruhe für den Arbeitsalltag empfangen. Die Besonderheit der neuen Brunneninstallation ist der überdimensionale Duschkopf in der 5. Etage. Durch die offene Bauweise ist es möglich, dass in ruhigen Abständen Tropfen bis in ein Becken im Foyer eintreten und sich konzentrische Kreise auf der Wasseroberfläche bilden, die mittels Halogenstrahler unter die Decke des Foyer projektiert werden. **Coal: The workplace of the past and Dortmund's foundation stone. Parks: The city's green areas – it is one of the greenest cities in the Ruhr area. BVB: Dortmund's soccer team. The city: A city for IT and trade fairs. Beer: Dortmund's economic past, but also present and future. In the reception area, the guest is welcomed with the theme »Arrive and Decelerate«. The atmosphere has just the right degree of peace for a regular day of work. The particularity of the new fountain installation is the oversized shower head on the fifth floor. Thanks to the open structure, drops of water quietly enter the pool in the reception area in calm sequences. The circles that are created on the surface of the water are projected onto the ceiling by using a halogen spotlight.**

Das Restaurant »Michelangelo« mit der Bar »da Vinci« wurde von unserer Gruppe neu benannt in »Davidis« und »Overbeck« und stellen somit einen erkennbaren regionalen Bezug zur Stadt Dortmund her. Als szenografisch inszenierte Vermittlerin fungiert die über die Stadtgrenzen hinaus bekannte Dortmunder Kochbuchautorin Henriette Davidis, die durch ihren dem Hotelrestaurant verliehenen Namen die Stadt Dortmund ins Hotel holt und damit den regionalen Hotelcharakter unterstreicht. Folglich verbindet sich mit der Namensnennung auch die grafische Gestaltung der Speisen- und Barkarte. **The restaurant Michelangelo with its bar called da Vinci was given a new name by our group and now goes by Davidis and Overbeck. This way, a recognisable regional connection to the city of Dortmund is created. Henriette Davidis, a local cook-book author, well known beyond city limits, is in charge of the scenographic realisation. By naming the restaurant after her, she draws the city of Dortmund into the hotel and thus underlines its character as a regional hotel. Consequently the graphic design of the menus at the bar and restaurant is renewed accordingly.**

13 Vitrinen mit »Dortmunder Originalen« Fundstücken vermitteln über dazugehörige Texte dem Gast Einblicke in die Stadtgeschichte, der somit eine aktive Rolle einnimmt. Dabei war die Positionierung der Vitrinen passend zum Exponat entscheidend, so dass jetzt beispielsweise die Vitrine mit dem original Trikot von Eric Zabel neben dem Heimtrainer im Fitnessbereich des Hotels steht. **Thirteen displays of ›original Dortmund‹ pieces with matching texts provide guests with insights of the city history and thus allow them to take part actively. The positioning of these displays is vital. The original uniform of Eric Zabel was placed next to the exercise machine in the hotel's fitness area.**

»Was für ein Typ!? – Wer verkörpert den Dortmunder des 21. Jahrhunderts? Aktion mit Gewinn-Chance« So lautete die Überschrift am 03.01.2008 in den Ruhr-Nachrichten Dortmund und gab den Startschuss an die »Dortmunder Bevölkerung«. »Die neuen Dortmunder« waren über diesen Aufruf schnell gefunden. Sie wurden von Falko Wübbecke im Fotostudio der FH Dortmund portraitiert und präsentieren sich nun lebensgroß und selbstbewusst im Pullman Dortmund. Ein kurzer Text im Bild verrät nicht nur, warum die jeweilige Person der »typische Dortmunder« ist, sondern vermittelt auch persönliche Lebenseinblicke. Erfahren Sie mehr über die Dortmunder im Pullmann Dortmund. **»What type of guy?! – Who epitomises the typical Dortmund local of the twenty-first century? An initiative with winning options«. This was the headline of the local newspaper Ruhr –Nachrichten Dortmund on 3 January 2008, which started a campaign asking the Dortmund locals to become active. The new »Dortmunders« were quickly found. They were portrayed by Falko Wübbecke in the photo studio of the University of Applied Sciences and Art Dortmund and are now presented confidently and in life size at the Pullman Dortmund. A short text not only reveals why this person is a »typical Dortmund local«, but also gives an insight into their life. Find out more… at the Pullman Dortmund.**

Die unmittelbare Nähe des Hotels zur Westfalenhalle und dem Westfalenstadion offenbart sich erst nach Betreten der Dachfläche, die nicht für jeden Gast zugänglich ist. Die Liveübertragung »Aussichten« überträgt den direkten Blick über drei Flachbildschirme ins Hotel. Diese sogenannte »Echtzeitpostkarte« holt die »Stadt ins Hotel« und zeigt immer ein aktuelles Stadtbild. **The direct proximity of the hotel to the convention hall Westfalenhalle and the stadium [Westfalenstadion] only really becomes obvious when entering the roof area, which is not accessible to all guests. The livestream Outlook, the roof top view, is shown on three flat-screen monitors in the hotel. The so-called »real-time postcard« draws the city into the hotel once more and always provides a current image of the city.**

Erleben Sie das Pullman Dortmund – den direkten Nachbarn der Fachhochschule Dortmund FB Design – mit seinen »Dortmunder Geschichten« und berichten Sie über Ihre Erlebnisse, so dass »Das Hotel in der Stadt« ist. **Experience the Pullman Dortmund – the direct neighbour of the Design Department of the University of Applied Sciences and Arts Dortmund – with its Dortmund stories and tell us about your adventures of how »the hotel is within the city«.**

»Chicken Lamp«
Student: Marcel Sikora | Semester theme: Glorification of a mundane object | Semester: 1, Graphic design
Type/Scope: Single image | Mentoring: Reinhard Rosendahl | Free submission

In meiner Serie »Effizienz« zeige ich das Objekt Automobil in einer ganz neuen Form. Es geht um seinen Stellenwert im 21. Jahrhundert und den Hinweis, wie verletzlich die Automobilindustrie ist. Durch die Streichung aller Attribute reduziere ich das Automobil auf das Wesentliche. Eine veränderbare Form, die nichts weiter als ein Fortbewegungsmittel ist. Ich bringe das Auto an Orte, an denen es losgelöst von seiner eigentlichen Funktion ist und somit zu etwas Neuem wird. Aussehen, Marke, Motorleistung werden verhüllt und daher irrelevant. Die eingepackten Autos bilden nun einen Teil der Landschaft. **In my series »Efficiency«, I show the automobile as an object in a completely new form. It is all about the automobile's significance in the twenty-first century and the reference to the vulnerability of the automotive industry. Through deletion of all its attributes, I reduce the automobile to its basics; a modifiable form, which is no more than a means of transport. I take the car to places where it is isolated from its actual function and thus is transformed into something new. Appearance, make, engine power are veiled and therefore irrelevant. The wrapped cars now become a part of the landscape.**

»Effizienz«
Student: Martin Mascheski | Semester theme: Transversale – The Magic of Objects | Semester: 5, Photo design
Type/Scope: 5 images | Mentoring: Prof. Caroline Dlugos

Die Serie »Trust me, it's a shortcut« greift auf das literarische und filmische Motiv der Abkürzung zurück. Das Abweichen von der geplanten Route, zugunsten einer Zeitersparnis erfordert stets eine Auseinandersetzung mit einer neuen, ungewohnten Umgebung. Wir suchen nach Hinweisen, die uns schneller unserem Ziel näher bringen sollen. Doch wo landen wir, wenn wir nur einen kurzen Moment unkonzentriert sind, die Natur uns überlistet und alle Hinweise auf Ort, Zeit und Ziel verschwinden? Angelehnt an den filmischen Effekt »day for night«, verschmelzen hier Tag und Nacht zu einer angespannten und ambivalenten Atmosphäre, die den Betrachter an seiner Entscheidung zweifeln lassen soll. Location: Portugal. **The series »Trust me, it's a short cut«** draws on the literary and cinematic motif of short cuts. The deviation from the planned route, to save time, always requires a confrontation with a new, unfamiliar environment. We look for signs that can bring us to our destination more quickly. But where do we end up if we lose concentration for just a moment, if nature outwits us and all signs of place, time and destination disappear? Following on the cinematic effect »day for night«, here day and night blend into a strained and ambivalent atmosphere, which is designed to make the observer doubt his decision. Location: Portugal.

»Shortcuts«
Student: Eugen Litwinow | Semester theme: Free subject | Semester: 2, Photo design
Type/Scope: 3 images | Mentoring: Prof. Susanne Brügger | Free submission

Porzellanfiguren sind der Inbegriff der Unschuld, sie zeigen Harmonie und Heile-Welt-Szenarien. Kombiniert und manipuliert man sie, bekommen sie eine völlig neue Bedeutung, die oft erst beim zweiten Hinsehen erkennbar wird – Broken Peaces also! Bei meiner Semesterarbeit habe ich gesammelte Porzellanfiguren zerbrochen, rearrangiert und übermalt. Für den Titel wurde Typografie per Hand aus Porzellan hergestellt. **Porcelain figurines are the epitome of innocence; they depict harmony and scenarios of an ideal world. If one combines and manipulates them, they attain a completely new meaning, which is often only recognised at second glance – namely, Broken Peaces! For my term paper, I broke collected porcelain figurines, rearranged them and painted over them. The typography for the title was created manually out of porcelain.**

»Broken Peaces«
Student: Katrin Rodegast | Semester theme: Free subject | Semester: 6, Graphic design
Type/Scope: 15 subjects | Mentoring: Thomas Linke | Free submission

DEIN IST DAS REICH
DIE PLANETEN-MANUFAKTUR

»Dein ist das Reich – Die Planeten-Manufaktur«
Student: Patrick Schröer | Semester theme: Diploma | Semester: 11, Graphic design
Type/Scope: Box with scion and humus, Book, 3 Campaigns, Website, etc. | Mentoring: Carsten Strübbe | Free submission

output

Wer träumt nicht ab und an davon, ein kleines bisschen eine eigene Welt zu erschaffen? Weder der Urknall noch eine höhere Macht sind für die Entstehung der Erde verantwortlich. Der Ursprung war ein kleiner Steckling des Ortusbaumes, dessen Frucht durch Insekten-Manipulation zu einem riesigen, von uns bewohnbaren Etwas wurde. Die Entdeckung des Stammes, an dem die Erde heran gewachsen ist, bietet nun die Möglichkeit, selbst Stecklinge zu nehmen und neue Planeten, im Einzelnen Planombu genannt, zu züchten. Der Manifest-Katalog und ein Steckling sind die Basis, anhand derer man sich seinen Planombu zusammenstellt. Ausgewählte Insekten manipulieren den Steckling so, dass aus seiner Frucht der gewünschte Planombu wird. Die Basis- und Haupteigenschaften werden im Kern gewählt. Auf ihm wächst das Fleisch in verschiedenen Geländeformen. Die Schale kann viele Strukturen entwickeln und die Geländeformen erweitern. Alles was darüber hinaus in der Atmosphäre geschieht, gehört zu den Raumerscheinungen. Der Fantasie sind dabei keine Grenzen gesetzt. Schöpfe aus den Möglichkeiten und schaffe für Dich, Deine Familie und Freunde oder Deine Stadt ein neues Reich, das einzigartig ist. Who does not dream of creating his or her own little world once in a while? Neither the Big Bang nor some higher power is responsible for the creation of planet Earth. The origin was a small shoot of the source tree whose fruit grew to become something huge and habitable thanks to insect manipulation. This is how Earth grew. The stem's discovery now makes it possible to take shoots and grow new planets, called Planombu. A declaration catalogue and a shoot are the base needed to create one's own Planombu. Selected insects manipulate the shoot such that the fruit turns into the desired Planombu. The basic and main characteristics are selected in the core – or pit, if you will. Around it grows the pulp in different textures. The skin may develop many different structures and amplify the textures. Beyond that, everything that happens in the atmosphere is part of the spatial phenomenon. Fantasy has no limits. Make use of options and create a new and unique kingdom for yourself, your family, your friends or your city.

Ein mobiler Shopaufbau für die Taschenmarke FREITAG. Schnell auf- und abgebaut, bietet der Indoor-Guerillastand für die Taschen aus LKW-Plane eine stimmige und durchdachte Präsentationsfläche. Fünf verschiedene Arten von Kupplungen und unterschiedlich lange Gerüststangen lassen sich zu einem modularen Shopsystem kombinieren. In der Formensprache von Baustellengerüsten und der ihnen eigenen Patina baut sich ein klares Raster auf, in dem die unterschiedlichen Taschen übersichtlich präsentiert werden. An Hängeregistern befestigt und aufgereiht, lassen sie sich durchblättern. Die Register werden auch als Halterung für die Einlegeböden aus Siebdruckplatte oder für Vitrinen genutzt. Die teils auf Rollen montierten Module können zusammen geschoben und mit LKW-Plane verschlossen werden. **A mobile shop for the handbag brand »FREITAG« [FRIDAY].** Easy to set up and take down, the indoor guerrilla stand offers a structured and carefully thought-out presentation area for the handbags made from trucks' tarpaulins. Five different types of clutches and scaffolding poles of varying lengths combine to make a modular shop system. From the design vocabulary of construction scaffolding and its unique patina, a clear grid emerges, where the different handbags can be clearly displayed. Arranged in rows on a hanging file system, they can be leafed through. The files are also used as support for the shelves of sealed plywood or for glass cabinets. The modules, which are partly mounted on casters, can be pushed together and bound together with truck tarpaulin.

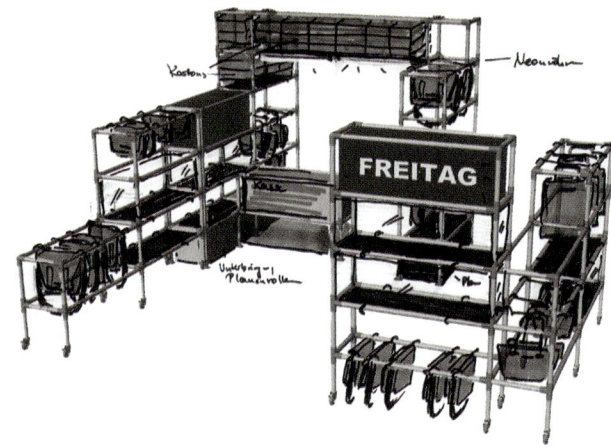

»Guerillashop für FREITAG«
Student: Larissa Prinz, Marie Träger | Semester theme: Retail design: guerilla shops | Semester: 7, Object and Interior design
Type/Scope: Trade show booth | Mentoring: Harald Steber | Free submission

Satirisches Märchenspiel in drei Akten von **Ephraim Kishon** / Premiere 12 August 2009 / **Stadttheater Dortmund**

Das Theaterstück handelt von schwarzen und weißen Mäusen, die sich gegenseitig hassen. Die weißen Mäuse fühlen sich den schwarzen durch ihre weiterentwickelte Lebensart überlegen und blicken auf sie herab. Die Bildidee war es, den Titel des Stückes mit Mäusen dar zu stellen, da sie ja die Hauptcharaktere sind. Die schwarzen Mäuse bilden die Worte »Schwarz auf Weiß«, die weißen Mäuse formieren sich um diese Worte herum. The play is all about black and white mice, which hate each other. Because of their more refined lifestyle, the white mice feel superior to the black mice and look down on them. The concept for the image was to present the play's title with mice – as they are the main characters. The black mice shape the words »Schwarz auf Weiß« [Black and White], the white mice are grouped around these words.

»Schwarz auf Weiß«
Student: Mailin Lemke | Semester theme: Hand-made | Semester: 5, Graphic design
Type/Scope: Poster | Mentoring: Prof. Dieter Ziegenfeuter

Verkehrsschilder – Nach Einschätzung des ADAC ist jedes dritte überflüssig. Sowohl durch ihre Masse als auch durch unnötige Anwendungen bieten sie dem Verkehrsteilnehmer keine Information mehr, sondern stiften lediglich Verwirrung. Dieses Buch soll als eine humorvolle, aber dennoch ernst zunehmende Kritik an dem Schilderwahn in Deutschland gesehen werden. Auf den aus Aluminiumplatten bestehenden Buchseiten findet der Leser verschiedene Möglichkeiten, die nutzlosen Verkehrsschilder zu ergänzen bzw. ihnen eine völlig neue, zum Teil auch abwegige Bedeutung geben zu können. Ihm sind Sprühfarben als auch Sprühvorlagen auf einem USB-Stick beigelegt. **There are more than 20 million traffic signs in Germany. According to the German automobile club [ADAC], a third of these is superfluous. Both through their quantity and their unnecessary application, they no longer offer the road user any information but only cause confusion. This book must be seen as a humoristic, but nevertheless serious, criticism of the road sign madness in Germany. On the book's pages made of aluminium plates, the reader will find different possibilities to supplement the useless traffic signs or to give them an entirely new meaning – at times even an outlandish one. Spray paint as well as spray samples on a USB memory stick are included.**

»Schilderwahn«
Student: Sarah Hruschka, Vivian Schmidt | Semester theme: Signs | Semester: 7, Graphic design
Type/Scope: Book, suitcase, buttons, spray templates | Mentoring: Stefan Claudius | Free submission

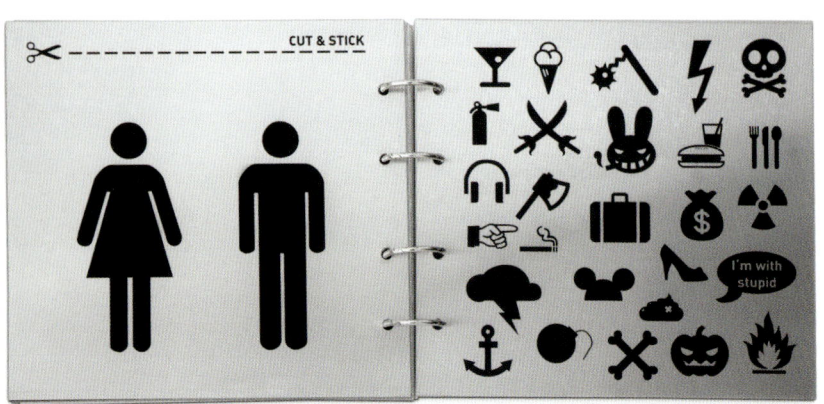

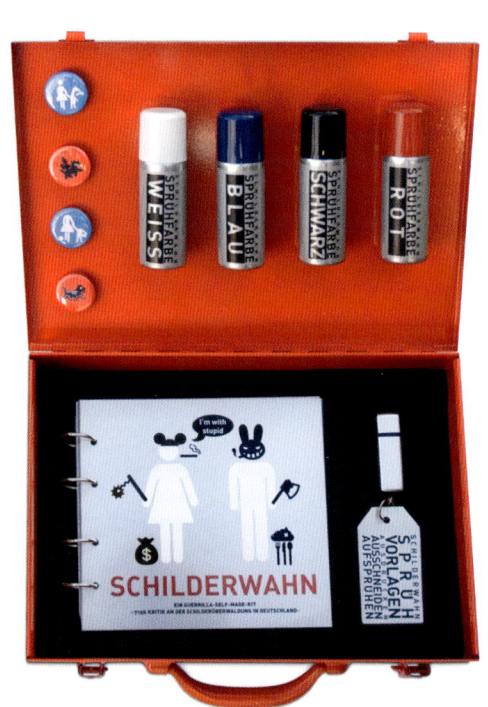

»Weiterbauen«
Student: Christine Steiner, Stefan Becker | Semester theme: Structural change | Semester: 10, 6,
Photo design, Graphic design | Type/Scope: Photo series | Mentoring: Barbara Burg | Free submission

Visuell liegt unser Fokus auf der entstandenen/entstehenden strukturellen Vielfalt und architektonischen Verschachtelung. Über die visuelle Ebene hinaus wirft dieses Phänomen eine Vielzahl von Fragen und Vermutungen auf, die sich durch das Sichtbar-Machen unweigerlich ins Bewusstsein drängen. »Man kann nicht nicht kommunizieren«, formulierte Paul Watzlawick in seiner Kommunikationstheorie. Und wenn jede Handlung kommunikativen Charakter hat, kann wohl auch die Gestaltung des Eigenheims etwas über die Bedürfnisse, Wünsche und Vorstellungen des Handelnden verraten. Gibt es Muster? Kann man anhand der architektonischen Struktur etwas über den sozialen Hintergrund der Bauenden erfahren? Wie ist der Begriff »Heimat« an die Fassade gekoppelt? Und inwiefern ist Architektur ein geeignetes Instrument der Gesellschaftsanalyse? In diesem Zusammenhang ergibt sich die Gelegenheit, die im Alltag nicht beachteten Fassaden mit anderen Augen wahrzunehmen. **Visually, our focus lies on structural diversity and architectural interlacing which has been/is being developed. This phenomenon raises a lot of questions and speculations beyond the visual aspect, which inevitably force themselves into one's consciousness. As Paul Watzlawick formulated it in his theory of communication: »One cannot not communicate«. And if each action has a communicative character, then even the design of one's own home will reveal something about the needs, wishes and imagination of the agent. Is there a pattern? Can one discover something about the social background of the builder on the basis of an architectural structure? How is the term »Heimat« [homeland] associated with the façade? And to what extent is architecture a suitable instrument to analyse society? In this connection, the opportunity arises to see commonly disregarded façades with different eyes.**

»péut-être...pas«
Student: Helen Sobiralski | Semester theme: Fashion Editorial »Fantastique« | Semester: 5, Photo design
Type/Scope: 8 images | Mentoring: Prof. Jörg Winde, Dietrich Halemeyer

In meiner Arbeit ergänzen sich Modelle, irreale Körper, Accessoires und scheinbar zusammenhanglose Elemente und Gegenstände zu »lebendigen Stillleben«. Die opulenten Motive sollen den Betrachter irritieren, ihm aber auch Räume für die eigene Imagination bieten. Durch die Komposition der einzelnen Elemente, die an klassischen Stillleben orientiert sind, ergeben sich Allegorien untereinander. Mensch und Ding werden eins. **In my work, models, unrealistic bodies, accessories and seemingly disconnected elements and objects combine to create »living still lifes«. The opulent subjects are designed to irritate the observer but also offer room for one's own imagination. Allegories develop amongst each other through the composition of the individual elements, which are based on traditional still lifes. Man and object become one.**

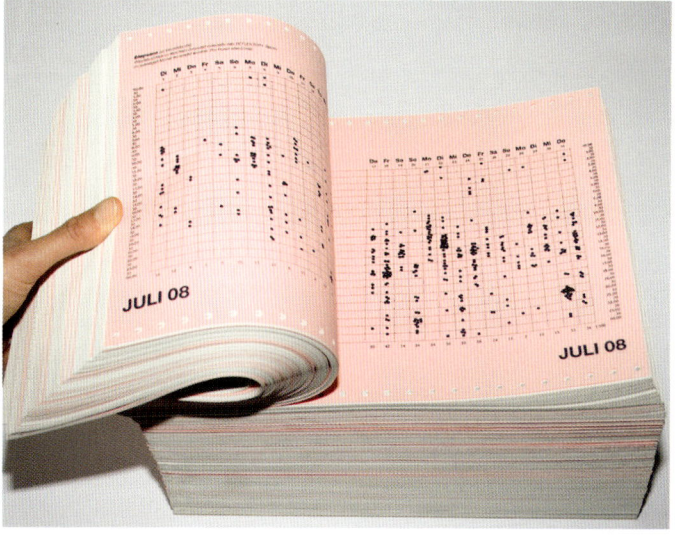

»e-book«
Student: Janina Kumpies | Semester theme: What do tomorrow's books look like?
Semester: 7, Graphic design | Type/Scope: Book | Mentoring: Prof. Sabine an Huef | Free submission

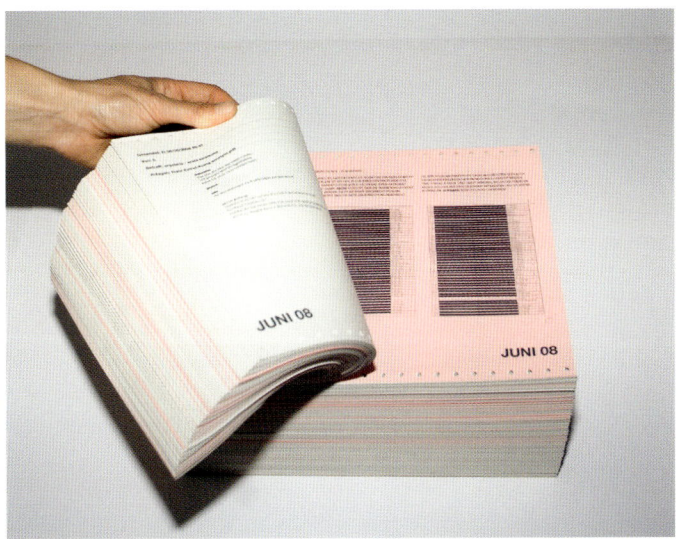

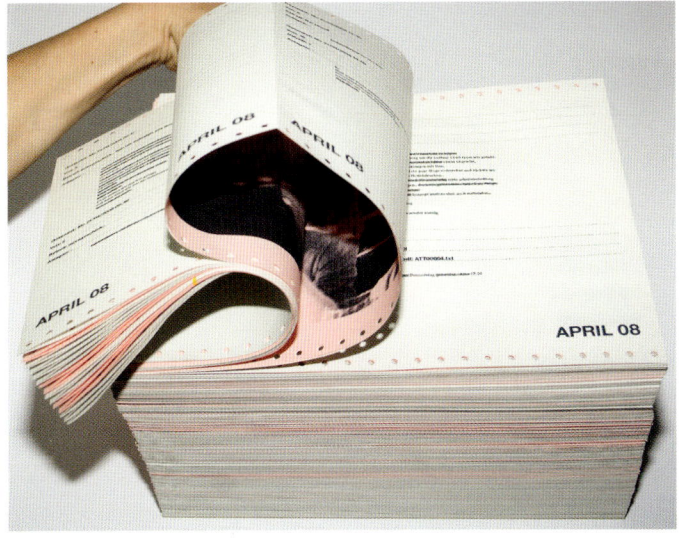

Intention »Zu schade, um weggeworfen zu werden. Zu aufschlussreich, um unbeachtet zu bleiben.« Das »e-book REFLEKTOR1« ist ein »Archiv« aller relevanten E-Mails aus dem angesammelten »E-Mail-Wahnsinn« des »Reflektor1« Teams 2008, der sich innerhalb neun monatiger effektiver Arbeit angesammelt hat. Der E-Mail-Verkehr, der innerhalb dieser Redaktionsarbeit sowie auch über die Grenzen des Teams hinaus, wie z.B. zwischen Autoren, Druckerei und Lektorat bis hin zum Verlag unternommen wurde, dokumentiert die unterschiedlichen redaktionellen Arbeitsschritte, die uns als Team für die Erarbeitung eines repräsentativen Jahrbuchs für den Fachbereich Design erforderlich schienen. Das Buch geht chronologisch in Monats-Schritten vor. Zu Beginn eines jeden Monats wird anhand eines Diagrammes visualisiert, wann genau und wieviele E-Mails verschickt wurden. Zusätzlich zu den chronologisch archivierten E-Mails befinden sich in diesem Archiv wichtige »Anhänge« genauso wie Fotografien, welche die Redaktionsarbeit dokumentieren. Die redaktionell irrelevanten Informationen und reinen »Briefinhalte« wurden so überdruckt, dass sie auf den ersten/zweiten Blick nicht lesbar, mit etwas Mühe jedoch durchaus entzifferbar sind. Das soll die relevanten Passagen im Text, die mit der Zeit inhaltlich immer wichtiger werden, separieren und hervorheben. **Intention »Too good to throw away. Too insightful to remain unnoticed.«** The »e-book REFLEKTOR1« is an archive of all the relevant e-mail messages that accumulated during the »e-mail frenzy« of the 2008 REFLEKTOR1 team in their nine-month period of work on the project. The e-mail traffic both within the editorial team and beyond it – between authors, the printing house and the editors, all the way to the publisher – documents the different editorial processes that we, as a team, deemed necessary for the creation of a representative yearbook for the design department. The book progresses month by month. At the start of each month, a diagram visualises when and how many e-mail messages were sent. In addition to the chronologically archived e-mail messages, this archive contains important »attachments«, as well as photographs documenting the editorial work. The information not relevant to the editorial process and the more personal content were overprinted, such that they would not be legible at first/second glance, but decipherable upon closer inspection. This was done to separate and highlight the relevant portions of text, which increased in importance as time went on.

XUYEN DAM, KAI RÖFFEN, TALENTS 161

DON'T BELIEVE ANYTHING. JUST DO IT AND SEE FOR YOURSELF.

Prof. Xuyen Dam

WARUM REFLEKTOR? Es war eine logische Folgerung. Im Jahr 2007 habe ich mit einem Studententeam die Publikation SEITE-EINS für den Fachbereich Design der Fachhochschule Dortmund initiiert und umgesetzt – mit kleinem Budget, dafür mit noch mehr Engagement und Motivation. Unser großes Ziel war, in erster Linie eine Dokumentation über Studentenarbeiten in ihrer reinsten Funktionalität umzusetzen. Es sollte ganz und gar nicht nach Dekor aussehen. Die Dokumentation sollte nicht verhübscht werden. Als Anfang 2008 eine Fortsetzung von SEITE-EINS zur Diskussion stand und sich die Möglichkeit auftat, mit dem Verlag ARNOLDSCHE Art Publishers aus Stuttgart zusammenzuarbeiten, wurde plötzlich alles nochmal sehr interessant und aufregend. Hier war auf einmal die unglaubliche Chance, die Auflage zu erhöhen, von einem Verlag professionell betreut zu werden, das Buch in Buchläden weltweit zu lancieren und dadurch den Fachbereich Design der Fachhochschule Dortmund noch bekannter zu machen. Das klang nach Herausforderung, Spaß und der Möglichkeit, etwas in Bewegung setzen zu können.

WAS HAT IHNEN AM MEISTEN SPASS GEMACHT AN DER REFLEKTOR-BETREUUNG? Grundsätzlich kann ich nie nein sagen, wenn engagierte Studenten auf der Matte stehen und was bewegen wollen. Ich glaube, für einen Lehrenden gibt es nichts besseres als Studenten, die etwas bewegen wollen. Wir haben es uns nicht leicht gemacht. Bei jedem Thema wollten wir das beste Ergebnis erreichen: Namensfindung, Bildsprache, Papierauswahl, Typografie, Jurierung der Studentenarbeiten, Präsentation auf der Buchmesse etc. Uns allen hat es sehr viel Spaß gemacht, den Entstehungsprozeß von REFLEKTOR1 zu erleben. Vor allem auch in der hochprofessionellen Zusammenarbeit mit dem Verlag ARNOLDSCHE Art Publishers. Und mir hat die Zusammenarbeit und die gemeinsame, intensive Zeit mit dem Team sehr viel bedeutet. Es war eine ganz, ganz tolle Truppe.

WAS WAR DAS EINFACHE UND DAS SCHWIERIGE BEIM ERSTEN REFLEKTOR? Die Herausforderung beim REFLEKTOR1 bestand darin, ganz anders als SEITE-EINS zu sein und gleichzeitig die große Qualität SEITE-EINS zu überbieten. Alles, was einfach aussieht, macht bekanntlich sehr viel Arbeit. Das trifft absolut auf die erste Ausgabe des REFLEKTOR1 zu.

Im Gestaltungsprozess pendelten wir permanent zwischen den Erwartungen vom ARNOLDSCHE Verlag, dem Fachbereich Design und unserem persönlichen Anspruch. Diverse Gestaltungspersönlichkeiten wie Philipp Teufel der Fachhochschule Düsseldorf oder Kurt Weidemann haben als Referenten für uns agiert. Der Rahmen wurde viel größer als bei SEITE-EINS, die Erwartungen und der Druck waren enorm.

Das Team bestand aus neun Studenten, die – zum großen Glück – ehrgeizig und gestalterisch kompetent sind. Die Diskussionen wurden aber dadurch nicht einfacher, die Arbeitstage und -nächte nicht kürzer. Und dann fiel der Hauptanteil der Arbeit in die vorlesungsfreie Zeit, so mussten die team-interne Kommunikation und die Korrekturen der Layouts zwischen München und Dortmund stets über E-Mails, Telefon und Skype stattfinden. Als das Projekt zu Ende ging, hatten wir uns mehr als 2.000 E-Mails geschrieben.

KÖNNTEN SIE FÜR UNS EIN RESÜMEE ÜBER DEN ERSTEN REFLEKTOR ZIEHEN? Erstmal: Ohne die großartige Unterstützung und das Vertrauen des Dekanats und vor allem von Martin Middelhauve und Ralf Junkers wäre REFLEKTOR1 nicht so geworden, wie REFLEKTOR1 geworden ist.

Ich bin immer noch sehr stolz auf unsere Leistung. Wir haben Impulse gegeben und Zeichen gesetzt. REFLEKTOR1 war ein wichtiges Signal. REFLEKTOR1 wird Maßstab für alle zukünftigen Publikationen der Fachhochschule Dortmund sein. Mit REFLEKTOR1 hat sich der Fachbereich Design der Fachhochschule Dortmund in der Hochschullandschaft Deutschlands nachhaltig positioniert.

WAS MACHT EINE/N »ECHTE/N« STUDENTEN/IN FÜR SIE AUS? Jemand, der gerne arbeitet, viel wissen und lernen will. Jemand, der die eigene Arbeit hinterfragt und keine Scheu hat, mit Fleiß und Disziplin das bestmögliche Ergebnis zu erreichen. **GIBT ES ARBEITEN VON STUDENTEN, DIE SIE BEEINDRUCKT HABEN UND DIE IHNEN IN ERINNERUNG GEBLIEBEN SIND?** Ja. es wäre absolut fatal, wenn es nicht so wäre. **LOHNT ES SICH NOCH DESIGN ETC. ZU STUDIEREN?** Es kommt auf die jeweilige Person und deren Definition von Design an. **WAS HAT SICH GEÄNDERT UND WAS AN DER FACHHOCHSCHULE?** Mehr: angewandte und praxisorientierte Gestaltung. Mehr: Design als Gestaltung von Inhalten nach funktionalen und formalen, insbesondere ästhetischen Kriterien. Mehr: gute Gestaltung im Sinne von ›sichtbar-werden-lassen‹ anhand klarer gestalterischer Konzepte, welche Funktionen und Formen sinnvoll miteinander verbinden. **WAS GEBEN SIE STUDIERENDEN MIT AUF DEN WEG?** Macht was! **WIE LANGE HABEN SIE DOZIERT? WO HABEN SIE DOZIERT? WO DOZIEREN SIE ZUKÜNFTIG?** Seit 1999 an der HFG Schwäbisch Gmünd. Ab 2006 an der Fachhochschule Dortmund. Ab 2009 an der Hochschule München. **WIE SIEHT IHR RÜCKBLICK-GEDANKE DAZU AUS?** Positiv und prägend. **WIE UND WO WOHNEN SIE?** Ich wohne und lebe sehr gut und sehr gern in München. München ist schön, lecker und leider sehr teuer. Aber lieber so als hässlich, schlecht und günstig. **WELCHE MUSIK INSPIRIERT SIE?** 1. Andante con Variazioni F-Moll - Joseph Haydn: Ragna Schirmer · 2. Premier Livre [1706] Sarabandes: Tzimon Barto · 3. Two-Part Invention in D minor: Gabriela Montero · 4. Italian Concerto in F, BWV 971 - 2. Andante: Angela Hewitt · 5. Leila au pays du carrousel: Anouar Brahem **WER INSPIRIERT SIE?** Daniel Eatock. Querdenker mit Eigensinn. **HÖREN SIE MUSIK BEIM ARBEITEN?** Nein. **WORAN ARBEITEN SIE GERADE?** Daran, nicht permanent vom Perfektionismus-Zwang malträtiert zu werden. **PLANEN SIE IMMER NUR EIN PROJEKT ODER IMMER SCHON DAS NÄCHSTE?** Das nächste und das übernächste. **ENTSTEHT BEI IHNEN ERST DAS WAS ODER DAS WIE?** Sowohl als auch. Es hängt vom Thema und dessen Umfang und Zielsetzung ab. **ARBEITEN SIE NOCH HANDWERKLICH ODER NUR DIGITAL?** Beides, zum Glück. **GIBT ES ETWAS BEI DER ARBEIT, WAS SIE HASSEN, ABER MACHEN MÜSSEN?** Spationieren, Grundlinienraster definieren. Projekte archivieren und dokumentieren. **GIBT ES ARBEITSMETHODEN, DIE IN VERGESSENHEIT GERATEN SIND?** Das Kopiergerät wird im Gestaltungsprozess oft unterschätzt. **HABEN SIE EINE GEOMETRISCHE LIEBLINGSFORM?** Die Linie. **NENNEN SIE IHR SCHÖNSTES SCHRIFTELEMENT.** Der Buchstabe X, die Zahl 8. **WO WÄREN SIE JETZT AM LIEBSTEN?** Ich bin jetzt gerne hier. **WAS AUF DER WELT HABEN SIE ALLES GESEHEN?** Man kann doch nicht alles genug gesehen haben? Als nächstes will ich mir die Anden anschauen. **EINE ERFAHRUNG, DIE DAS LEBEN BESCHREIBT?** Es sind nie die Veränderungen, die wir uns wünschen, durch die alles anders wird. **WAS HÄLT IHRER MEINUNG NACH JUNG? WAS HÄLT SIE JUNG?** Ich bin jung. **SIND SIE OFFEN FÜR NEUE KONTAKTE?** Nein. Es ist kein Unglück. Aber großes Glück ist es auch nicht. **HAT IHNEN SCHON MAL VITAMIN B GEHOLFEN BZW. EIN KONTAKT?** Netzwerke sind enorm wichtig. Vertrauen auch. Vor allem im beruflichen Umfeld. **WOFÜR GEBEN SIE AM LIEBSTEN GELD AUS?** Ich bin ein sparsamer Mensch, sagen meine Freunde. **WIE VIEL BUDGET BRAUCHEN SIE FÜR IHR TRAUMPROJEKT?** Wie viel kostet es, ein Haus zu bauen? Mit Flachdach, Sichtbeton, am Starnberger See? **WAS BEDEUTET IHR JOB UND DIE UMGEBUNG FÜR SIE?** Eine schöne, interessante Umgebung beeinflusst und steigert die Lust zum Arbeiten. **WELCHES SIND IHRE FÜNF LIEBLINGSWÖRTER?** Prägend, Konsens, Gedanke, Niederkomplex, Vision. **WELCHE FÜNF BÜCHER STUFEN SIE ALS WICHTIG EIN?** 1. Pre-specifics – Komparatistische Beiträge zur Forschung in Design und Kunst. 2. Laboratorium – is the answer · 3. Der Lob des Schattens – Tanizaki Junichiro · 4. Design as Art. Bruno Munari · 5. Wagashi. The Graphics of Japanese Confection. **WELCHE FRAGE HABEN WIR VERGESSEN?** Spielen Design und Gestaltung im Alltag eine wichtigere Rolle? · Kann es Gestaltung ohne Konzept überhaupt geben? · Wann kommt die nächste Gestaltungs-Revolution? · Ist es nicht mal dringend Zeit für eine Anarchie in der Gestaltung? · Welche Rolle spielen im Studenten-Dasein Vilem Flusser, Peter Sloterdijk und Norbert Bolz? · Brauchen wir eine neue Form von Gestaltungsschulen? · Brauchen wir Konzepte, die der Problemstellung gerecht werden? · Wie können die neuen Denkmodelle von Schulen aussehen? · Ist die Gesellschaftstheorie tot? · Wo sind die neuen Grenzen der Lesbarkeit? · Muss ein guter Designer auch ein guter Jurist, ein guter Priester oder ein guter Koch sein? · Haben wir alle ein Recht auf gute Gestaltung? · Wie geht es mit dem traditionellen Design weiter? **WENN SIE SICH JETZT WAS WÜNSCHEN KÖNNTEN, WAS WÄRE ES?** Alle Sneakers dieser Welt in meiner Schuhgrösse!

DON'T BELIEVE ANYTHING. JUST DO IT AND SEE FOR YOURSELF.

Prof. Xuyen Dam

WHY REFLEKTOR? It was a logical conclusion. In 2007, I initiated and published the magazine SEITE-EINS with the help of a team of students for the design department of the University of Applied Sciences and Arts in Dortmund – on a small budget, but with more commitment and motivation. Above all, our goal was to create purely functional documentation of student projects. There was to be nothing decorative about it. Nor was it supposed to look lavished at all.

In early 2008, we were discussing a sequel to SEITE-EINS, and the opportunity presented itself to cooperate with the Stuttgart-based ARNOLDSCHE Art Publishers; just like that, everything became much more interesting and exciting. All of a sudden, here was the chance to increase the number of copies published, get the professional support of a publisher, launch the book in bookshops around the world and thus spread the word about the university's design department even further. This sounded like a fun challenge, and the chance to start something amazing.

WHICH ASPECT OF MANAGING THE REFLEKTOR PROJECT DID YOU LIKE BEST? I can almost never say no when dedicated students come up to me and want to set something in motion. From the point of view of a teacher, I don't think there is anything better than students who want to set something in motion. We have not been easy on ourselves. We wanted to achieve the best results in every aspect: choosing a name, imagery, paper quality, typography, evaluating the student submissions, presenting the project at the book fair, etc.

We all really enjoyed witnessing the creation of REFLEKTOR1, especially in the extremely professional collaboration with ARNOLDSCHE Art Publishers. The collaboration and the exciting time spent working with the whole team meant a great deal to me. They were an excellent, excellent crowd.

WHAT WERE THE EASY PARTS IN THE FIRST REFLEKTOR, AND WHAT WERE THE HARD PARTS? The challenge for REFLEKTOR1 consisted in representing something completely different from SEITE-EINS and at the same time surpassing its excellent quality. After all, everything that looks easy is always a lot of work. This could not be truer than the first issue of REFLEKTOR1. In designing the book, we were constantly going back and forth between the expectations of ARNOLDSCHE Art Publishers, those of the design department and our own. Several notable design personalities, like Philipp Teufel of the University of Applied Sciences in Düsseldorf and Kurt Weidemann, agreed to act as speakers for us. The scope of things was much larger than with SEITE-EINS; the expectations and the pressure were extremely high.

The team consisted of nine students, who – very fortunately – were ambitious and competent designers. But this did not make the discussions any easier, nor the working days and nights any shorter. And the lion's share of the work took place during the semester break, so communication with other team members and layout corrections had to be orchestrated between Munich and Dortmund via e-mail, phone and Skype. When the project went to end, we had been written more than 2.000 emails.

COULD YOU SUMMARISE YOUR EXPERIENCE WITH THE FIRST REFLEKTOR FOR US? First off: without the faith and the support from the Dean, and most importantly from Martin Middelhauve and Ralf Junkers, REFLEKTOR1 would not have become REFLEKTOR1. I still feel very proud of what we have achieved. We have stirred things up and raised the bar. REFLEKTOR1 was an important signal; it set the standard for all future publications by the University of Applied Sciences and Arts Dortmund. With REFLEKTOR1, the Design Department of the University of Applied Sciences and Arts Dortmund created a lasting name for itself.

FOR YOU, WHAT ARE THE HALLMARKS OF A »GOOD« STUDENT? Someone who likes to work, who is curious and eager to learn. Someone who takes a critical view of his or her own work and who is not afraid to put in the diligence and discipline it takes to achieve the best results possible. **WERE THERE ANY STUDENT PROJECTS THAT STRUCK YOU, THAT MADE A LASTING IMPRESSION?** Yes. It would be absolutely dreadful if there were none. **IS IT STILL WORTHWHILE TO STUDY DESIGN, ETC.?** It depends on the individual person and their definition of design. **WHAT IS DIFFERENT NOW IN DESIGN AND AT THE UNIVERSITY?** More: applied and real-life-oriented design. More: design as the shaping of ideas according to functional, formal, and above all aesthetic criteria. More: good design in the sense of ›letting things emerge‹ using precise design concepts that combine form and function in a meaningful way. **WHAT DO YOU TELL YOUR STUDENTS?** Do something! **HOW LONG HAVE YOU BEEN A PROFESSOR? AND WHERE? WHERE WILL YOU GO IN THE FUTURE?** I started at the design university in Schwäbisch Gmünd in 1999. At the University of Applied Sciences and Arts Dortmund from 2006 onwards. At the University of Applied Sciences and Arts in Munich since 2009. **HOW WOULD YOU DESCRIBE THIS PROCESS IN RETROSPECT?** Positive and formative. **HOW AND WHERE DO YOU LIVE?** I live in Munich, where I really like it. I can't complain. Munich is beautiful, there's good food, but unfortunately it's very expensive. But I'd rather have it like that than ugly, bad and cheap. **WHAT KIND OF MUSIC INSPIRES YOU?** 1. Andante con Variazioni in F minor - Joseph Haydn: Ragna Schirmer · 2. Premier Livre [1706] Sarabandes: Tzimon Barto · 3. Two-Part Invention in D minor: Gabriela Montero · 4. Italian Concerto in F major, BWV 971 — 2. Andante: Angela Hewitt · 5. Leila au pays du carrousel: Anouar Brahem **WHO INSPIRES YOU?** Daniel Eatock. Unconventional thinkers. **DO YOU LISTEN TO MUSIC WHILE WORKING?** No. **WHAT ARE YOU WORKING ON AT THE MOMENT?** On not letting myself constantly be abused by the dictates of perfectionism. **DO YOU ONLY PLAN ONE PROJECT AT A TIME, OR DO YOU ALWAYS THINK ABOUT THE NEXT ONE?** The next one and the one after that. **IN YOUR WORK, WHAT COMES FIRST: THE WHAT OR THE HOW?** Both. It depends on the subject matter, its scope and aim. **DO YOU STILL WORK MANUALLY OR ONLY DIGITALLY?** Both, fortunately. **IS THERE SOMETHING IN YOUR JOB THAT YOU HATE BUT STILL CAN'T AVOID DOING?** Letter-spacing, defining baseline grids. Archiving and documenting projects. **ARE THERE ANY PROCEDURES OR METHODS THAT HAVE BEEN FORGOTTEN?** The photocopier is often underestimated in the design process. **DO YOU HAVE A FAVORITE GEOMETRICAL FORM?** The line.

TELL US YOUR FAVORITE CHARACTER OR NUMBER. The letter X, the number 8. **WHERE WOULD YOU LIKE TO BE RIGHT NOW?** I like being right here, right now. **HOW MUCH OF THE WORLD HAVE YOU SEEN?** Can you ever see anything enough? I want to see the Andes next. **A LESSON YOU LEARNED FROM PERSONAL EXPERIENCE?** It is never the changes we wish to see that change everything. **WHAT KEEPS PEOPLE YOUNG? WHAT KEEPS YOU YOUNG?** I am young. **ARE YOU MUCH OF A NETWORKER?** No. It's not a disaster. But it's not very fortunate either. **HAVE YOU EVER BENEFITED FROM KNOWING THE RIGHT PEOPLE?** Networks are absolutely essential. As is trust. Especially on the job. **WHAT DO YOU PREFER TO SPEND YOUR MONEY ON?** I am an economical person, according to my friends. **WHAT SORT OF A BUDGET DO YOU NEED FOR YOUR DREAM PROJECT?** How much do I need to build a house? Flat-roofed, with fair-faced concrete, on Lake Starnberg? **WHAT DO YOUR JOB AND YOUR ENVIRONMENT MEAN TO YOU?** A pleasant, interesting environment influences and increases the willingness to work. **WHAT ARE YOUR FIVE FAVORITE WORDS?** Prägend [formative], Konsens [consensus], Gedanke [thought], Niederkomplex [of low complexity], Vision [vision]. **WHICH FIVE BOOKS DO YOU CONSIDER IMPORTANT?** 1. Pre-specifics — Some Comparatistic Investigations on Research in Design and Art · 2. Laboratorium — is the answer · 3. In Praise of Shadows. Tanizaki Junichiro · 4. Design as Art. Bruno Munari · 5. Wagashi. The Graphics of Japanese Confection. **WHAT DID WE FORGET TO ASK?** Does design play a major part in everyday life? · Is design without concept even possible? · When will the next design revolution come? · Isn't it high time for anarchy to seize the world of design? · How important are Vilem Flusser, Peter Sloterdijk and Norbert Bolz to the lives of students? · Do we need a new form of design school? · Do we need concepts that do justice to the challenge? · What could the new philosophies for schools be like? · Is the theory of society dead? · Where are the new limits of readability? · Does a good designer also need to be a good legal expert, a good priest or a good cook? Do we all have a right to good design? What will the future hold for traditional design? **IF YOU COULD HAVE ONE WISH GRANTED RIGHT NOW, WHAT WOULD THAT BE?** Every trainer in the world in my shoe size!

ZWISCHEN MARKE UND MENSCH
GIBT ES MEHR ALS 30-SEKÜNDER UND DOPPELSEITEN.

MARKEN BRAUCHEN DEN KONTAKT ZU MENSCHEN. KLAR, SONST KENNT SIE NIEMAND. OPTIMALERWEISE IST IHRE KONTAKTAUFNAHME SO FASZINIEREND, DASS DIE MENSCHEN IHRERSEITS DEN KONTAKT ZUR MARKE SUCHEN. AM BESTEN IN FORM VON SYMPATHIE, INSPIRATION, BEGEISTERUNG UND – DA MACHEN WIR UNS MAL NICHTS VOR – LETZTEN ENDES AUCH IN FORM VON GELD. DIE GESTALTUNG DIESES KONTAKTS VON MARKEN UND MENSCHEN IST EINE DER AUFREGENDSTEN SPIELWIESEN DES KOMMUNIKATIONSDESIGNS. WER JEDOCH IN DIE WERBUNG WILL, UM ALS CREATIVE DIRECTOR FÜR DIE IMAGE-KAMPAGNE DES JAHRES VERANTWORTLICH ZU ZEICHNEN, SEINE TVCS IN DER PRIMETIME UND SEINE DOPPELSEITEN IN DEN GROSSEN PUBLIKUMSZEITUNGEN ZU SEHEN, DEM SEI GESAGT: DAS IST DAS AUSLAUFMODELL EINES WERBE-KREATIVEN.

KAI RÖFFEN
Executive Creative Director & Managing Director [TBWA\Düsseldorf]
Vorstandsmitglied des Art Directors Club in Deutschland
Mitglied des Medienbeirats NRW
Mitglied des One Club NY

EIN BEITRAG ÜBER DEN ANSPRUCH AN KREATIVE VON HEUTE UND WAS DER WAHRE NERVENKITZEL DER BRANCHE IST.

Nichts gegen Image-Kampagnen. Es gibt immernoch TVCs, die einem gehörig Gänsehaut machen. Auch Printkampagnen, vor denen man aus Ehrfurcht vor der exzellenten Art Direktion niederknien will, gibt es einige. Das gilt übrigens nicht nur für Image-Kampagnen, auch Produktinszenierungen sind in der brillianten Ausführung zu Genüge vorhanden. Gerade bei Award-Shows merkt man jedoch, dass die Arbeiten, die einem den Herzschlag wirklich hochtreiben, immer häufiger nicht in der Klassik geboren werden.

Zum Beispiel die Kampagne »The Best job in the World« von Tourism Queensland. Um die Region bei Reisewilligen bekannt zu machen, brauchte man hier nicht mehr als eine Stellenanzeige. Ausgeschrieben war ein Vertrag über sechs Monate. Der Einsatzort war eine Villa auf Hamilton Island im Great Barrier Reef. Job-Description: »Island Caretaker« inklusive Pool-Pflege, Schnorcheln und ein wenig Bloggen über die Traumgegend. Gehalt: 150.000 australische Dollar, was etwa 80.000 Euro entspricht. Die Anreise war inklusive. Der Run auf den Job war immens, von der medialen Welle in der Öffentlichkeit ganz zu schweigen. Eine Kampagne mit vergleichbarem Medievolumen hätte das Tourismboard von Queensland in Jahrzehnten nicht bezahlen können.

Ähnliche Wirkung zeigte eine Whopper Kampagne von Burger King. Anstatt den Whopper in den Fokus einer Produktkampagne zu stellen und zu erzählen, wie männlich und lecker er ist, nahm man ihn einfach raus – aus dem Sortiment. Dieses kleine Experiment führte man in einer Filiale durch und filmte die entsetzte Kundschaft, die Reaktionen zwischen Ungläubigkeit und Wut zeigte. Der als »The Whopper Freakout« bekannt gewordene Film kursierte im Internet und erzählte zwar nichts von »männlich und lecker«, jedoch machte er einer breiten Öffentlichkeit eines sehr deutlich: Der wahre Wert des Whopper ist viel größer als knappe dreieinhalb Euro. Den gleichen Beweis trat eine weitere Aktion an. Bei »The Whopper Sacrifice« lud Burger King Facebook-User dazu ein, 10 ihrer Facebook-Freunde von ihrer Liste zu streichen und sie gegen einen Gratis-Whopper einzutauschen. Über 200.000 Freundschaften mussten bisher dran glauben.

Ebenso wirksam waren Oasis, die ihre neue Platte »Dig out your Soul« durch Straßenmusikanten in der New Yorker U-Bahn, vor den Augen schreibwilliger Pressevertreter haben uraufführen lassen. Oder Adidas, die mit der Brücke in Form von Oliver Kahn über eine Münchener Autobahn ein Bild geschaffen haben, das während der WM 2006 um den Globus ging. Diese Kampagnen haben Awards beim ADC und anderswo abgeräumt. Aber nicht, weil sie sauber exekutiert und schön sind.

Diese Kampagnen haben alle einen anderen Schlüssel zum Erfolg. Sie schaffen substanziellen Mehrwert mit einem kleinen aber intelligenten Einsatz: Kreativität. Denn Kreativität ist kein Selbstzweck. Kreativität ist ein Mittel zum Zweck. Der Zweck hier heißt innovative Wertschöpfung, und zwar gleichermaßen in den Köpfen der Menschen wie in den Kassen der Markenbesitzer. Mit anderen Worten: Kreativität darf nicht nur der Schönheit der Kommuniktation dienen. Kreativität schafft Ideen, mit denen Marken viel bewegen können.

Um viel in Bewegung zu setzen, müssen Marken nachhaltig geführt sein. Sie brauchen eine relevante, differenzierende und glaubwürdige Markenstrategie, die in einer konsequenten, involvierenden und aktivierenden Kreation mündet. Starke Marken schlagen die Brücke von Strategie zur Kreation, in dem sie eine Marken-Überzeugung verinnerlichen, eine tiefsitzende Motivation, die ihr Handeln treibt. Je konsequenter eine Marke nach ihrer Überzeugung handelt, desto größer die Wirkung auf ihr Umfeld. Um ein entsprechendes Momentum aufzubauen braucht man große Ideen, die das Verhalten der Marke prägen und somit ihre Manifestation in der Gesellschaft. Ideen wie »The Best Job« [= dream holiday destination] oder »Oliver Kahn« [= Impossible is Nothing] sind solche Manifestationen einer Marke. Markenverhalten ist mehr als Kommunikation. Es ist Handeln, das dem Konsumenten die Überzeugung der Marke unter Beweis stellt.

Gute Markenideen brauchen auch keinen Mediaplan. Wenn Menschen etwas wirklich interessiert, dann suchen sie es sich schon selbst, egal über welches Medium. Daher ist es essenziell, dass Ideen aus Insights entwickelt werden. Nur wer Freud und Leid seiner Audience kennt, weiß, wonach sie wirklich sucht. Dieses Agieren nach dem Interessenprinzip macht Marken nicht nur relevant, es macht sie involvierend und bringt die Menschen dazu, sich zu engagieren. Das hat eine viel höhere Kontaktqualität zwischen Marken und Menschen zur Folge als ein 30 Sekunden TVC jemals leisten kann. Da hilft es auch nicht, wenn man seine Kampagne auf alle Formate der sich immer noch weiter fragmentierenden Medienwelt adaptiert. Dann ist es immer noch Werbung und Werbung nervt. Starke Ideen machen sich Medien als Erfüllungsgehilfe zu nutze. Das kann auch klassisch TV sein. Aber die klassischen Media-Formate zählen weniger in einer Welt, wo alles Medium sein kann. Es zählen Ideen, die den gewollten Kontakt mit Menschen herbeiführen.

Wir sind also nicht in der Werbewirtschaft, wir sind in der Ideenwirtschaft. Das ist kein neues Glaubensbekenntnis der Markenkommunikation, sondern die Erkenntnis der Kommunikations-Realität. Das Spielfeld für Kommunikationsdesign ist größer geworden, die Regeln weniger. Kreative von heute sind keine Mediengestalter. Kreative von heute sind Ideenschöpfer. Gute Exekution ist die Grundvorausetzung für gutes Kommunikationsdesign. Für gute Markenarbeit ist mehr gefragt: strategisches Denken und die Fähigkeit Ideen zu generieren, an denen sich Kommunikation und Markenhandeln ausrichten kann. Kreative sind endlich Kreative, nicht nur Exekutierende. Grafikdesign, Fotodesign, Objektdesign, Raumdesign, Film – die Mauern der Disziplinen und Formate gehören niedergerissen! Kreative müssen größer denken, ganzheitlicher und vor allem mutiger. Die Idee steht im Mittelpunkt, nicht Filme oder Printmotive. Ideen gewinnen nachhaltig und bewegen Menschen. Und das ist es doch eigentlich, was den Nervenkitzel ausmacht.

Ein gut arbeitendes Beispiel für diese neue Nervenkitzel-Kreation kommt aus der gefühlt verstaubten Regierungskommunikation. Ein Gesundheitsministerium in den baltischen Staaten benötigte eine Kampagne für die Hygiene bei Kindern. Seit Jahrzehnten versuchen Eltern und Aufklärungskampagnen Kindern einzutrichtern, sich regelmäßig die Hände zu waschen. Das Problem: Die Kinder interessiert es »einen Dreck«. Die Idee: Eine transparente Seife, die im Kern ein Spielzeug einschließt. Natürlich! Die Idee ist nicht neu. In Cornflakes-Packungen war schon immer Spielzeug. Aber sie ist einfach, schnell und wirksam. Sie hat die richtige Mechanik und damit die Lösung für das Problem parat. Sie hat die Verhaltensänderung bei Kindern zur Folge, ebenso wie das Interesse der Medien und Eltern. Eine große Kampagne. Und die Werbemittel dafür? Nie gesehen.

THERE IS MORE BETWEEN
BRANDS AND MAN
THAN 30-SECOND SPOTS AND DOUBLE PAGES.

BRANDS NEED TO COME INTO CONTACT WITH PEOPLE; OTHERWISE, IT IS CLEAR THAT NO ONE WILL KNOW ABOUT THEM. IDEALLY, THE PROCESS OF MAKING CONTACT IS SO FASCINATING THAT PEOPLE IN TURN SEEK CONTACT WITH THEM. THE BEST WAY IS THROUGH EMPATHY, INSPIRATION, ENTHUSIASM AND – THERE'S NO DENYING IT – THROUGH MONEY. THE DESIGN OF SUCH CONTACT BETWEEN BRANDS AND PEOPLE IS ONE OF THE MOST EXCITING PLAYGROUNDS IN COMMUNICATION DESIGN. HOWEVER, LET THIS BE A WARNING TO THOSE WHO WANT TO GO INTO ADVERTISING, TO WORK AS CREATIVE DIRECTORS FOR THE IMAGE CAMPAIGN OF THE YEAR, TO SEE THEIR TVCS DURING PRIME TIME AND THEIR DOUBLE PAGES IN THE BIG NEWSPAPERS: THIS IS AN OUTDATED MODEL OF A CREATIVE MIND IN ADVERTISEMENT.

KAI RÖFFEN
Executive Creative Director & Managing Director [TBWA\Düsseldorf]
Board Member of the Art Directors Club in Germany
Member of the Board of Advisers at NRW

THIS ARTICLE IS ABOUT WHAT TODAY'S CREATIVE MINDS NEED TO HAVE AND WHAT THE REAL THRILL OF THIS INDUSTRY IS.

Nothing against image campaigns. There are still TVCs out there that give you goose bumps. There are also various print campaigns that make you want to kneel down in awe of the excellent work of the respective art directors. This is not limited to image campaigns only; there are also a large number of product presentations that are brilliantly performed. Especially during award shows, though, we notice that the projects that make your heart beat faster are usually not the classic campaigns.

Let's take, for example, the campaign for »The Best Job in the World« by Tourism Queensland. This group needed just one ad to raise awareness of its region with people who are fond of travelling. It involved posting a six-month contract for a job at a villa on Hamilton Island, located on the Great Barrier Reef. Job description: »Island caretaker«, including pool maintenance, snorkelling and a few blog posts related to this paradise area. Salary: 150,000 Australian dollars, which is equal to roughly 80,000 euros. The travel costs were included. The job attracted an immense amount of applicants, not to mention the subsequent wave of publicity. Not even with decades of funding could the Queensland tourism board have financed a campaign with a comparable media volume.

A similar phenomenon was seen in the Whopper campaign by Burger King. Instead of focusing on the Whopper in their product campaign and showing how manly and yummy it is, they simply took it out of their assortment. This little experiment was conducted in one chain store and the shocked customers were filmed; their reactions, ranging from disbelief to anger, were shown. The spot known as »The Whopper Freakout« circulated on the internet, and even though it said nothing about »manly and yummy«, it made one point very clear to the public at large: the real value of a Whopper is far greater than three and a half euros. The same was proven through another ad. »The Whopper Sacrifice« invited Burger King Facebook users to delete 10 friends from Facebook for a free Whopper. Over 200,000 friendships have been cancelled so far.

Another successful campaign was done by Oasis, who had the debut of their new album »Dig Out Your Soul« performed by street musicians on the New York subway in front of keen press reporters. Adidas, meanwhile, created an image that went around the world during the 2006 World Cup: a bridge above a Munich motorway in the shape of Oliver Kahn, goalkeeper of the German national football team at the time. These campaigns have won awards at the ADC and other places, and not because they were cleanly conducted or because they were beautiful in the classic sense.

All these campaigns had a different key to success. They created substantial added value with little, but intelligent input: creativity. Creativity has no end in itself. Creativity is a means to an end. The end, here, is innovative added value, in people's heads as well as in the pockets of brand owners. In other words, creativity should not only serve the beauty of communication. Creativity brings ideas about that enable brands to make a point and bring a message across.

In order to set this in motion, brands need sustainable management. They need a relevant, differentiating and trustworthy brand strategy that leads to dedicated, inclusive and stimulating creation. Strong brands bridge the gap between strategy and creation by internalising a deep motivation that drives their actions. The more consistent a brand acts according to its values and beliefs, the bigger the effect on its environment. In order to create such momentum, great ideas are needed to mark the brand's behaviour and thus its manifestation in society. Ideas like the »The Best Job« [= dream holiday destination] or »Oliver Kahn« [= nothing is impossible] are examples for such brand manifestations. Brand behaviour is far more than communication. The brand proves to the consumer how convincing it is by taking action.

Good brand ideas do not need a media plan. If people are really interested in something, then they will look for it on their own by any available means. For that reason, it is essential to develop ideas that come from insights. Only those familiar with their audience's happiness and sorrow know what they really seek. Based on the principle of interest, this proactiveness makes brands not only relevant, but also involving, and drives people to become active themselves. The result is a much higher quality of brand contact than a 30-second TVC could ever achieve. It does not even make a difference if the campaign has been adapted to all possible formats in this constantly fragmenting media world. It will still be »only« advertising and advertising is annoying. Strong ideas exploit media as a means of self-fulfillment. This can be realised in a classic way through television, but the traditional media formats do not have as much value in a world where everything can be a tool. The ideas that bring about the desire for contact in people are those that count.

Nicht nur der Kontakt zwischen Mensch und Mensch ist nötig, sondern auch der Kontakt zwischen Mensch und Medien, damit Werbung überhaupt funktioniert. Hier stellt sich für uns die Frage: "Hat sich der Mensch entwickelt? Oder hat Werbung sich verändert? Oder wieso ist plötzlich alles anders?" Unter diesem Aspekt berichtet Kai Röffen/TBWA und diesjähriger Referent des Pink Saturday ADC/Berlin über den Bund zwischen Mensch, Marke und Momenten. **Not only contact between people is vital, contact between man and media is necessary, too, in order to make advertising work at all. This gives rise to a number of questions: "Has man developed? Or has advertising changed? Or why is everything different all of a sudden?" Kai Röffen/ TBWA and this year's speaker for the Pink Saturday ADC/ Berlin talks about this and the bond between people, brands and moments.**

Thus, we are not part of the advertising economy – we are living in the idea economy. This is no new creed for brand communication; it is knowing the reality of communication. The playground of communication design has become larger, but with fewer rules. The creative minds of today are no media designers. Good implementation is a basic requirement of good communication design. Good work with brands needs strategic thinking and the ability to generate ideas that communication and brand behaviour can lean on. After all, creative minds are best at creation, not execution. Graphic design, photography design, object design, interior design, film – the walls of disciplines and formats shall be taken down! Creative minds need to think bigger and, especially, more daringly. The idea is the centre, not films or print images. Ideas produce long-term results and move people. In the end, that is what causes the real thrill.

A good example for this new, thrilling creation comes from the world of government communication. The ministry of health of one of the Baltic states needed a campaign for teaching the importance of hygiene to children. For decades parents and educational campaigns have tried to instill into children's minds that they should wash their hands regularly. The problem: kids could not care less. The idea: a toy encased in a transparent soap. Of course! The idea is hardly new: Cornflake boxes have long included toys inside, but it is a simple, fast and effective idea. It uses the right mechanisms and thus leads to solving the problem. It results in a change in child behaviour and also affects the interest of the media and parents. A great campaign, and I don't recall seeing a single means of advertising…

HABEN SIE TALENT? ARE YOU TALENTED?

Genau wegen dieser Frage sind wir mit den, vom ADC ausgezeichneten Talenten in Kontakt getreten und haben mal nachgefragt, ob sie uns Ihr Talent auch unter Beweis stellen können. **We used precisely this question to make contact with talents recognised by the ADC and asked them to show us what they are talented in.**

Bist du Kopf-Mensch oder Bauch-Mensch? **Are you a cerebral person, or do you follow your gut feelings?** GROSSE HOVEST: Zu dieser Frage habe ich erstmal gleich einen Test im World Wide Web gefunden, und hier ist mein Ergebnis: »Sie sind ein Mischtyp: Sie sind weder ein eindeutiger Bauch-, noch ein klarer Kopftyp, sondern eine gelungene Mischung aus beidem. Sie handeln meistens klug, überlegt und nicht überstürzt, können sich in brenzligen Situationen jedoch auch auf Ihren Bauch verlassen, der Ihnen eine lange Pro- und Contraliste abnimmt. Mit Ihrer Art können Sie sich den jeweiligen Gegebenheiten prima anpassen: Sie zeigen Ihre Gefühle und wirken sehr authentisch, lassen sie jedoch auch nicht die Oberhand gewinnen, sondern bewahren einen kühlen Kopf.« **I actually found a test on this on the World Wide Web, and here's my result: »You are a hybrid: You are neither clearly the cerebral nor the instinctive type, but a healthy mix of the two. Most of the time, you act intelligently and deliberately and don't rush into things, but in crunch time you can rely on your instincts, which relieve you from the tedious weighing of pros and cons. Your attitude lets you adapt to new situations easily: you show your emotions and come across as authentic and genuine, but you don't let yourself get carried away by your emotions and always manage to keep your head.«** DOMINGUEZ: Gibt's da immer eine klare Trennung? Ich versuche beides zuzulassen. Ansonsten Kopfmensch mit zuviel Bauch... **Can you ever really separate the two? I try to combine them. But if I had to choose: cerebral person with too much gut...** GÖTTLING: Ich bin wohl eher der Bauch-Mensch. **I'm leaning more towards the gut feeling.** MICHAILIDIS: Ich glaube, für andere sieht das nach Bauchmensch aus [und damit meine ich nicht die Pfunde, die ich infolge des Diplomstresses in letzter Zeit weiter zugelegt habe]. Ich bin aber relativ sicher, dass Kopfmensch eher der Fall ist. **I think to others it looks like I'm all about the gut [and I don't mean those pounds that I have kept putting on during the stressful final exam period]. But I am fairly certain that I'm more the cerebral type.** BALICKI: Kopf. **Cerebral person.** Deine Lieblingsfarbe ist? **Your favorite colour is?** GROSSE HOVEST: Schwarzweiß. **Black and white** DOMINGUEZ: Schwarz. **Black.** GÖTTLING: Irgendwas zwischen Apfelblau und Zitronenrot. **Something between apple-blue and lemon-red.** Orange und Cyan subtraktiv gemischt. **Orange and cyan subtractively mixed.** BALICKI: Die Nicht-Farbe. **The non-color.**

Zu welcher Zeit arbeitest du am liebsten? **At what time of day do you prefer to work?** GROSSE HOVEST: Nachts. **At night.** DOMINGUEZ: Vormittags und abends. Aber kann man sich das als Arbeitnehmer aussuchen? **In the mornings and evenings. But do you have a choice as an employee?** GÖTTLING: morgens. **In the morning.** MICHAILIDIS: Von 10.00 bis 15.00 Uhr, von 18.00 bis 00.00 Uhr und in der Zeit dazwischen, davor und danach. **From 10 a.m. to 3 p.m., from 6 p.m. until midnight and during the time in between, before and after.** BALICKI: Eigentlich nachts, wenn es schön ruhig ist. Dabei ist die Ruhe wichtiger als die Nacht ;] **To be honest, at night when it is nice and quiet. Although the quiet is more important than the night ;]** Welche Musik inspiriert dich? **What kind of music inspires you?** GROSSE HOVEST: Schöne Musik [Damien Rice, Eliott Smith, Radiohead, etc.]. **Good music [Damien Rice, Elliott Smith, Radiohead, etc.].** GÖTTLING: Häufig melancholische und traurige Musik. **A lot of the time melancholy and sad music.** BALICKI: Trans Am, Tortoise, The Redneck Manifesto, Ken Ishii. **Trans Am, Tortoise, The Redneck Manifesto, Ken Ishii.** Was ist dein Durchhalte-Mittel? **What keeps you going?** GROSSE HOVEST: Kaffee und Spaß. **Coffee and fun.** DOMINGUEZ: Cola und Musik. **Coca-Cola and music.** MICHAILIDIS: Freude an der Arbeit. **Enjoying what I do.** BALICKI: Wasser. **Water.** Wer inspiriert dich? **Who inspires you?** DOMINGUEZ: Gott und die Welt. **Anyone and anything.** GÖTTLING: Da gibt's schon einige. Brad Bird, James Jean, Tomer und Asaf Hanuka, Studio Soi, John Lasseter, House Industries. **There are quite a few. Brad Bird, James Jean, Tomer and Asaf Hanuka, Studio Soi, John Lasseter, House Industries.** BALICKI: Studio Ghibli. **Studio Ghibli.** Welche Zeitung liest du? **Which newspaper do you read?** BALICKI: Spiegel-Online. **Spiegel-Online.** MICHAILIDIS: Google Reader. **Google Reader.** Stell uns eine Frage. **Ask us a question.** GÖTTLING: Kennt ihr eigentlich noch Mila Ayuhara? **Do you still remember Mila Ayuhara?** MICHAILIDIS: Ihr habt neun Kugeln gleicher Farbe und Größe. Eine Kugel ist jedoch schwerer. Wie findet ihr heraus, welche die schwerere ist, wenn ihr nur zwei Mal mit einer Apothekerwaage wiegen dürft? **You have nine balls of the same colour and size. One ball is heavier. How do you find out which one is the heavier one if you are only allowed to use a balance scale twice?** BALICKI: Wusstet ihr, dass Holzhacken deshalb so beliebt ist, weil man bei dieser Tätigkeit den Erfolg sofort sieht? **Did you know that chopping wood is so popular because you can immediately see the results of your work?** Was wolltest du schon immer mal beantworten bzw. gefragt werden? **What have you always wanted to answer or to be asked?** BALICKI: Die 1.000.000 Dollar Frage. **The 1,000,000-dollar question.**

CHRISTOPH GROSSE HOVEST

DIE.ART

Wie bist du zu dem Thema deiner Arbeit gekommen? Bzw. zu deiner Idee? **How did you come up with the central theme for your submission? What gave you the idea?** Ausschlaggebend waren die Realbildaufnahmen, die an einigen Wochenenden mit der Hilfe von Christian Kalbhenn [Ex-Kamera Student der Fachhochschule] entstanden sind. Schon beim Dreh auf dem Phoenix Gelände in Dortmund Hörde entwickelte ich einige Ideen, wie man diesen alten Stahlkomplex auf eine abstrakte und experimentelle Art und Weise wieder Leben einhauchen kann. Diese Ideen entwickelte ich unabhängig von den Aufnahmen weiter, und so entstanden die Lebensformen, die letztendlich ihren Platz in dem alten Stahlwerkkomplex fanden. **The thing that started it all was the footage taken during several weekends with the help of Christian Kalbhenn [former camera student at the University of Applied Sciences and Arts Dortmund]. Already during shooting in the Phoenix area of Dortmund Hörde, some ideas developed about how to bring this old steel complex back to life in an abstract and experimental way. I further developed these ideas separately from the actual footage, and thus the life forms were created that, in the end, were placed in the old steel mill.** Wo sammelst du Ideen? **Where do new ideas come to you?** Ideen sammle ich immer und überall, wichtig ist dabei Alltägliches einmal anders zu betrachten, sich auf ungewöhnliche Blickwinkel einzulassen und Dinge auch einfach mal aus ihrem Zusammenhang zu reißen. Des Weiteren findet man natürlich Inspiration in einigen Internetforen, die sich mit Design und Kunst beschäftigen. Auch in guten Büchern, im Fernsehen und bei Ausstellungen kann man Ideen finden. **Anytime and anywhere. The important thing is to take a second look at the mundane, everyday things, to try and adopt unusual perspectives, and to take things out of their normal context. Other than that, of course, several Internet forums dealing with design and art provide inspiration. Ideas can also be found in good books, on television and at exhibitions.** Wie lange hast du für die Umsetzung deiner Idee gebraucht? **How long did it take you to realise your idea?** Insgesamt waren es ca. 4 Monate, in denen ich fast jeden Tag 10 bis 16 Stunden an der Produktion meines Diploms gearbeitet habe. **Approximately four months all in all; four months in which I worked on my project for 10 to 16 hours a day, almost every day.** Gibt es jemanden, dem du den Preis zu verdanken hast? **Is there anybody to whom you owe winning this award?** Allen Leuten, die mich während meines Diploms unterstützt haben. **Everyone who helped and supported me during those months.** Hat dir der Preis Vorteile verschafft? **Have you benefited from the award?** Ja, auf jeden Fall, nach dem ich den ADC-Nachwuchswettbewerb gewonnen hatte, bekam meine Arbeit eine sehr grosse Öffentlichkeit. **I have indeed: after winning the ADC student award, my project received a lot of publicity.** Gab es Jobangebote und Anfragen danach? **Did you get any job offers or inquiries after that?** Ja, es gab einige Jobangebote, meist für eine Festanstellung. Da ich aber schon während des Studiums als freiberuflicher Grafiker gearbeitet habe, bin ich auch nur auf Angebote eingegangen, bei denen ich auch als Freiberufler gebucht wurde, aber selbst da gab es genug. **Yes, I got several offers, most of them for permanent positions. But since I had already worked as a freelance graphic designer while at university, I only responded to offers where I would be contracted as a freelancer; and there was no shortage of those either.** Wo arbeitest du jetzt? **Where do you work now?** Ich bin als Freiberufler tätig, vorwiegend im Bereich »Motion-Design«. Teilweise arbeite ich von meinem eigenem Büro aus, teilweise werde ich von Agenturen für Projekte vor Ort gebucht. **I am a freelancer working mostly in »motion design«. Sometimes I work from my own office; sometimes agencies contract me for in-house projects.** Hast du schon mehrere Preise gewonnen? **Have you won any other awards so far?** Andere Preise habe ich nicht gewonnen, aber ich habe meine Arbeit auch nicht bei vielen anderen Wettbewerben eingereicht. Bei den Animago Award wurde ich noch in der Kategorie »Beste technische Realisierung« nominiert. **I haven't won any other prizes, but I haven't submitted my work to many other contests either. But I was nominated at the Animago Awards in the category of »Best Technical Realisation«.** Musstest du beim Einreichen deiner Arbeit etwas bezahlen? **Did you have to pay a submission fee?** Ja, man musste Gebühren zahlen. Es waren bei mir ca. 100 Euro. Aber dafür gab es dann ja auch Ruhm und Ehre! **Yes, there was a fee. I paid approximately € 100, but it got me publicity and fame, so that's okay.** Was gibst du anderen mit auf den Weg? **What recommendations would you give to others?** Fleissig sein, neugierig bleiben und viel experimentieren. **Work hard, retain your curiosity and experiment a lot.**

»watch movie!«

»Talent des Jahres«
Abschlussarbeiten 2007
Mentoring: Prof. HD Schrader

PETER BALICKI
BLACK BOX – STATIONS OF A FLIGHT

Wie bist du zu dem Thema deiner Arbeit gekommen? Bzw. zu deiner Idee? **How did you come up with the central theme for your submission? What gave you the idea?** Flugreisen haben seit jeher eine gewisse Faszination auf mich ausgeübt. Zudem reizte mich die strikt kühle Berechnung und Protokollierung, die innerhalb eines Flugschreibers stattfindet im Kontrast zu den überaus emotionalen Vorgängen, die Menschen bei einer Flugreise durchleben. Umgehend begeisterte mich die Idee, diese beiden konträren Aspekte zu vereinen. **Airplane travel has always held a certain fascination for me, as well as the strictly unemotional calculation and recording that go on inside a flight recorder, in contrast to the utterly emotional processes that people go through when travelling by plane. I was immediately enthralled by the idea of combining those two contrary aspects.** Wie motivierst du dich? **Where do you get your motivation from?** Ich mag Neues. Neues kommt nur, wenn man Altes zu Ende bringt. **I like anything new. New things only start when you bring old things to an end.** Wie lange hast du für die Umsetzung deiner Idee gebraucht? **How long did it take you to realise your idea?** Die theoretische Vorlaufzeit, in der die Idee wuchs, betrug ungefähr drei Monate. Die Arbeit an sich habe ich in einem Semester fertig stellen können. **The theoretical warm-up phase, in which the idea took shape, was approximately three months. The project itself took me all of one semester to finish.** Was blieb während deines Projektes auf der Strecke? **Which elements of the project got lost on the way?** In den letzten drei Monaten vor Abgabe: Alles. **In the last three months leading up to the deadline: everything.**

Gibt es Kreativitätstechniken, die du benutzt? Hast du eigene entwickelt? **Are there any techniques for creative thinking that you use? Have you developed any of your own?** Ich horche in mich hinein, welches Gefühl ich mit meiner Arbeit vermitteln bzw. umsetzen will. Dazu suche ich dann passende Musik. Anschließend sammle ich massig viel zum Thema passendes Material und fange dann an auszusortieren und eigene erste Entwürfe anzufertigen. Während dieses Vorgangs verknüpft sich das ursprüngliche Gefühl mit der erschlossenen Bildwelt und fördert etwas Neues, Eigenständiges zutage. **I listen to my inner voice to »hear« which emotions I want to convey or realise with my work. Then I look for music to match that emotion. After that, I amass anything and everything related to my subject and start to sort through the material and prepare the first drafts. In this process the original emotion merges with the developed imagery and creates something new and unique.** Gibt es jemanden, dem du den Preis zu verdanken hast? **Is there anybody to whom you owe winning this award?** Im Diplom-Kurs habe ich Christoph Grosse Hovest kennengelernt. Wir waren mit gleichem Elan bei der Sache und dabei ständig online. So konnten wir uns jederzeit kleine Schnipsel unserer Arbeiten hin- und herschicken und diese besprechen. Es ist extrem wichtig, sich mit anderen über seine Arbeit auszutauschen. Ein zweiter Standpunkt lässt einem den eigenen festigen oder überdenken – was nie schaden kann. Danke Christoph! **During the last semester, I met Christoph Grosse Hovest. We showed the same enthusiasm for our work and were always online. That way we were able to send each other small snippets of our work and discuss them. It is extremely important to discuss your project with others. A second opinion helps to strengthen one's own or to revise it – which can never hurt. Thank you, Christoph!** Gab es Jobangebote und Anfragen danach? **Did you get any job offers or inquiries after that?** Die Auszeichnung hat mir bei Agenturen die Tür ein großes Stück weiter geöffnet. Nach dem Diplom habe ich 2 Jahre lang als freier Mitarbeiter bei verschiedenen Agenturen in ganz Deutschland an interessanten Projekten arbeiten können. **The award has flung the door wide open for me with agencies. After graduating from university, I was able to collaborate on interesting projects as a freelancer for different agencies for two years.** Wo arbeitest du jetzt? **Where do you work now?** Mittlerweile festangestellt bei Sehsucht in Hamburg. Eine Motion-Design Agentur mit einem sehr, sehr netten Team. **I am an employee at Sehsucht in Hamburg, which is a motion design agency with a team of very nice people.** Gibt es Kommunikationsweisen die dir fehlen? Die es geben sollte? **Are there any means of communication that you miss? That should exist?** Sich ohne Worte verstehen – leider durch die Schnelllebigkeit sehr selten geworden. **Understanding each other without speaking – this has unfortunately become very rare in our fast-moving world.**

 »watch movie!«

»Auszeichnung«
Abschlussarbeiten 2007
Mentoring: Prof. HD Schrader

DENNIS DOMINGUEZ
STEREOTYPE

Wie bist du zu dem Thema deiner Arbeit gekommen? Bzw. zu deiner Idee? **How did you come up with the central theme for your submission? What gave you the idea?** Da meine Eltern aus zwei verschiedenen Ländern kommen [Spanien und Slowenien] und ich in Deutschland aufgewachsen bin, brodelten die Themen »Vorurteile« und »nationale Stereotype« wohl schon lange in mir. Im Auslandssemester in Ljubljana wurde es dann etwas konkreter. **I guess the two themes »prejudices« and »national stereotypes« had been fermenting inside me for a long time because my parents are from two different countries [Spain and Slovenia] and I grew up in Germany. My exchange semester in Ljubljana gave the idea a more concrete shape.** Wie motivierst du dich? **Where do you get your motivation from?** Den Anspruch zu haben, dass die nächste Arbeit besser sein muss als die letzte. Damit meine ich nicht alleine das Ergebnis, sondern auch wie man dorthin gekommen ist. **From my desire to always have the next piece of work be better than the last. And I don't mean just the results; I also mean how I got there.** Wie lange hast du für die Umsetzung deiner Idee gebraucht? **How long did it take you to realise your idea?** Sechs Monate insgesamt. Wobei die ersten beiden vor allem dazu dienten, mit anderen Ideen abzuschließen. Dann sicher ein bis zwei Monate, in denen das Konzept und der Stil entstanden, und zwei Monate in der Umsetzung. **Six months all in all. But the first two were mostly spent finalising other ideas. Then came one or two months where the concept and the style took shape, and two months of realising the concept.** Gibt es jemanden, dem du den Preis zu verdanken hast? **Is there anybody to whom you owe winning this award?** Professor Johannes Graf hat mich während des Seminars toll unterstützt. Gerade in der Konzeptphase war das sehr wichtig. **Professor Johannes Graf offered me valuable support during the seminar. That was very important, especially during the concept phase.** Wo arbeitest du jetzt? **Where do you work now?** Bei Claus Koch in Düsseldorf. **With Claus Koch in Düsseldorf.** Hast du schon mehrere Preise gewonnen? **Have you won any other awards so far?** Die Diplomarbeit hat beim ADC einen Preis gewonnen, dann bei den European Design Awards und ist kürzlich mit einem red dot: »best of the best« ausgezeichnet worden. Davor habe ich einmal beim ADC und einmal beim output eine Auszeichnung erhalten [beides Teamarbeiten mit Sven Franke]. **My final thesis won an award from the ADC, another one at the European Design Awards and it was recently awarded a red dot as »best of the best«. Before that, I won an award from the ADC and another one at OUTPUT [both in collaboration with Sven Franke].**

Musstest du beim Einreichen deiner Arbeit etwas bezahlen? **Did you have to pay a submission fee?** Ja, außer bei den European Design Awards. Dort habe ich über die Novum eine Wildcard bekommen. Es lohnt sich also auch seine Arbeiten zu den Magazinen zu schicken. Das kostet auch nichts! **Yes, except at the European Design Awards, for which I managed to get a wildcard through Novum. So it's worth submitting your projects to magazines. There is no fee for that either.** Hast du viele neue Kontakte geknüpft? **Did you make any new contracts?** Einige Kontakte schon. Man kommt aber natürlich generell einfacher mit Agenturen ins Gespräch, wenn die Mappe stimmt und zusätzlich Arbeiten ausgezeichnet wurden. **A few, yes. Of course, contacting agencies is always easier with a good portfolio and a few awards.** Wie trittst du mit anderen in Kontakt? [Internet, Telefon...] **How do you contact them? [Internet, phone...]** Meistens schicke ich eine Mail mit einer kleinen Auswahl meiner besten Arbeiten als PDF. Wenn eine Agentur Interesse hat, kann auch mal eine halbe Stunde später das Telefon klingeln. Manchmal kommt aber auch gar nix. Dann kann man ruhig mal anrufen. **In most cases, I send an e-mail with a PDF file containing a selection of my best works attached. Sometimes, if the agency is interested, I get a phone call half an hour later. But sometimes I get no response whatsoever. In that case I usually call them.**

reddot design award winner 2009 · EDAWARDS · »Auszeichnung« Abschlussarbeiten 2008 Mentoring: Prof. Johannes Graf

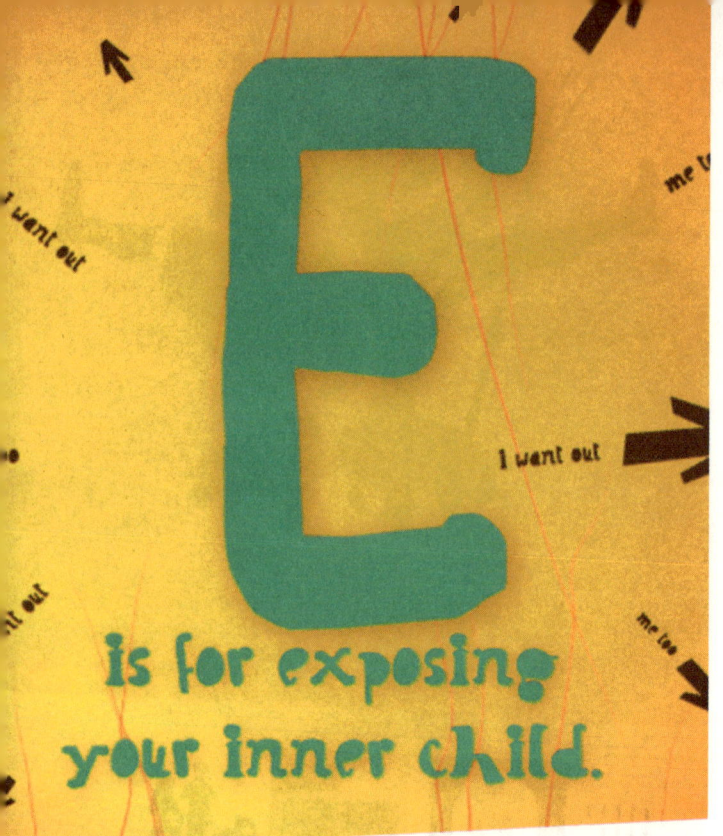

DANIEL GÖTTLING
WELCOME TO FONTMESS

Wie bist du zu dem Thema deiner Arbeit gekommen? Bzw. zu deiner Idee? **How did you come up with the central theme for your submission? What gave you the idea?** Zum Thema meiner Arbeit bin ich erst nach einiger Zeit gekommen. Ich hatte erst überlegt, etwas komplett anderes zu machen. Aber es war dann für mich naheliegend, etwas zu machen, mit dem ich mich voll und ganz identifizieren konnte. Was in meinem Fall meine Fonts und Animation und Illustration waren. **I arrived at the theme only after a while. I had first envisaged doing something completely different. But then it seemed more natural for me to do something I could completely identify with, which in my case were my fonts and animation and illustration.** Wo sammelst du Ideen? **Where do new ideas come to you?** Ideen kommen, wie bei jedem denke ich, eigentlich überall. Auf'm Klo, auf'm Weg zur Arbeit, beim Arbeiten generell. Ich habe da keinen besonderen Platz, um Ideen zu sammeln. **I think anyone would agree that ideas come all the time – on the toilet, on the way to work, while working in general. I don't really have a particular place where I go to get ideas.** Wie lange hast du für die Umsetzung deiner Arbeit gebraucht? **How long did it take you to realise your project?** Alles in Allem würde ich sagen, saß ich ein gutes halbes Jahr an der Umsetzung meiner Arbeit. **All in all, I would say I spent a little over six months working on the realisation of my project.** Was blieb während deines Projektes auf der Strecke? **Which elements of the project got lost on the way?** Nichts! Ich konnte mich wirklich total austoben. Über Schriftdesign, Illustration, Buch und Plakatgestaltung, Webdesign und schließlich Animation war wirklich alles dabei, was Spaß macht. Ich kann mich also nicht beklagen. **None! I had absolutely free reign. From font design, illustration, and book and poster design to web design and finally animation, everything that I've found fun, was there. So I really can't complain.**

Gibt es jemanden, dem du den Preis zu verdanken hast? **Is there anybody to whom you owe winning this award?** Es gab schon einige Leute, die mir sehr geholfen haben. Meine Freundin hat mich sehr stark unterstützt. Beim Sounddesign für meine Filme habe ich sehr große Unterstützung von Jonas Förster [Sound] und Steve Taylor [Voiceover] bekommen. Und natürlich von Prof. HD Schrader. **There are definitely a few people who have helped me a great deal. My girlfriend was a great support. Jonas Förster [sound] and Steve Taylor [voice-over] were a great help in the sound design for my films. And of course, Prof. HD Schrader.** Wo arbeitest du jetzt? **Where do you work now?** Bei der Schönheitsfarm Postproduction in Hamburg. **At the post-production studio Schönheitsfarm in Hamburg.** Bist du selber darauf gekommen deine Arbeit einzureichen? **Did you submit your project of your own accord?** Ja, die Idee kam von mir. Ich denke auch, das jeder Diplomand seine Arbeit bei so vielen Wettbewerben wie möglich einreichen sollte. **Yes, that was my idea. And I think that every graduate-to-be should submit his or her final project to as many competitions as possible.** Hast du viele neue Kontakte geknüpft? **Did you make any new contracts?** Auf Grund des Preises eigentlich nicht. Eher durch meinen Job. **Not because of the award, no. I did, however, through my job.** Wie trittst du mit anderen in Kontakt? [Internet, Telefon...] **How do you contact others? [Internet, phone...]** Viel läuft bei mir über E-Mail und Internet. Ich rede aber lieber mit den Menschen. **I use e-mail and the internet a lot. But I actually prefer to talk to people.** Dein Vorschlag zur Verbesserung der Welt? **Your idea on how to make the world a better place?** Ist das hier eine Misswahl? **Is this a beauty contest?** Was gibst du anderen mit auf den Weg? **What recommendations would you give to others?** Macht, worauf Ihr Lust habt! Alles andere ist Zeitverschwendung und bringt Euch nicht weiter. Achtet auf gutes Essen, genügend Schlaf, viel Vitamin C, immer einen angespitzten Bleistift in der Tasche, und das Wichtigste, glaubt an Euch selbst! Aus eigener Erfahrung, weiß ich, dass das sehr schwer ist. **Do whatever you feel like! Anything else is a waste of time and will get you nowhere. Take care to eat healthy, get enough sleep and enough vitamin C, always carry a sharp pencil in your pocket, and the most important thing: always believe in yourself! I know from experience that that is very hard to do.** Was bedeutet dein Job und die Umgebung für dich? **What do your job and your environment mean to you?** Sehr viel. Ich denke, dass es sehr wichtig ist, in einer Umgebung zu arbeiten, in der man sich wohlfühlt. Man verbringt ja schon die meiste Zeit bei der Arbeit, und da sollte meiner Meinung nach alles stimmen. Da zählt für mich auch nicht das Geldargument. Wenn das Umfeld nicht passt, bringt mir viel Geld gar nichts. **Very much. I think it is very important to work in an environment where you feel at home. After all, you spend most of your time at work, so I think everything there should be just right. And I won't hear financial arguments against this: if I don't like my environment, a lot of money won't help.**

»Talent des Jahres«
Abschlussarbeiten 2008
Mentoring: Prof. HD Schrader

 »watch movie!«

SEBASTIAN MICHAILIDIS
DRAHT

Wie bist du zu dem Thema deiner Arbeit gekommen? Bzw. zu deiner Idee? **How did you come up with the central theme for your submission? What gave you the idea?** Die Semesteraufgabe bestand darin, ein Corporate Design mit begleitenden Medien für ein Museum der eigenen Wahl zu erstellen. Ich hatte mich für ein Computermuseum entschieden und in diesem Zuge unter anderem verschiedene Plakate ausgemacht für Sonderausstellungen. Eines der Plakate bewarb eine Ausstellung über Netzwerke. Es hieß »Draht« und stellte in seiner ersten Rohfassung ein Gesicht grafisch stilisiert in einem Liniennetzwerk dar. Es bot sich an, dieses Plakat in eine Animation zu überführen. Der Film ist also mehr oder weniger eigendynamisch aus einer Bildidee entstanden. **The assignment for the semester consisted in creating a corporate design with accompanying media for a museum of my choice. I had chosen a computer museum and had, among other things, created different posters advertising special exhibitions. One of the posters advertised an exhibition on networks. It was called »Draht« [Wire] and, in its first draft, depicted a graphically stylised face in a network of lines. The poster just begged to be transposed into an animation. So the film's evolution from a pictorial idea was pretty much a process with its own momentum.** Wo sammelst du Ideen? **Where do new ideas come to you?** Beim Autofahren und auf dem Sofa. In jedem Fall fern des Computers, wenn ich nicht ohnehin nur experimentiere. Der PC verleitet sehr dazu, sich in der Umsetzung halb garer Ideen zu verlieren. **In the car and on the sofa. Anywhere that's far away from the computer, when I'm not just experimenting anyway. In front of a PC, you are too tempted to lose yourself trying to realise half-finished ideas.** Wie motivierst du dich? **Where do you get your motivation from?** Ich versuche immer, verschiedene Dinge parallel zu tun zu haben. Ich mache dann jeweils das, worauf ich gerade am meisten Lust habe, sofern Deadlines und der Gesamtzeitplan diese Vorgehensweise erlauben. Im Resultat arbeite ich gewöhnlich insgesamt viel schneller und natürlich macht die Arbeit auch mehr Spaß. **I always try to have several things to do at the same time. And then I work on whatever I feel like at the moment, provided that deadlines and the overall time frame permit this sort of approach. If they do, I end up working much faster, and of course, the work is always more fun that way.** Wie lange hast für die Umsetzung deiner Idee gebraucht? **How long did it take you to realise your idea?** Die Umsetzung ging erstaunlich schnell. Theoretisch hätte der Film trotz seiner 2-minütigen Länge sicherlich in zwei Wochen komplett fertig sein können, wenn ich nicht immer wieder die Illustrationen überarbeitet und ausgetauscht hätte. **A surprisingly short time. In theory, I'm sure that the film could have been completed within two weeks, despite it being two minutes long, had I not continually revised and replaced the illustrations.** Gibt es Kreativitätstechniken, die du benutzt? Hast du eigene entwickelt? **Are there any techniques for creative thinking that you use? Have you developed any of your own?** Mindmaps einerseits, um gezielt Ideen zu finden, und das Abschalten aller äußeren Reize andererseits, um ungezielt Ideen entstehen zu lassen. **First, mind maps to actively find ideas; second, shutting out all external stimuli to get ideas flowing of their own accord.** Gibt es jemanden, dem du den Preis zu verdanken hast? **Is there anybody to whom you owe winning this award?** Carsten Strübbe hat mir sicherlich, wie schon in anderen Seminaren, durch seine immer motivierende und vor Irrwegen schützende, gestalterisch offene Betreuung sehr gut zur Seite gestanden. **As in previous seminars, Carsten Strübbe has certainly lent me valuable and creatively encouraging support while preventing me from going astray in his ever-motivating manner.** Hat dir der Preis Vorteile verschafft? **Have you benefited from the award?** Ich gehe davon aus und hoffe, dass sich der eigentliche Nutzen solcher Preise zeigen wird, wenn man das Studium verlassen haben wird und in die Berufswelt aufbricht. **I believe and hope that the true benefit of awards like these will emerge when I graduate from university and start a career.** Hast du schon mehrere Preise gewonnen? **Have you won any other awards so far?** Es ist inzwischen ein Red Dot Award für das Payback Projekt hinzugekommen, das sich auch in dieser Ausgabe des Jahrbuches findet. **The Payback project, which also appears in this issue of the yearbook, has since won a red dot award.** Was gab es als Preis für deine Arbeit? **What did you get for your submission?** Etwas öffentliche Aufmerksamkeit, eine sehr schöne Urkunde, das Sushi Buch, in dem meine Arbeit veröffentlicht worden ist und einen kleinen zackigen rosa Kreis, den ich mir demnächst ins Portfolio kleben darf, um in der Folge hoffentlich reizvolle Jobs zu bekommen. **Some publicity, a very nice-looking certificate, the Sushi book in which my submission was published and a little jagged pink star that I will be allowed to add to my portfolio; with that star, I hope to get some exciting job offers in the future.**

 »watch movie!«

»Auszeichnung«
Semesterarbeiten 2008
Mentoring: Carsten Strübbe

CHRONICLE, 33PT 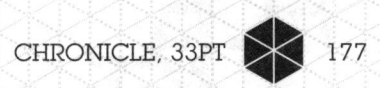 177

20. - 22. August 2008
SONDERLINGE in der Heldenbar
Studierende der Fachhochschule Dortmund präsentieren
12 fotografische Arbeiten aus dem Sommersemester 2008
Heldenbar im Grillo Theater, Essen

28. - 29. Oktober 2008
effet 2008 – elektronische Nacht
Eine Co-Produktion zwischen der Fachhochschule Dortmund
und dem Zeiss-Großplanetarium in Berlin
Leitung: Prof. Cindy Gates, Dipl.-Des. Rocco Helmchen

12. November 2008
REFLEKTOR-RELEASE
Präsentation & Buchausgabe des REFLEKTOR1
im Foyer des Fachbereich Design

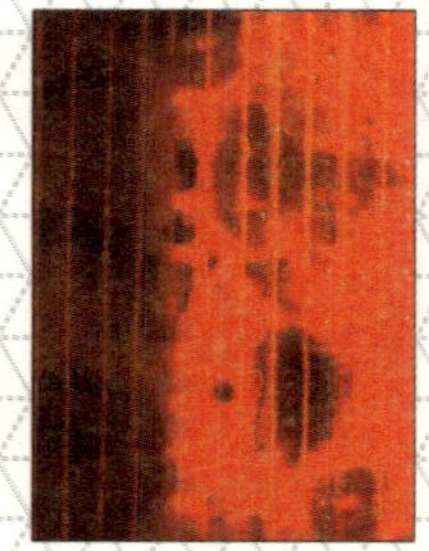

14. Januar - 15. Februar 2009
»transluzide«
Arbeiten von Prof. Margareta Hesse
Galerie des Fachbereich Design

31. Januar – 1. Februar 2009
I, OBJECT
Portraitfotografien der Studierenden des Fachbereich Design
Eröffnung: Prof. Dr. Ralf Bohn
Gloriahalle Düsseldorf

13. – 15. Februar 2009
Schauraum »YES WE CAN«
Studierende des Fachbereich Design präsentieren ihre Abschlussarbeiten
Fachbereich Design der Fachhochschule Dortmund

13. Februar – 3. April 2009
DIE MAGIE DER DINGE
Eine Ausstellung von Studierenden der Fachhochschule Dortmund, Fachbereich Design in Kooperation mit der RWE Westfalen-Weser-Ems AG, RWE Tower Dortmund zur Dortmunder Ausstellungsreihe TRANSVERSALE
Künstlerische Leitung: Prof. Caroline Dlugos, Prof. Margareta Hesse
[Ausstellungskatalog, Dortmund: Fachbereich Design 2009]

13. Februar – 7. Juni 2009
TRIUMPH: DER FLIEGENDE TEPPICH
Eine Kunstinstallation an der Schnittstelle von Kunst und Design
Museum für Kunst und Kulturgeschichte Dortmund
Künstlerischer Kurator: Prof. Ovis Wende

24. - 26. März 2009
Podest 09.1 »GANZ WIE ANDERS«
Der Diplomstudiengang Kommunikationsdesign und der Bachelor-studiengang Design Medien Kommunikation präsentieren dreidimensionale Arbeiten aus dem Wintersemester 2008/09
Fachbereich Design der Fachhochschule Dortmund

3. - 4. April 2009
33pt. Eskapade – Beiträge zur Typografie
Typografie-Symposium
Aula Fachbereich Design

Mai 2009: Book Launch
Inszenierung und Ereignis
Ralf Bohn & Heiner Wilharm [Hg.], Beiträge zur Theorie und Praxis der Szenografie [Bielefeld: transcript 2009], 410 Seiten, kart., zahlreiche z. T. farbige Abbildungen, ISBN 978-3-8376-1152-6; 29,80 €

9. Mai 2009
ADC PINK SATURDAY
Vortragsreihe für Studenten zur Berührung mit der Werbe-Praxis
Fachbereich Design der Fachhochschule Dortmund
Leitung: Referenten und Mitglieder des ADC e.V.

26. - 28. Mai 2009
Buchwoche am Fachbereich Design
Vorträge, Workshops, Buchausstellung
Fachbereich Design der Fachhochschule Dortmund

3. - 26. Juni 2009
»Hundefutter-Verpackungen«
Ausstellung von Seminararbeiten der Studienrichtung Grafikdesign
Galerie Fachbereich Design
Leitung: Prof. Johannes Graf

7. Juni - 15. November 2009
Herrscher der Lüfte
Ausstellungsgestaltung im Museum für Naturkunde Dortmund
Eröffnung: Prof. Martin Middelhauve

19. Juni - 14. August 2009
137° – Fotografien aus der Gummistiefelfabrik Novesta in Zlín
von Studierenden und Lehrenden der Fachhochschule Dortmund und der Tomas Bata Universität Zlín, Tschechien Wissenschaftspark Gelsenkirchen
Leitung: Prof. Jörg Winde, MgA. Jaroslav Prokop und MgA. Jan Jindra [Zlín]

1. – 19. Juli 2009
Halbe Gespräche
Arbeiten von Prof. Nora Fuchs
Galerie Fachbereich Design

4. Juli – 9. August 2009
REVISITED
Fotografie und Archiv
Museum für Kunst und Kulturgeschichte Dortmund
Leitung: Prof. Jörg Winde und Bernd Dicke

13. Juli 2009
Poesie und Drama – Inspiration – Theater
Fotografieausstellung der Studierenden der Fachhochschule Dortmund
Fachbereich Design der Fachhochschule Dortmund

16. – 20. Juli 2009
Schauraum
Präsentation von Abschlussarbeiten
Fachbereich Design der Fachhochschule Dortmund

2. - 16. August 2009
SCHEIN ODER SEIN
Fotografische Arbeiten von Studierenden
des Fachbereich Design
Maschinenhalle Zeche Scherlebeck

7. - 29. August 2009
ABBILDUNG ÄHNLICH
Fotografien und Filme Studierender des Fachbereich Design
TZR Galerie in Düsseldorf

Ruhrtriennale 2009 - 2011
Bühnenbild für die Literaturreihe in der Jahrhunderthalle Bochum
Nachfolgeauftrag der GRUPPE TRIUMPH für die Ruhrtriennale 2009 - 2011
Leitung: Prof. Ovis Wende

10. - 13. Dezember 2009
2nd Scenographers' Symposium
»Vertrauen ist der Anfang von Allem«
Aula der Fachhochschule Dortmund
Leitung: Prof. Dr. Ralf Bohn, Prof. Dr. Heiner Wilharm,
Prof. Dr. Pamela C. Scorzin M.A.

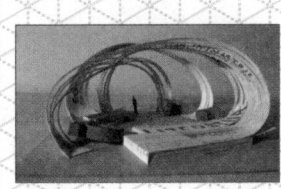

33pt. Eskapade
TYPOGRAFIE SYMPOSIUM

TYPOGRAFIE IST EMOTIONAL

Manch einer mag denken, die Typografie sei eine trockene, gar emotionslose Disziplin. Genau das Gegenteil ist in Wahrheit der Fall. Die Typografie ist hoch emotional und sensibel. Dies gilt für jede konzentrierte Beschäftigung mit der Typografie, aber auch und vor allem für die Lehre dieser Disziplin. Typografie lehren ist sehr anspruchsvoll und sehr schön zugleich [dies trifft wahrscheinlich auf alle interessanten Dinge des Lebens zu]. Anspruchsvoll, da natürlich längst nicht alle Studierende unsere Liebe und Leidenschaft für Schrift teilen, ja diese noch nicht einmal nachvollziehen können. Schön, da natürlich auch einige dieser jungen Menschen unsere Liebe und Leidenschaft für die Typografie nicht nur teilen, sondern diese mit ihrer Hingabe sogar übertreffen.

Dieser zweiten Gruppe junger Menschen gehören die Initiatoren der Symposiumsreihe 33pt. — Beiträge zur Typografie[1] an. Alle sind oder waren Studierende[2] des Fachbereich Design der Fachhochschule Dortmund und alle teilen unsere Begeisterung und unsere Leidenschaft für Schrift und Typografie. Die Symposiumsreihe 33pt. — Beiträge zur Typografie[1] ist ein ausgewiesen studentisches Projekt. Die Idee, die Konzeption und die Gestaltung sind studentischer Initiative zu verdanken. Die zweite Veranstaltung 33pt. Eskapade[3] wurde in einer Seminararbeit im WS 2008/09 entwickelt und realisiert. Nun mag man meinen, das mache die Sache leicht. Nur engagierte und motivierte Schriftliebhaber finden sich in einem Seminar zusammen. Das scheint ja geradezu paradiesisch zu werden für alle Beteiligten: Studierende wie Lehrende. Dies ist leider mitnichten der Fall. Denn, wie gesagt: Die Typografie ist hoch emotional und sensibel und die meisten Typografen sind es auch.

sich die vielen Diskussionen und Kompromisse erst lohnen? Und hier schließt sich einmal mehr die Verbindung zur Typografie und Gestaltung von und mit Schrift. Die Typografie bedarf der absoluten Konzentration auf das Wesentliche. Eine Konzentration auf kleinste, von den meisten kaum wahrnehmbare Details, ohne jedoch das Ziel, die Idee, die Gesamtheit aus dem Auge zu verlieren. Eine Schrift entsteht zwar aus vielen unterschiedlichsten Überlegungen und Detailfragen, ergänzt sich aber in ihrer Gesamtheit zu weitaus mehr als der Summe ihrer Details. Erst die Haltung, aus der heraus eine typografische Formensprache entwickelt wird, macht sie zu einer autonomen Schrift.

Wie unterschiedlich diese Ideen und Haltungen sein können, haben alle Referenten von 33pt. Eskapade in vorbildlicher [und von uns inszenierter] Art und Weise in ihrer Vorstellung gezeigt. Und damit fügt sich in die Idee von Individualität [die Initiatoren und Teilnehmer] und dem großen gemeinsamen Projekt [das Symposium] noch eine Komponente, nämlich die Realität. Mit allen ihren großen und kleinen Unbekannten, Irritationen und Überraschungen.

Seminare werden grundsätzlich sehr sorgfältig geplant und vorbereitet, dennoch haben alle Seminare ein spezifisches Eigenleben und eine ganz individuelle Dynamik. Diese Energie heißt es positiv und kreativ zu nutzen und damit den Verlauf der Seminare konstruktiv zu lenken. Unser Seminar unterschied sich jedoch zusätzlich noch gravierend von den üblichen Lehrangeboten, nämlich in dem angestrebten Ergebnis: der Konzeption, Planung und Gestaltung unseres Symposiums. Wohlbemerkt: Unser Symposium. Soll heißen: unser dezidiertes Ziel war ein gemeinsames Projekt, in dem wir uns alle möglichst gleichwertig wieder finden, ohne das Gesamtkonzept aus dem Auge zu verlieren. Ein scheinbar unmögliches Unterfangen, denn ich erinnere nochmals, dass wir hier von einem unkontrollierbaren Haufen von emotionalisierten und sensiblen, teilweise leicht exzentrischen Gestaltern und Typografen sprechen [die beiden Betreuer selbstverständlich eingeschlossen]. Doch vielleicht beschreiben ja genau diese beiden Pole den Schlüssel des Erfolges einer solchen studentischen Initiative? Vielleicht braucht ein gemeinsam schwer erarbeitetes und kontrovers diskutiertes Projekt ja gerade diese emotionalen und sensiblen Individuen... und vielleicht braucht jeder Einzelkämpfer solch eine gemeinsame große Idee für die

IST REALITÄT PLANBAR?

Ja und Nein. Ein überzeugendes Konzept [und der unabdingbare Glaube daran], gute Vorbereitung [Übung macht wirklich in vielen Dingen den Meister] und, daraus resultierend, Vertrauen [in den Einzelnen und das Team] machen sicherlich das eine oder andere planbar. Dennoch und Gott sei Dank ist natürlich die Realität [der Moment, der in der Planung ja noch in der Zukunft liegt] nicht wirklich vorhersehbar und daher planbar.

WENN PLANUNG AUF REALITÄT STÖSST, SIND WIR LIVE DABEI.

Ab dem Moment verschieben sich Wahrnehmungs- und Zeitebenen miteinander. Das ist ein wirklich bemerkenswerter und zu benennender Aspekt, der wiederum auf den Umgang mit Typografie und Schrift zurückführt. So ist der Umgang mit Typografie und typografischer Gestaltung mit der massiven Präsenz von Internetseiten und Blogs ein grundsätzlich anderer geworden. Alles ist jederzeit verfügbar [zumindest im Bild] und verändert unsere Wahrnehmung merklich. Wir meinen alles zu kennen, zu wissen, zu diskutieren und zu kopieren, meist ohne die Kenntnis des Originals bzw. eines theoretischen oder gar wissenschaftlichen Hintergrundes. Ich befürchte, der Riesenanteil des studentischen Workload[4] [zumindest in unserem Fachbereich] berechnet sich weder vor der Lektüre oder vor dem Exponat, gar vor den eigenen Arbeiten [oder in der Diskussion über diese], sondern vor bekannten und weit verbreitenden Internetpräsenzen.

Vor diesem Hintergrund begrüßen wir entschieden die nicht planbare Realität und die authentische Erfahrung [sowohl im persönlichen als auch im fachlichen Sinne] dieser zwei Tage im April. Für uns, für die Referenten[5], für die Besucher und vor allem für die Studierenden. Und hier schließt sich dann auch der Kreis, denn wir möchten keinesfalls, dass sich die Typografie zu einer trockenen, gar emotionslosen Disziplin entwickeln könnte.

Am 05. April 2009 um 06:33 Uhr postete Peter [aus unserem Team] auf dem Blog 33pt. Eskapade in der Kategorie Allgemein unter der Überschrift Glücklich: WIR waren GROSS!!!

TYPOGRAFEN SIND EBEN HOCH EMOTIONAL UND SENSIBEL UND DIE TYPOGRAFIE IST ES AUCH.

Sabine an Huef

www.33pt.de

[1] Das erste Symposium in der Reihe fand im Dezember 2006 in der Fachhochschule Dortmund im Fachbereich Design zum Thema Musik statt. Referenten waren u.a.: Peter Bruhn, Malmö; Verena Gerlach, Berlin; Walter Pamminger, Wien; 3deluxe, Wiesbaden; Dirk Uhlenbrock, Essen; Natascha Dell, Aachen; Jörg Hemker, Hamburg; Filip Blazek, Prag und Peter Bilak, Den Haag.

[2] Ich hoffe inständig, dass alle studentischen Akteure dieser Veranstaltung ihr Studium mittlerweile erfolgreich abgeschlossen haben.

[3] Das Symposium 33pt. Eskapade fand am 3. und 4. April 2009 in der Fachhochschule Dortmund im Fachbereich Design statt. Referenten aus folgenden Bereichen: Falk Haberkorn, Leipzig [Kunst]; Barbara Hahn und Christine Zimmermann, Von B und C, Bern; Sven Voelker, Karlsruhe/Berlin; Phil Baines, London; Siggi Eggertsson, Berlin [Typografie in der Anwendung]; Autobahn, Utrecht; Jos Buivenga, Arnhem; Martin Majoor, Arnhem [Typografie und Schriftgestaltung]; Sven Ehmann, Gestalten Verlag, Berlin [Verwertung/Verlag]; David Crow, Manchester [Wissenschaft/Theorie]; Roob Meek und Frank Müller, Berlin [Typografie in Bewegung] und Typeradio, Den Haag [Interview und Aktion].

[4] Der Workload ist der in Zeitstunden ausgedrückte erwartete studentische Arbeitsaufwand, der für einen erfolgreich absolvierten Studienabschnitt notwendig ist. Der Arbeitsaufwand wird in Zeitstunden gemessen und setzt sich aus verschiedenen Faktoren zusammen.

[5] The Questa project is a type project of Jos Buivenga and Martin Majoor. It all began after we met at the 33pt. Symposium in Dortmund, both giving a lecture. We knew each other from the Academy of Fine Arts in Arnhem, but we had not seen each other for about 25 years. We renewed our contact and after a few meetings we decided that we wanted to do a type design project together. [www.thequestaproject.com]

TYPOGRAPHY IS EMOTIONAL

Some might think typography is a dry and unemotional discipline. Actually, it is the exact opposite. Typography is highly emotional and sensitive. This is true of each concentrated activity with typography, but especially of teaching this discipline. Typography is challenging and beautiful at the same time [this is probably the case for all interesting things in life]. Challenging, of course, because not all students share our love and passion for script. To be honest, some cannot even relate to it. Beautiful, well, because some young people not only share our love and passion for typography, but even outdo us in their devotion to it.

This second group of young people encompasses those who initiated the series of symposia 33pt. – Beiträge zur Typografie[1] [33pt. – Input to Typography]. All of them are or were students[2] of design at the University of Applied Sciences and Arts Dortmund and all share our enthusiasm and passion for script and typography. The series of symposia 33pt. – Beiträge zur Typografie[1] is a student designated project. The idea, the concept, and the design came from the students' initiative. The second event, 33pt. Eskapade[3] [33pt. Escapade], was originally developed and realised within a seminar project paper in the winter term of 2008/09. Now, one may think that this makes things easier. Only committed and motivated script aficionados take part in seminars. These should be ideal conditions for all of the participants, students, and teachers. Unfortunately, this is by no means the case; remember, typography is highly emotional and sensitive and this applies to most typographers as well.

Seminars are always thoroughly planned and well prepared, but nevertheless each has its own way of doing things and an individual drive and energy. This energy has to be used positively and creatively and thus gear the seminars' course constructively. On top of that, our seminar was entirely different from regular classes in its focus: the concept, planning and design of our symposium. Mark it well: our symposium. In other words, our determined goal was a joint project that all of us would identify with to the same degree without losing sight of the overall concept. A mission seemingly impossible: again, we deal with an uncontrollable bunch of emotional and sensitive, sometimes slightly eccentric designers and typographers [the two seminar mentors included, of course]. However, perhaps it is these two extremes that are the key to success of such student initiatives. Maybe a hard-earned and controversial project like this needs such emotional and sensitive individuals... and maybe every lone warrior needs such a common great idea to make all discussions and compromises worthwhile. Here, the connection between typography and design of and with script comes into play once more. Typography requires full concentration on the essence. It means concentrating on small details most people barely perceive without losing sight of the target itself – the idea, the whole of the project. A script derives from many varying thoughts and detailed questions, but as a whole its result is far more than the sum of its parts. It is the attitude with which a typographic language of forms is developed that makes it an autonomous script.

Ideas and attitudes can be very diverse. This was exemplified by all speakers of 33pt. Eskapade in their presentations [put into scene by us]. This is where, along with the idea of individuality [the initiators and participants] and the great common project [the symposium], another component comes into play: reality, with all its irritations, surprises, and unknown aspects great and small.

CAN REALITY BE ANTICIPATED?

Yes and no. A convincing concept [and the indispensable belief in it], good preparation [skill often really does come with practice] and the resulting trust [trust in the individual team member and the team itself] surely make some things predictable. Nevertheless – and thankfully so! – reality [the moment that still lies in the future when planning for it] is by nature really only predictable in its unpredictability.

WHEN PLANNING MEETS REALITY, WE EXPERIENCE IT »LIVE«.

From that moment on, perception and time levels shift. This really is a remarkable aspect, and it takes us back to our way of dealing with typography and script. Dealing with typography and typographic design has drastically changed due to the massive presence of websites and blogs. Everything is available at all times [at least as an image] and that changes our perception noticeably. We think we know it all; we discuss and copy it, mostly without any knowledge of the original or of the theoretical or even scientific background. I am afraid that a huge part of students' workload[4] [at least in our field of work] consists not so much of reading or exhibiting – to say nothing of creating or discussing their own works – but much rather of popular and widely spread internet sites.

Knowing this, we wholeheartedly welcome the unpredictable reality and the authentic experience [as much personal as technical] of these two days in April – for us, the speakers[5], the visitors, and particularly for the students. This is also where we come full circle in our aim to at any cost prevent typography from developing into a dry or even emotion-free discipline.

On 5 April 2009 at 6.33 a.m., Peter [from our team] posted an article on the blog 33pt. Eskapade in the category General with the headline Happy: WE were GREAT!!!

Typographers simply are highly emotional and sensitive, as is typography itself.

Sabine an Huef

www.33pt.de

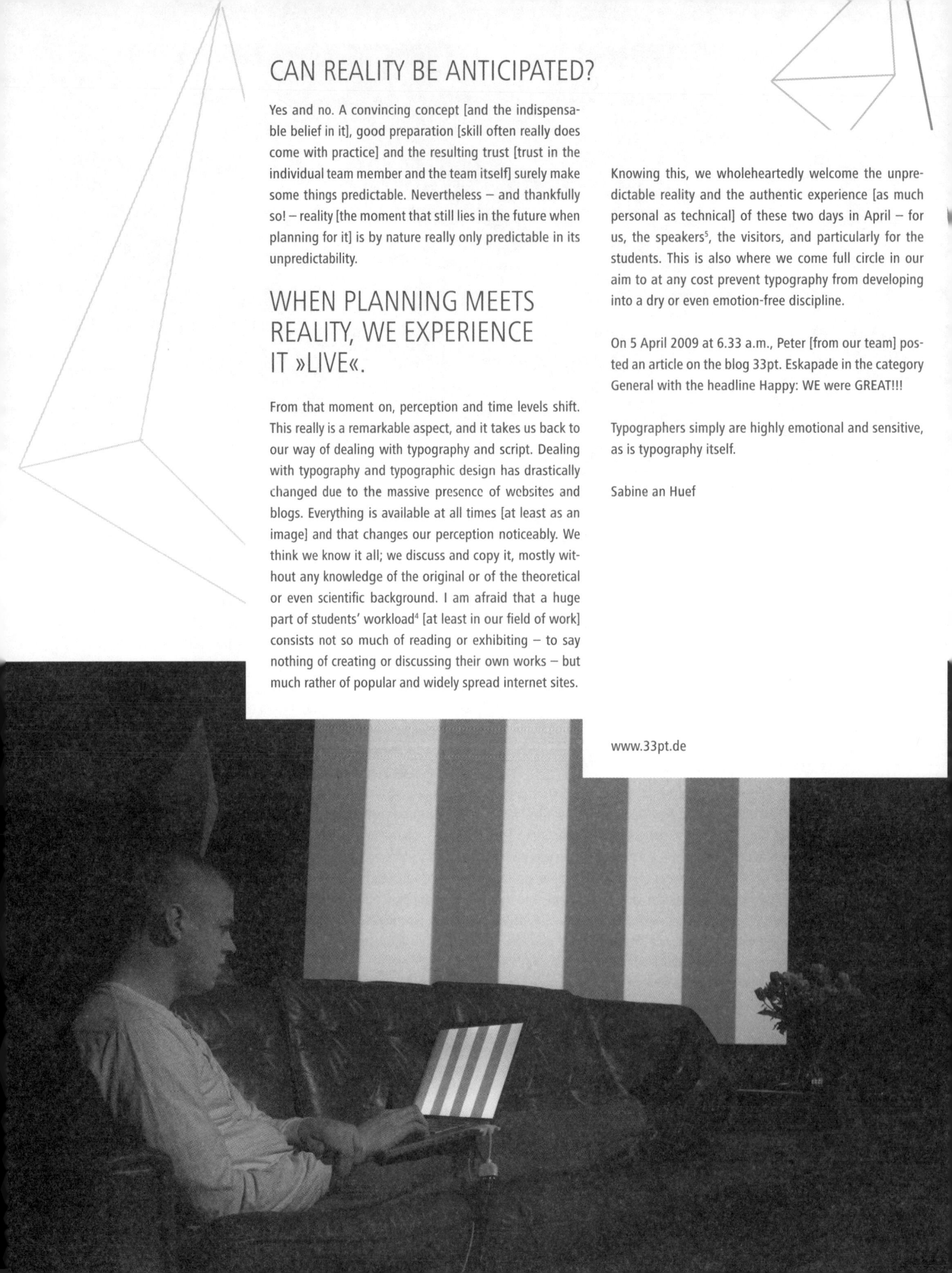

[1] The first symposium of this series took place on the topic of music in December 2006 at the University of Applied Sciences and Arts Dortmund in the field of design. Some of the speakers were: Peter Bruhn, Malmö; Verena Gerlach, Berlin; Walter Pamminger, Vienna; 3deluxe, Wiesbaden; Dirk Uhlenbrock, Essen; Natascha Dell, Aachen; Jörg Hemker, Hamburg; Filip Blazek, Prague; and Peter Bilak, The Hague.

[2] I really hope that all student participants in this event have finished their studies successfully by now.

[3] The Symposium 33pt. Eskapade took place on 3 and 4 April 2009 at the University of Applied Sciences and Arts Dortmund in the field of design. The speakers and their respective fields of work were: Falk Haberkorn, Leipzig [arts]; Barbara Hahn and Christine Zimmermann, About B and C, Bern; Sven Voelker, Karlsruhe/ Berlin; Phil Baines, London; Siggi Eggertsson, Berlin [applied typography]; Autobahn, Utrecht; Jos Buivenga, Arnhem; Martin Majoor, Arnhem [typography and script design]; Sven Ehmann, Gestalten Verlag, Berlin [application/publishers]; David Crow, Manchester [science/theory]; Roob Meek and Frank Müller, Berlin [typography in motion] and Typeradio, The Hague [interview and action].

[4] Workload is the expected amount of work needed for students to successfully complete a particular part of their studies. Workload is measured in hours and consists of various coefficients.

[5] The Questa project is a type project of Jos Buivenga and Martin Majoor. It all began after we met at the 33pt. Symposium in Dortmund, where we were both giving a lecture. We knew each other from the Academy of Fine Arts in Arnhem, but we had not seen each other for about twenty-five years. We renewed our contact and after a few meetings decided that we wanted to do a type design project together. [www.thequestaproject.com]

TYPOGRAPHERS SIMPLY ARE HIGHLY EMOTIONAL AND SENSITIVE, AS IS TYPOGRAPHY ITSELF.

IMPRESSUM
IMPRINT

KONZEPTIONELLE BEARBEITUNG UND ENTWURF / CONCEPTUAL DEVELOPMENT AND DRAFT
Aram Adjamian
Katharina Blasik
Matthias Oel
Max Poertgen
Eva Rücker
Matthias Smukal
Simon Sommer
Simone Wanzke
Marco Werner

BETREUUNG / SUPPORT
Prof. Dr. Pamela C. Scorzin M.A.
Prof. Willi Otremba

© 2009 ARNOLDSCHE ART PUBLISHERS, STUTTGART UND DIE AUTOREN / AND THE AUTHORS

Alle Rechte vorbehalten. Vervielfältigung und Wiedergabe auf jegliche Weise (grafisch, elektronisch und fotomechanisch sowie der Gebrauch von Systemen zur Datenrückgewinnung) — auch in Auszügen — nur mit schriftlicher Genehmigung der ARNOLDSCHEN Art Publishers, Liststraße 9, D-70180 Stuttgart.

All rights reserved. No part of this work may be reproduced or used in any forms or by any means (graphic, electronic or mechanical, including photocopying or information storage and retrieval systems) without written permission from the copyright holder. ARNOLDSCHEN Art Publishers, Liststraße 9, D-70180 Stuttgart.

AUTOREN / AUTHORS
Kai Röffen
Prof. Sabine an Huef

MITARBEIT REPROS / REPROS WITH THE HELP OF
Christian Twittenhoff

ÜBERSETZUNG / TRANSLATION
Miriam Levy, X-LS extended language services, Heidelberg

SCHRIFTEN / FONTS
Frutiger Next LT
ITC Lubalin Graph

PAPIER / PAPER
Pamo Art, 90 g/m², 1,5-faches Volumen
Luxo Magic, 150 g/m²
Schleipen, 90 g/m², 1,75-faches Volumen

OFFSET REPRODUKTION / OFFSET REPRODUCTIONS

srt & werbeagentur GmbH,
D-59439 Holzwickede
www.srt-werbeagentur.de

DRUCK / PRINTED BY
raff holding gmbh
D-72585 Riederich
www.raff-holding.de
Dieses Buch wurde gedruckt auf 100 % chlorfrei gebleichtem Papier und entspricht damit dem TCF-Standard. This book has been printed on paper that is 100 % free of chlorine bleach in conformity with TCF standards.

WIR DANKEN FÜR DIE UNTERSTÜTZUNG / WE WOULD LIKE TO THANK

Arctic Paper Mochenwangen GmbH
D-88284 Mochenwangen
www.arcticpaper.com

Cordier Spezialpapier GmbH,
D-67098 Bad Dürkheim
www.cordier-paper.de

Holger Nils Pohl
Elena Schneider
Hannes Woidich

BILDNACHWEIS / PHOTO CREDITS
© Jan Hoet, Foto: Hans Schröder [S 057]
© Ansicht Museum MARTa Herford
Foto: Thomas Mayer [S 059]
© ZKM, Foto: ONUK [S 051]
© ZKM, Foto: Fabry [S 052]
ZKM Foyer mit Marie Sesters
»Access«, 2001-2003/2005
Foto: Franz Wamhof [S 055]
© THS/ Moritz [S 115]
Rendering Turmaufbau: THS-Hauptverwaltung, ehemalige Zeche Nordstern, Gelsenkirchen: Projekt »NT2« – Aufstockung des Turms von Schacht 2 mit einer Skulptur von Markus Lüpertz, Architekt: Karl-Heinz Petzinka mit Nathalie Ness und René Clasen, Gelsenkirchen [S 118]
© Jochen Gerz: Projekt 2-3 Straßen
[S 110, 112]

BIBLIOGRAPHISCHE INFORMATION/ BIBLIOGRAPHICAL INFORMATION
Die Deutsche Bibliothek verzeichnet diese Publikation in der Deutschen Nationalbibliografie; detaillierte bibliografische Daten sind im Internet über http://dnb.ddb.de abrufbar. Die Deutsche Bibliothek lists this publication in the Deutsche Nationalbibliografie; detailed bibliographical data are available on the Internet at http://dnb.ddb.de

ISBN 978-3-89790-315-9
Made in Germany, 2009

FACHHOCHSCHULE / UNIVERSITY OF APPLIED SCIENES AND ARTS
Fachbereichsrat der Fachhochschule Dortmund Fachbereich Design
Fasta der Fachhochschule Dortmund Fachbereich Design
REFLEKTOR1 Team
Florian Backhaus
Bernd Dicke
Prof. Cindy Gates
Sonja Göllner
Ralf Junkers
Johannes Klais
Sebastian Klebe
Prof. Jörg Lensing
Prof. Martin Middelhauve
Prof. Dr. Wilhelm Schwick
Cengiz Sunter
Angelina Weizmann

INTERVIEWS
Prof. Dr. h.c. Peter Weibel
Prof. Dr. h.c. Jan Hoet
Prof. Jochen Gerz
Prof. Dipl.-Ing. Karl-Heinz Petzinka
Prof. Xuyen Dam
Christoph Grosse Hovest
Peter Balicki
Dennis Dominguez
Daniel Göttling
Sebastian Michailidis

ARNOLDSCHE ART BOOKS ARE AVAILABLE INTERNATIONALLY AT SELECTED BOOKSTORES AND FROM THE FOLLOWING DISTRIBUTION PARTNERS
USA – ACC/USA, Easthampton, MA, sales@antiquecc.com
CANADA – NBN Canada, Toronto, lpetriw@nbnbooks.com
UK – ACC/GB, Woodbridge, Suffolk, sales@antique-acc.com
FRANCE – Fischbacher International Distribution, Paris, libfisch@wanadoo.fr
BENELUX – Coen Sligting Bookimport, Amsterdam, sligting@xs4all.nl
SWITZERLAND – OLF S.A., Fribourg, information@olf.ch
JAPAN – UPS United Publishers Services, Tokyo, general@ups.co.jp
THAILAND – Paragon Asia Co., Ltd, Bangkok, info@paragonasia.com
AUSTRALIA / NEW ZEALAND – Bookwise International, Wingfield, customer.service@bookwise.com
RUSSIA – MAGMA, Moscow, magmabooks@mail.ru
CHINA – Book Art Trade Co., Shanghai, alice.jin@bookart.com.cn

For general questions, please contact ARNOLDSCHE Art Publishers directly at art@arnoldsche.com, or visit our homepage at www.arnoldsche.com for further information.

Besuchen Sie uns im Internet
Please visit our homepage
www.reflektor-dortmund.de
www.fh-dortmund.de
www.arnoldsche.com

ISBN 978-3-89790-315-9